CARLYLE

CARLYLE

By **LOUIS CAZAMIAN** Professor
of English Literature at the University of Paris

Translated by
E. K. BROWN

ARCHON BOOKS
1966

THIS EDITION FIRST PUBLISHED 1932

REPRINTED UNABRIDGED 1966 WITH PERMISSION

LIBRARY OF CONGRESS CATALOG CARD NUMBER: 66-25186
PRINTED IN THE UNITED STATES OF AMERICA

FOREWORD TO THE AMERICAN EDITION

This book was first published in the happy, unconscious summer of 1913, and soon found itself, along with much else, part of the flotsam of a submerged world. It was destined to have, nevertheless, more than its normal share of luck, since it is thought worthy, after such an interval, to be republished in English. I am under a very special obligation to Professor E. K. Brown, who not only took the initiative, but bore the strain of a translation—how heavy a strain, I clearly and remorsefully realise; and who devoted to the task an industry which he might have turned to excellent use for his own ends. My thanks are due as well to Messrs. Macmillan, who have endorsed the hope that the view of Carlyle here put forth may not have grown out of date in the intervening years.

During that lapse of time, the literature of the subject has not ceased to grow. New documents have come out; at least one monumental biography has been pushed near completion; side-lights have been thrown on many aspects of Carlyle's personality, work and doctrine. It might have seemed imperative to revise the present survey with the help of an increased or, on some points, of a corrected evidence. But the aim of this brief appraisal was from the first too modest, or too ambitious, to incur the obligations which devolve upon more thorough studies. It was an attempt toward an interpretation of Carlyle as a whole; leaving out all minor issues, it fastened on the leading traits, so as to build, if possible, a coherent picture; content even to draw a somewhat simplified sketch, provided the grouping of the features and their proportions were not untrue. The unity of an eminently forcible character, the substance of an influential body of thought, the common spirit and design running through its various parts, the individual accent of the voice that proclaimed it, such were the objects to which everything was made subservient. Of the special problems inevitably arising out of all considerations of Carlyle, two only were given any prominence: the relation of his thought to the philosophy of Germany; and the psychological tangle of his domestic life. Whether all those aims were attained, it is not for me to say; but I may perhaps feel assured that they remain of particular interest at the present day; and that recent scholarship has not materially added to the main texts and data upon which a general study of Carlyle must rest.

However, even if the figure of the man, the thinker and the writer, should appear to us in the same light as it did twenty years ago, we may well ask ourselves, whether time has made no difference with the message. Since this little book was written, the human mind has been shaken by the mightiest of earthquakes, and few are the values of the past that have borne the shock unchanged. What need has the twentieth century, hastening from its stormy youth, under lowering skies, to an apparently grim future, of the angry seer's denunciations; and can the young men and women of to-day be expected to hear with gratitude the scolding which their grandfathers listened to in awe?

If the prophet is to be tested by the event, the faith of Carlyle has been amply justified. Where he only voiced some of the deepest necessities of conduct, he erred not.

FOREWORD

In the midst of a softening world, he stressed the duties of hardness, courage, and work; he warned his age that the occasion for sacrifice, for a virile strength of purpose, would never cease to be. The men whose fathers had imbibed those lessons were called upon to look death in the face. A form of hero-worship was made the national religion: the hero was the nation itself. Not only the fighters, but every human being, in the Old World and in part of the New, had to brace themselves, and to endure. It proved true, as Carlyle had said, that life was a battle. The army stood for a while as a pattern for all human endeavor.

But from the ordeal the nations arose with fierce indignant hearts; and the prophet had been signally justified, but the world determined that the future should belie him. His message was fraught with the fatalities of the past: what if man, rising above his dead self, should win through to freedom by the sheer force of his despair? Had the seer made allowance for the creative power of the spirit?

He had had glimpses, at times, of the beyond that stretched outside the horizon of the old, familiar wisdom; but he had not led the way to explore it; his aim was to fasten on the known, the sure; his teaching emphasised only tried certainties. The soul of man, moved to its depth by the wreck of a world, and stirring with the premonition of another era, cannot rest and be nourished on the finality of Carlyle's message.

We find fault with the teacher as with the doctrine. To us, the very loudness of his assertion betrays the uneasy sense of an alloy in his faith—a lurking doubt. In the light of the new psychology, Carlyle's anger fails to move us, because we see through his denunciations, to the personal urge of his subconscious self. Through his own applications of his principles, he was fallible; his scale to portion out right and wrong between races, nations and men, was subjective; he was a good judge of moral laws, but his perception of moral facts could be singularly warped. The Empires which Carlyle extolled as conquests of right are found, when probed more searchingly, to be built largely upon might; and the identity of might with right has ceased to be acceptable, since the Providential government of the universe is no longer regarded as a simple matter and an obvious truth.

Again, he put under a ban too many of the powers of man. The intelligence is coming into its own once more; not Carlyle's "intellect"—a mystic perception of things unseen—but the processes of reason and science. The problems of to-day have to be worked out, if mankind is to live; and the sage of Chelsea believed only in the solutions which could be achieved at once; in the solutions which were already achieved.

And so the justification of his gospel may have marked the turning point at which the race was passing beyond the stage where his gospel was all-sufficient. He did voice vital needs, even more than he knew, but otherwise than he knew; and since the claims of life gave his teaching its urgency, other claims, equally valid, may to-day call for another doctrine. The claims of life, as such, are no longer sacred to us, unless they approve themselves to a sense of justice more exacting than the will to live; and those systems which Carlyle derided or cursed—the theories of science and reason—have proved to be, no less than his, expressions of supreme human needs. The new ethics tries to rise on a wider basis. We are waiting for another intuition, one more birth of ideas, beyond Nietzsche, who already superseded Carlyle; a synthesis that must reconcile life with the idealism of thought, through some broader relationship and association than the rough imperious control which Carlyle seized upon, and ceaselessly emphasised.

Thus outgrown in the field of spiritual revelation, Carlyle's work remains a prominent landmark of the past; neither the literary history of Britain, nor the social development of the nineteenth century, can be considered without him; history will never cease to be busy with his name. And the artist, unique as he was though limited, loses nothing of his appeal to us. His broken, interrupted utterance was the forerunner of our short, implicit, impatient style; he taught us first to think in disconnected fragments. And the flashes of his visionary imagination have prepared us for the flickering of images on the various screens—those of our hurried life, or those of all pictorial representations—where our mental energy gathers more and more of its materials. But here again, Carlyle does not give us all—what artist does? He has no classicism in him. Should the craving for artistic balance, for harmony and a superior order come decidedly to the front, other masters than he would be sought for the virtue of their example.

That Carlyle should no longer be read by the common man for the inspiration of his message, but by the student, the scholar, the cultivated few, for his historical meaning and the eloquence of his word, is a shrewd and a not unkind retort of fate to the great contemner of logic and beauty.

CONTENTS

	PAGE
FOREWORD TO THE AMERICAN EDITION	v

BOOK I
YOUTH AND MORAL FORMATION

CHAPTER
I.	MORAL FORMATION	3
II.	GERMAN INFLUENCE	29
III.	CRAIGENPUTTOCK	56
IV.	EARLY ESSAYS	86
V.	SARTOR RESARTUS	100

BOOK II
THE PROPHET AND HIS AGE

I.	CHEYNE ROW	137
II.	THE PHILOSOPHY OF HISTORY	153
III.	SOCIAL PHILOSOPHY	182

BOOK III
THE VEHEMENT REITERATIONS

I.	CROMWELL AND FREDERICK	213
II.	SERMONS AND SATIRES	240
III.	LAST YEARS	265
	CONCLUSION	275
	INDEX	287

BOOK I
YOUTH AND MORAL FORMATION

CHAPTER I

MORAL FORMATION

I

THE first impression that Carlyle makes upon a reader is that of a proud and lonely rebel; and the final impression that his great personality leaves is much the same, the impression of an indignant prophet, dominating the age he spent his life in denouncing. But by the ties of race, family and religion he was bound to his age; like other mortals he was under the sway of those absolute modalities, time and space, whose mysterious tyranny haunted his quivering imagination. The shape and quality of his moral being, if not all its traits, were those of Scottish Puritanism. The first and strongest influences upon him, the influences which engraved the deepest marks upon his spirit were those of his childhood, the home in which he grew up, the severe, peculiar ways of his parents, the temper of life in his native village. It is impossible to exaggerate the importance of his belonging as a child to a stable race, to a social organisation which was essentially traditional; for by this connection he was in sympathy with the collective will before in his maturity he came to oppose it. Besides, the very cast of his opposition, the very energy with which he sustained it, he owed to the remote and tacit will of the race to which he belonged, a will which he did not reject, but whose scope he merely extended.

Carlyle was born on the 4th of December, 1795, at

Ecclefechan, a village in that Border country, where the jealous age-old rivalry of English and Scots had resulted in a folk more savage, and more pertinacious, than could be found anywhere else in Britain. His father, James Carlyle, a stone-mason, had by Margaret Aitken, his second wife, nine children, five daughters and four sons, of which Thomas was the eldest child. A simple, pious woman, Carlyle's mother concentrated her life in her keen intelligent affection for her children; and tempered the stern Biblical severity of her husband who, notwithstanding his manifold virtues, was wanting in tenderness. She foresaw how her eldest son would develop; and, believing in his genius, she was a great support to him through the trials of his long years of uncertainty and quest. As long as she lived, to her he most liked to confide his hopes and disappointments; if he gave the deepest of his mind to his wife, to his mother he seems to have given the most genuine and spontaneous of his affections.

To understand the childhood of Carlyle, one must conceive the simple, frugal and yet comfortable life of a country household, awed by a spirit of Puritan gravity; a village made up of grey houses straggling along a road; a green landscape of hills and streams; the usual background of the Lowlands, quite without the marvelous and fascinating originality of the Highlands but with an austere charm, expressing a certain nobility, and once loved never to be forgotten. Moreover, the neighborhood of Ecclefechan was specially favored; not far from there the Firth of Solway might be seen and the distant hills of the lake country. The combined delicacy and immensity of this landscape fired his rugged genius and set it dreaming.

MORAL FORMATION

Ecclefechan is on the main highway from England to the west of Scotland. In this country, broken into minute divisions, and with each division a distinct entity, Carlyle's birthplace has all the specific qualities of Annandale, the valley of the river Annan. At the end of the 18th century the inhabitants of this valley retained all the folkways of primitive Scotland. At peace since the Union of England and Scotland, Annandale had not changed, had not been stirred to a new life by the new industrial civilisation which has since transformed the country and accelerated the pace of living. Here civilisation was still patriarchal, and the family was the social unit, necessary and absolute. Religion, as potent in the home as in the church, was the sole instructor of man and gave to life a solemn, imperious, unforgettable background. In all the people of the valley—although some were more rigorous and enthusiastic than others—one faith was the principle of their dignity and their obedience. Carlyle never lost his sense of a close and clannish relation to his relatives: to the end he thought of himself as a member or a chief of a clan. He helped his brothers with advice, or support, or money. He kept up an affectionate correspondence with his mother; his less intimate relation with his father left him with the inconsolable regret which falls upon those who have delayed too long in the revelation of their souls. The touching tribute to his father in the *Reminiscences* is among the essential texts for the understanding of Carlyle. In his full maturity he liked to return in thought to his humble beginnings and his first instructors. The emphatic characteristics of his work and personality, his doctrine, the tone of his preaching, everything, points back to his family tradition and his inherited instincts; and untameably independent as his personality was, its most personal achievements were, unknown to Carlyle, but expressions of tendencies older than he.

His very independence of spirit, indeed, and the indomitable energy which was the mainspring of his life, were part of his inheritance; it was the religion of his parents which modelled his soul for action; and it was the precept and the example of his home which fixed at the centre of his being the need and the command to work. So strict in James Carlyle and his wife was the instinct of personal religion, that they rejected the parish and its minister: their Calvinism was deeper than that of the Church of Scotland; they adhered to a stricter sect, *The Seceders*, and, by the fact of their dissent, their religion became more zealous. The march of his mind brought Carlyle far beyond the precise particulars of his parents' faith; but the impress of their spirit was never effaced from his. His letters to his mother reveal the depth and the endurance of this impress; writing to her as to the teacher who had taught him the rudiments of the Bible, he achieves a communion in the austere faith so dear to both their hearts.

For such a faith, the world is but a field where God has placed man to fear and serve him; against the revolts of nature and sin the will must combat with eternal vigilance; the passions, pride and sloth, are the devil's snares; the substance of grace is to discover one's daily task; upon the renunciation of self in effort man is to build day after day toward the painful victory of salvation. The law of love has little place in this gospel of penitence and effort; entirely Hebraic and Puritan, the religion of the Carlyles was in close sympathy with the principle of their family spirit; it narrowed the word of God and the sympathy of human creatures. In compensation it gave to the soul the marvelous resisting power and elasticity of steel. No wound of fate could weaken the spirits which were nourished by such bread as this. Rather did they interpret misfortune as a benefit showered upon them by Providence. The flésh is weak indeed and has an unutterable yearning after happiness; but this yearning is a shameful and contemptible thing; the only valid joy is in the obstinate fulfilment of duty. In his later years, Carlyle was to preach a doctrine scarcely distinguishable from this.

Religious faith, in this conception, was to issue and fructify in action; this faith was the supreme and infallible guide and guard to action; this faith was a formulation of the prodigious labor of experience and intuition by which the race had adapted itself to the mysterious laws of the invisible world; this faith clothed with the prestige of divine revelation the requisites of balance and effectiveness legible in the very structure of man.

Action was likewise the purport of all the example and precept to be found in the more superficial and homely side of the Carlyles' mode of life. The same will to survive and to acquire which had led the Carlyle family from of old to such a passionate adherence to the preestablished laws of moral hygiene, exhibited itself now in a robust craving for physical health and for success; success on the material plane, on that of intellectual and literary achievement also. The spirit of Carlyle's ancestors had for two generations been seeking to realise itself, to rise to the luminous state of complete and lofty expression; in the labors and the works of the glorious child were to come the longed-for and definitive self-realisation, and the full satisfaction of the craving for success. The grandfather, born in poverty, had known privation and the shame of an unregulated life, and then he had undertaken the painful and thankless task of making a homestead; with his own hands the father had built the house in which his progeny was born; a laborious artisan, he had brought discipline into his life, and risen to an honest comfort, sweetened by the consideration of his fellows and the propriety of his mode of life; in his later years he rose even higher and became a farmer. Of his four sons, John, the third, became a doctor, and combined with the prestige of a profession, some reputation in letters; but with a sound presentiment, the whole family recognised in Thomas the chieftain and the promise of the clan. From him, his brothers like his mother, expected some great achievement; and Thomas was aware of the expectation. Poor, unknown, ailing, he felt himself summoned to a great task; his youthful letters are filled with an obscure but certain feeling that he is destined for some mysterious vocation; and he never failed to sustain, in his mind, a collaboration with the dead in the magnificent structure of his fame. His father, he wrote, was the unseen, sunken pillar upon which he himself rested.

Fortified by the collective desire of his family, consecrated by his religious faith, the instinct for self-preservation and expansion reached in Carlyle the point where a heroic individualism becomes egotism. His rich and rugged personality was unable to accommodate itself to the necessities of life in society, as it was incapable of making a delicate adjustment to the susceptibilities of another being; for all his treasures of sincere affection, he had the infinite hardness of a character which was unaware of its own hardness. Preoccupied to conquer himself and to con-

MORAL FORMATION

quer ideas, he so strained his energies that he was able to relax far too seldom; the great riddle and the grief of his life had their source in the very principle of his strength and triumph. Bent upon beating into submission a rebellious temperament, upon curing himself of a tenacious disease, the wretched pain of his body and the enervation which comes from pain, he allowed his craving for health to take a preponderant and undue place in the direction of his life. Following upon the uncertainties and agonies of his youth, came a maturity in which his activity was certain of its goal and its value, and in which he enjoyed a health which, if never robust, was dependable; and yet his old age, so long and so glorious, was sombre when it could have been serene, and sombre because he had taken too much to heart the lesson his race had taught him. He had to pay to a law, human or divine, to a law which his religious conscience had not perceived, a retribution for a success which had been too complete; his head had to bow before a strange Nemesis, the fear of which he could not learn from all the wisdom of all his ancestors. He was too late in learning that the disinterested imprudence that love excites is greater than all the salutary properties of prudence; all that nature wishes is the survival of life, so that nature need attach no penalty to the hardening of the self by a too-powerful will to live and gain; but the heart of man has its distinct laws and needs, quite apart from the utilitarian laws of nature and morality; and ignorance of these laws can lead to suffering, if not to death.

II

From his early childhood, Carlyle's mother intended him for the ministry. It seemed there could be no greater, no more satisfying, career for his precocious intelligence.

As a schoolboy, by his tenacious memory and his insatiable desire for knowledge, he made rapid progress. At the village school he learned the elements of English and in the same years, by the kindness of the minister of the dissenting sect to which his parents belonged, he learned the rudiments of Latin. When he was eleven years old, in 1806, he left Ecclefechan to attend the Academy (or high school) of Annan, the nearest town. Here he continued his study of Latin and acquired the bare rudiments of Greek. But, of much greater importance, his aptitude for mathematics now revealed itself and Carlyle became a very estimable mathematician. Meanwhile the lines of his character had become evident; already he was proud, solitary and meditative, with a gravity beyond his years. He seldom cared to play with his classmates, and he had much to bear from their riotous ways. Little as he resembled the dreaming, imaginative nature of Shelley, his schooldays were not unlike Shelley's, embittered by contact with the cruelty of his associates. One day, indeed, driven beyond endurance, he broke the promise he had made to his mother and fought back. Twenty years later in an attempt at a novel he represented the schooldays of his hero, Wotton Reinfred, in the light of his own; and the biography of Teufelsdröckh, the philosopher of *Sartor Resartus*, reproduced in many details, and with the simple transpositions which the change of place required, Carlyle's own first impressions of life. He too had admired the sunsets in which the future Professor Teufelsdröckh was to distinguish against the gold of the sky the vague outlines of bluish hills.

In 1809, as a stage in his preparation for the ministry, he set off on foot to go to Edinburgh and enroll in the university of that city. He was then thirteen years of age. In Edinburgh the students do not live in college as they do at Oxford and Cambridge; and Carlyle had to rent a little room in the city. Every month he received from his family a box of provisions, containing butter, eggs and oatmeal. As an undergraduate he vindicated by his conduct the high hopes he had awakened in high school—he was diligent, earnest, in a word, irreproachable; but, except in mathematics where he won his professor's regard, he failed to distinguish himself in his studies. His failure to do so may in part be ascribed to the antiquated and pedantic education to which he was subjected; but, in part at least, it was the natural outcome of his unyielding character. If it is fair to say that there is some satirical exaggeration in the bitter representation of Edinburgh in *Sartor Resartus*, it is also fair to say that Carlyle got little from his teachers. He was an auditor at the last lectures Dugald Stewart gave, lectures thronged by English students as well as Scottish; but Dugald Stewart was not the man to initiate Carlyle into the study of philosophy. In later years Carlyle spoke of the Scottish school of philosophy with respect but without enthusiasm. Whatever leisure he did not give to theology he gave to a very catholic reading, literary rather than historical or philosophical.

The long summer vacations he would spend in the family home, and refresh himself there after his all but solitary life in the great city. From a distance he watched the active intellectual life of Edinburgh, where the recently founded *Edinburgh Review* was then the centre of a fascinating group of mordant essayists. Carlyle had few friends and his life was a life of the mind and spirit. In

Wotton Reinfred he has unconsciously revealed the secret of his loneliness. Of his hero there he writes, "A keen and painful feeling of his own weakness, added to a certain gloomy consciousness of his real intrinsic superiority, rendered him at once suspicious and contemptuous of others." All the elements of romanticism are here in Carlyle's youth; and, indeed, it was because he himself had suffered from its symptoms that he could, in curing himself, direct his contemporaries to a cure.

His health was still unimpaired. His frame and features had already become quite mature: tall and gaunt, but muscular, with his cheeks reddened by the bracing climate of Ecclefechan, he wore his dark hair long and tangled, as he was always to do.

Four years in Edinburgh satisfied the minimum residence rule in theology: when these were past, Carlyle was obliged to present himself in Edinburgh but once a year for the purpose of test examinations before the faculty in theology. Eager as he was to relieve his parents as soon as possible of the burden of his support, he jumped at the first opportunity of earning a living: in 1814 he was appointed mathematical instructor in the Academy at Annan, his own old school. The following year his father gave up being a mason to become a farmer; and the family moved to Mainhill not far from Ecclefechan. Carlyle was in the neighborhood of his home and continued to go there as often as before. His life in this period might well have been a fairly happy one; the sadness which ran through it, and which was darkened beyond the fact when he came to write of it in his *Reminiscences*, is to be ascribed to the long birth pangs of his

MORAL FORMATION 13

genius, to the awakening of his mind as much as to his disappointed ambition.

Another life, parallel to his own might already have stirred him to emulation if not to jealousy, the life of a countryman of his, a little older than Carlyle and like Carlyle intended for the Church. Edward Irving, even when a brilliant student at Annan, had been hailed by his masters and fellows as a rising star. When Carlyle returned to Annan, he was met with the tale of Irving's more recent successes. They had previously met in Edinburgh and at that first meeting, a potential opposition had been discernible. Chance threw them into the position of rivals. After teaching at Haddington where Jane Welsh, who was to be Carlyle's wife, had been one of his pupils, Irving had been appointed schoolmaster at Kirkcaldy. Some parents who were dissatisfied with his teaching grouped themselves to organise a rival school, and to it, on the recommendation of his former professors at Edinburgh, Carlyle was appointed. A pious enthusiast, as eloquent as he was sincere, but futile none the less, Irving is a weakened impoverished image of what, with the consent of fate, Carlyle might have become; his talent was a readier one than Carlyle's, and all he lacked was genius and a depth of personality. Mastered by a mystical enthusiasm he followed the downward path of popular success, —hysterical preaching, the electrification of crowds, the attempt to perform miracles and to work upon the nerves of his followers. His was a superficial form of the same religious regeneration which was deepened in Carlyle by the flow of profound and spiritual sources. The ephemeral notoriety of Irving, his subsequent misfortunes and his premature death are in the most striking contrast with the slow ascent of Carlyle to a solid influence which stretched farther and farther, growing greater and more fruitful with the years.

The conduct of Irving was however, very generous, generous enough in more than one way to win the gratitude of Carlyle and all whom his fate concerns. He welcomed his rival, showed no animosity and indeed became his best friend. On many occasions he was of invaluable help to Carlyle. Forgetting the conflict in their interests, the two schoolmasters frequently met for long friendly conversations. However important was Carlyle's influence upon Irving's life, it was not to modify his destiny. The influence of Irving upon Carlyle was more important: Irving was his senior, he was more polished, more familiar with the usages of society, and he was able to moderate Carlyle's fierce dislike of the ways of the world. Carlyle borrowed books from him; it was Irving's copy of Gibbon in which he read the great history of Rome. The critical rationalism of Gibbon was among the stimuli to a decision toward which he had long been moving. One day, going to Edinburgh for an annual test, he found that the professor who was to interrogate him was away; and in his absence Carlyle detected an omen and never returned. The last tie which bound his future to the Church of Scotland was thus quietly loosed. The native independence of his genius and the boldness of his now maturing thought made him recoil from any constraint upon his freedom of mind; the state of his religious convictions was not compatible with ecclesiastical discipline, or with the strict literalness with which he thought a minister should interpret the Christian beliefs. To the

MORAL FORMATION

very depths of his being, Carlyle was to remain impregnated with the Hebraic Christianity of his family; as long as his mother lived he left with her an impression that he continued to share her faith. But from the day of this quiet decision, his religion tended more and more to be simply a personal one.

In this period occurred an event which has been the subject of much dispute. Among Irving's pupils was a young girl of good family and cultivated mind—Miss Margaret Gordon. Carlyle met her some months before he left Kirkcaldy. The evidence that we have authorises the opinion that there was a real affection between them; but circumstances and the interposition of Miss Gordon's aunt, who was likewise her guardian, brought about their separation. It is probable, too, that Miss Gordon had a previous attachment; at all events, they parted. She wrote him a letter in which a spirit of the noblest friendship is combined with an extraordinary penetration into his character: with very fine perception of his genius, she foretold the glory he was to achieve and begged him for his own happiness to moderate the fierce energy of his temperament and to try to make himself a more loveable being. Carlyle was to meet her once more, in London, twenty years later, meet her as a happy married woman. Is there an undercurrent of regret in the cautious words in which he evokes his memory of her? Was she still in the foreground of his mind when he had given his heart to another woman? Is she the model of Blumine, the heroine of Teufelsdröckh's romantic love? It would be as rash to state this as a fact as to reject it absolutely. It is highly probable that this first attachment of Carlyle was merely superficial, just the awakening of his imagination; that his love for Miss Gordon left no indelible traces on his heart; that when he fell in love with Jane Welsh he was able to give her the whole of it. Margaret Gordon may nevertheless have provided him with certain of the traits he ascribed to Blumine; and the pathetic end of his adventure with her harmonised with the dramatic theme of *Sartor Resartus.* Some critics have contended that Mrs. Carlyle and she alone was the original of Blumine. Without adopting this position, one may say that in so far as the emotion of Teufelsdröckh is genuine and vital despite its apparent irony, it was in the immediate reality of his love for his young wife that Carlyle found its source. The portrait of his heroine may have been composite, without any division of his heart as he composed it.

Neither Irving's school nor Carlyle's prospered; their methods and their curricula incurred the same reproaches. Tired of their profession, and encouraging each other to break with it, they decided to go up to Edinburgh to seek their fortune. Irving would hope to find some post in the ministry which should be worthy of his talent; and Carlyle would live by giving private lessons and take up the study of the law. They got to Edinburgh in December, 1818. There was nothing in the practice of law to excite Carlyle to enthusiasm; and before long he felt out of his element in the atmosphere of the courts. But all his plans had been upset and his future was uncertain; his was a stubborn nature and he persevered. The period 1819-1822 was a decisive one in his life, a period in which he suffered in body and soul, in which his character completed its formation and his intelligence found in this formation a new force. A moral crisis meanwhile threatened the very balance of his personality, and in its solu-

MORAL FORMATION

tion left him with the structure of his beliefs built on strengthened foundations, the foundation of the deepest energies of his being.

III

The bitter discontent which darkened the youth of Carlyle had many ingredients. There was first of all the lack of consonance between his instincts and the occupations to which he was constrained. And there was a sense that the uncertainty of his projects was a grave disappointment to his family as well as to his personal ambition. His father and mother had stoically acquiesced in his abandonment of the ministry; and they continued to have faith in him even in the darkest hour through which his destiny led him. After all his high hopes and theirs, what was to be his future? He went through "sour days of wounded vanity."

The bar was a possibility, although the preparation for it was a costly prospect. Carlyle set himself vigorously to work, followed lectures and read authorities. But only to find that the principle of Scottish law, like that of English, was one of compromise and routine, calling in its practitioners for no more than prosaic common sense and sceptical prudence; there was no lofty systematic principle here, no indefatigable quest for absolute equity, nothing but a tangled mass of precedents and traditions. Carlyle was too independent, too aspiring, to accommodate himself to what he found; and he definitively gave up the law. Very gradually another prospect was seducing him and here the very depths of his nature were captivated. The vocation of literature was before him too; should he answer its appeal? A perilous future was part of the price he would have to pay, and coupled with that was the contingency of failure. Very slowly Carlyle responded to the appeal. As early as 1819 he was able to find some hack work by which to eke out his scanty resources; his collaboration was accepted by the publisher of the *Edinburgh Encyclopaedia*. For that compilation he wrote between 1819 and 1823 no less than fifteen articles all meticulous and impersonal. Although these beginnings were not in themselves discouraging, the kind of work to which they pointed was barren and thankless. A confused sense of discord between his occupations and his desires continued to dominate Carlyle and with it went an anxiety which was to brood over him for many a year.

Along with his uncertainties, his physical suffering, now from illness and now from overwork, preyed upon his mind. Carlyle set himself the impossible task of continuing to read widely and to write, while he studied law and gave lessons in mathematics. The exertion was too great. He refused to heed the protests of his body; and in spite of the provisions and the allowance from his family, there was more than enough to ruin his health in his crowded days and long vigils, in the continued tension under which he lived and in his anxiety for the future. He fell a victim to insomnia and dyspepsia. His crises of indigestion, frequent and painful already, affected his character and his emotional life in the usual way, and Carlyle became melancholy. So great was the repercussion of his malady upon his nervous system that it is not excessive to describe him as a neurasthenic. At any rate he had all the symptoms of neurasthenia,—a weakened vitality, a deep-seated melancholy and a susceptibility to obsessions. In his *Reminiscences* he pictures Irving and his other friends,

MORAL FORMATION

unaware of his malady, making sport of his woe-begone airs and ways; and the recollection of the bitter misery which had in those early years overwhelmed him, stirred him even in his old age to a great sadness. Young as he then was, the nature of his upbringing, the austerity of the religion to which he had adhered, and his brooding upon death had moulded his soul to be sad rather than happy; in his earlier youth the resilience of his physical constitution had been great enough for him to react and to find in his sheer vitality a source of gaiety; he had even been, at certain times, happy. Henceforward he was to be the prey of black thoughts; and the bitter ironic cast of his mind was to be confirmed and to enclose him all his life.

At the centre of all his sufferings, perhaps at their very source, was the upheaval in Carlyle's religious convictions. Carlyle was one of those who cannot conceive of life without a religion which should provide him with a faith by which he could live. Now his faith had been shaken. Whither, and how far, would doubt conduct him? His spirit, hitherto sheltered in a familiar calm harbor, was spreading over unknown seas. The will to believe was at variance with his critical reason. He had already cut loose from the clergy; now he was cutting loose from the common body of believers. One unforgettable evening he admitted to Irving: "that I did not think as he did of the Christian religion and that it was in vain for me to expect I ever could or should." In his mother's letters, careful as she was not to call him to account for his new attitude, he could divine her regrets; and such a discovery added to his torture. Was it the devil who was tempting him, was it intellectual pride which impelled him, or was it the authentic voice of conscience? Must he, passing from denial to denial, decline to the odious and despicable state of the sceptic? The church offered him a sure future, easy honors, and peace of spirit; many a man to secure her bounties had stifled scruples far graver than his. The spiritual temptation of Carlyle was really the choice of vocation which was now before him; his decision was not difficult; for it was not the material but the spiritual uncertainty and disaster which threatened him, of which he was chiefly afraid. The sum of these spiritual sufferings and perturbations brought about a weakening of Carlyle's energies; there flowed through his spirit a confused but powerful tide of anguish, quenching the fire of his will to live and of his hope in the future. Carlyle was in the Valley of Despair. Of these years he could never speak without a poignant pity for his past anguish, without a sharp contraction of his heart. "*Acti labores*," he writes fifty years later; "yes, but of such a futile, dismal, lonely, dim and chaotic kind, in a scene all ghastly-chaos to one, sad dim and ugly as the shores of Styx and Phlegethon, as a nightmare-dream, become real!" Whither was he going? No fear seemed excessive. The forces of evil were fastening upon him in the form to which his nature was most vulnerable. Cased in the impenetrable mail of their faith, his ancestors had been able to defy the world and its pains and all the snares of the Evil One; but the armour of Carlyle had been shattered and fate had him by the throat; from its shameful degrading grasp he was madly struggling to escape. Was the romantic spirit to conquer yet another great soul, to intoxicate him with its base and bitter joys, the ignoble joys which a wounded soul draws from its own wound? Carlyle was still too strong for such a fate; he collected his forces; the deep-

MORAL FORMATION

est craving of his temperament was not to weaken but to struggle and to conquer. If he would conquer, the full weight of his will must come into play, his whole energy must leap into immediate action, and confront the advance of the malady with a passionate denial. As one might have foretold, the vehement moral upheaval in Carlyle took a religious turn.

The dramatic faculty of Carlyle singled out three great moments in which to centre the stages of his moral crisis. Every reader of his work is familiar with the mystical cycle through which in *Sartor Resartus* the philosopher's mind passes: and every reader knows that the philosopher's experience is a dramatisation of his creator's. *The Everlasting No, The Centre of Indifference, The Everlasting Yea*, in these striking names Carlyle suggests the stages of that progress in which the heroic soul passes from morbid despair to joy and peace. There is a formula here, universally applicable, and specially effective for the man who would be cured of romantic pessimism. Carlyle has foreshortened and simplified the actual story of his spiritual development. The second and third stages are not really elements in his crisis: they follow and complete its solution. It is difficult to discover in his biography any exact correspondences with what they contain, it is difficult to isolate and localise them. In truth they comprehend a great number of transitions, and dramatise what was in fact a gradual process, and not the experience of single days. *The Everlasting No* is the essential element in the crisis: from it the others derive. And *The Everlasting No* corresponds with a particular episode in Carlyle's life, one of such importance that on it we must pause.

Religions have always turned to their own account

those exceptional manifestations of spiritual life which are like an impetuous revolution or a sudden loss of balance. In them they perceive a fruitful, if mysterious, source of spiritual advancement. And the study of normal psychology vindicates their position in a very large measure, although in doing so it tends to deprive these manifestations of any supernatural character. The human personality, the joint product of nature, heredity and environment, has not often achieved a stable equilibrium, a dependable and consistent conception of itself or of the world of objects, by the time when it must come to grips with life; it is suddenly summoned to make new adaptations, and the primary impulse in their formation comes from the instinctive forces of the subconscious. The adolescent, habituated as he has been to an artificial atmosphere, is not really capable of social life, or if he is, divergent tendencies, irreconcilable tendencies, within him, develop intramental conflicts which impede him in the struggle for life. Some transformation is almost always imperative, although its necessity may be felt only in an obscure way. In most persons a succession of gradual adaptations is the mode in which personality and character are definitely shaped and ordered. In some the personal life is too feeble or too vacillating, and no unification is ever achieved. In a third kind of persons, there is a sudden shock, with a violent disturbance, bringing either spiritual elation or spiritual distress or a combination of the two, and producing the effect of a rapid mysterious illumination of the soul. In a few instances, by processes comparable to the dissolution and crystallisation of material elements, the elements of the self are dispersed and rearranged. The new order is sometimes, too, so perma-

MORAL FORMATION

nent as to be indestructible. There are temperaments which are completely renewed; in them ruling passions are annihilated; other passions make their appearance; so coherent, so permanent, in these cases, is the new order of being, that it seems to have been formed previously, and the person so affected is inclined to say that he was not until now aware of his true disposition, and has but now found it. The Catholic Church ascribes such renovation to the operation of divine grace; in Protestant religions it is known as regeneration and accepted as a law of moral life. It is permissible to say that such manifestations—far from being as yet susceptible of clear and complete explanation—no longer appear to the psychologist to suppose a supernatural origin. In the psychologist's view they do not endow the soul with alien energies; they but mark the advance into activity of energies always potential in its life.

This explanation is probably valid for Carlyle. But his moment of supreme crisis is not a regeneration of his personality; it is rather a confirmation of it. His crisis is a negative adaptation, a reaction against the world and himself, undertaken in favor of a deeper self which in this opposition affirms its character. The stable equilibrium to which Carlyle now came was an equilibrium between beliefs already long present in his spirit. Of the moral faith he now achieved he had long borne the seed. Nevertheless *The Everlasting No* was a sudden turn, a "fire baptism." Here was a revolt of Carlyle's will to live, taking arms against the enemy which had been preying upon the very sources of his life, and triumphing over his sufferings by denying their existence. To express this from the religious point of view, the point from which Carlyle envisaged it, his soul purified by renunciation and total disinterestedness, joining in the protest of regenerated humanity against the spirit of everlasting denial, persistently refusing to recognise the dominion of the Evil One over it, escaped from that dominion. "The Everlasting No had said: 'Behold, thou art fatherless, outcast, and the Universe is mine (the Devil's);' to which my whole Me now made answer: '*I* am not thine, but Free and forever hate thee!'"

Nowhere in literature is there a deeper tragic intensity than in this page of *Sartor Resartus*. In the guise of his hero the philosopher, Carlyle has described the essence of his own anguish in the Valley of the Shadow of Death, the bitterness of his agony, the ruin of his hopes and happiness: "The heart within me, unvisited by any heavenly dewdrop, was smouldering in sulphurous, slow-consuming fire. . . . I lived in a continual, indefinite, pining fear; tremulous, pusillanimous, apprehensive of I knew not what; . . . as if the Heavens and the Earth were but boundless jaws of a devouring monster, wherein I, palpitating, waited to be devoured. . . ." One day at last, one sultry Dog-day, the Wanderer was toiling, in the French Capital, "along the dirty little *Rue Saint-Thomas de l'Enfer*, when, all at once, there rose a Thought in me, and I asked myself: 'What *art* thou afraid of? Wherefore, a coward, dost thou forever pip and whimper and go cowering and trembling? Despicable biped! What is the sum-total of the worst that lies before thee? Death? Well, Death; and say the pangs of Tophet too, and all that the Devil and Man may, will or can do against thee! Hast thou not a heart; canst thou not suffer whatso it be; and, as a Child of Freedom, though outcast, trample

MORAL FORMATION 25

Tophet itself under thy feet, while it consumes thee? Let it come, then; I will meet it and defy it!' And as I so thought, there rushed like a stream of fire over my whole soul; and I shook base Fear away from me forever. I was strong, of unknown strength; a spirit, almost a god. Ever from that time, the temper of my misery was changed: not Fear or whining Sorrow saw it, but Indignation and grim fire-eyed Defiance."

Such is the fiction and it differs but little from the fact. Instead of Paris, put Edinburgh and for the Rue Saint-Thomas de l'Enfer substitute Leith Walk. It is a plausible conjecture that Carlyle underwent the experience in the summer of 1822, in July or the early days of August. At this time he was altogether unable to sleep. Every day, going from Moray St., where he lived, to bathe in the Firth of Forth, he passed along Leith Walk. The first meeting between Carlyle and Jane Welsh had come in May, 1821; he had fallen in love with her and they kept up a frequent interchange of letters. His passion, threatened by many obstacles and interrupted by many disagreements, had quickened his moral life and sharpened his consciousness of his unfortunate position. It is impossible not to believe that this passion had swollen that tide of desperate energy which coursed up from his subconscious being. Certain students of his life have proposed a physiological explanation of the crisis; these persons would find in his affirmation of *The Everlasting No*, a moment of reprieve from his digestive troubles. It is likely enough that a craving for physical health did play a part in the revolt of his entire personality in this crisis; and from *The Everlasting No*, his body as well as his soul were to benefit. But there was still ahead of him much physical suffering and many a relapse, and there was no particular moment in which his bodily health markedly improved The materialistic hypothesis is a simplification of the facts, and one with no basis in evidence.

The Everlasting No was a negation of a negation; with it Carlyle denied the Devil, the spirit of falsehood and unbelief; and in this negation there is a potential affirmation. With it his spirit accepted the worst possibilities of fate, and so freed itself from the spell of fear: just as renouncing man's stubborn craving for happiness, sacrificing itself, this soul escaped from the dominion of pain and harm and in its despair achieved a strange peace. Hence the passage by way of *The Centre of Indifference* is just a transition which already points to *The Everlasting Yea*. When we come to the study of *Sartor Resartus*, we shall examine the content of these symbolic phrases, and investigate the life of Carlyle to discover the events with which they correspond. But we have now reached the moment in which the preliminary stage of Carlyle's development is complete; and the first stage in his crisis determined the tendency of his future. In Carlyle will had affirmed itself as an absolute and autonomous force, superior to every force that might oppose it; henceforward his will was free to seek fields for its activity, and was to find its shape and form in the instincts, needs and habits of his inherited temperament. Once this will is reestablished in harmony with adequate positive doctrines, it will supply the centre for the controlling tendencies of Carlyle's temperament, and fix the objective of the new life which without it would have been impossible. *The Everlasting No* may be conceived as a *coup d'état* operated by the vital energy of the man and di-

MORAL FORMATION

rected against all the morbid elements of his soul, against his egocentric sensibility, so prone to grief and inquietude, and against his impotent reason, capable only of doubt and destruction. *The Everlasting No* is a philosophical version of Christian asceticism or, more precisely, of the Puritan primacy of will over understanding. At first sight it seems to have scaled the loftiest heights of Stoicism, to achieve an impassive acceptance of the idea of death and damnation. But if in this supreme decision of Carlyle's conscience there is an essence of heroism and renunciation, it is a volatile essence which was speedily to evaporate. As Carlyle came to conceive it, in the logic of his thought and of his life, this challenge flung by human despair in the face of the threat of eternal destiny was but the violent affirmation of an individual will seeking to know itself, and prepared, in the quest of this knowledge, to ruin all else. The period between 1822 and 1825, the years in which Carlyle wooed and won Jane Welsh are the noblest, the most magnanimous, in his life; for when his belief crystallised there followed a narrowing of his mind and a contraction of his heart. Suddenly restored to the natural line of its development, his personality drew from the annihilation of itself a higher force of resistance and expansion. Courage returned as Carlyle forgot the danger; and in its track joy was not far behind.

This new source of energy, spurting so suddenly and never to dry up, was to fertilise every power in Carlyle's spirit, and his genius was at the contact of this marvelous water to spring into life. Henceforward his character and his doctrine are determined and stable: the central flow, the principle, of all his beliefs and all his efforts was never to be quenched. The substance of his thoughts, in large part dictated by the imperious tendencies of his temperament, was in its remainder to come to him from the literature and philosophy of Germany.

CHAPTER II

GERMAN INFLUENCE

I

CARLYLE learned to read French in his early youth. During his stay with Irving at Kirkcaldy in 1816 he read "the small Didot French classics in quantity." Among the articles he prepared for the *Edinburgh Encyclopaedia* were those on Montaigne, Montesquieu, Necker and Pascal. In 1819 he was reading d'Alembert and quoting him with approval. In January, 1820, he tried in vain to dispose to the *Edinburgh Review* of a criticism of the Swiss scholar Pictet's theory of gravitation. In 1822 he translated a mathematical treatise of the geometer Legendre. He spoke French, however, without fluency and with a marked foreign accent, as he discovered when he visited Paris in 1824; but even then his imagination was greatly stirred by the monuments and reminders of the Revolution, and he walked about the theatre in which that great drama had been played, with the most alert curiosity. And before he undertook to write its history, among his early essays, he composed studies of Voltaire and Diderot. Without being able to determine exactly what he may have read, we may say that his acquaintance with things French was extensive enough. The great writers of the seventeenth century appear to have left him indifferent; but the Encyclopaedists and their Scottish and English followers affected his mind to a degree. The French writers of the eighteenth century reinforced Hume and Gibbon in their tendency to strip Carlyle of a belief in dogmatic Christianity. Another influence, working to the same ends but more obscurely, should be mentioned: in 1830 Carlyle translated the pamphlet of Saint-Simon on the "Nouveau Christianisme" and declared that in it there were "several strange ideas, not without a large spice of truth." At that time he was already engaged upon *Sartor Resartus*.

What did Carlyle owe to Rousseau? A debt more precise, certainly, than those we have indicated. In the lectures on Heroes Rousseau has his place along with Johnson and Burns. It must have been with many reservations that Carlyle admired Rousseau, believing as he did that Rousseau's doctrine was that of a madman, and that the Revolution toward which it pointed was the work of the mad. Nevertheless he found in Rousseau a spark of the celestial fire, the supreme virtue of earnestness, and an ability to reach in certain matters the rockbed of reality. While the hearts and minds of his contemporaries were drying into a purely artificial state, Rousseau believed in the natural, and freed himself from the deceptive fumes of intellectual pride. In his appeal to elemental forces, he struck in Carlyle a sympathetic chord.

Through his defects, Rousseau perfectly exemplifies the French mind; through his virtues he is not merely isolated from the French mind, but its direct opposite. Carlyle admires him as an exception with no power to soften his attitude toward the French. This is not the place to develop the history of Carlyle's relations with the French mind—to show how his hasty comprehensive judgments upon France grew and were nourished. It is enough to state that along with almost all his British contemporaries he saw in France the embodiment of the spirit of rational negation. It did not occur to him to cherish for France any gratitude for the part French thought had played in enabling him to cast off the shackles of dogma; he was content to let France bear the brunt of the passionate reaction which threw him back toward some positive belief. As he built up his doctrine upon a series of absolutist moral affirmations, he became aware that directly opposed to this doctrine was a whole movement toward the analysis of ideas, a movement of which the English Utilitarians were the immediate representatives, but of which the French thinkers of the 18th century were the chief sources. From this awareness flowed the persistently aggressive expression of his enmity toward French thought and culture, an enmity in which his temperament was at one with his doctrine. In the French mind he found one of the terms of an antithesis which is omnipresent in nature and life: it is the negative term, almost identical with evil, error and sin. The destructive activity of this mind is a weapon of Providence: but even in its periods of great effectiveness, it is a sorry thing. The French worship of logic and tinsel condemns it to worldly philosophy and rhetoric, and seduces it into rendering to the understanding the homage which is due to the reason alone. Carlyle in these opinions is echoing the old German controversy in which Teutonic solidity was opposed to Gallic frivolity. Carlyle, as in so many matters, failed to elaborate his own ideas in respect of France: he merely assimilated those that others had discovered, fortifying them with the vigor of his emphasis, the originality of his temperament, and the tremendous force which comes from overwhelming sincerity.

In Germany Carlyle found the true home of his mind. After his Puritan inheritance, the German influence was the most important element in his moral development. From the very first, he was conscious of profound instinctive attraction to Germany, and not once was this attraction, which grew steadily more compulsive, broken. Carlyle learned German between 1819 and 1821, at Edinburgh and Mainhill, during the darkest years of his youth. His self-appointed task was not easy: his teacher was a mere makeshift and it was hard to get books. German was a very rare accomplishment in Great Britain. One could have counted on one's fingers the number of literary men who could read it—Coleridge, Scott, William Taylor and a very few more. Carlyle's interest in German was aroused by Madame de Staël's treatise and by certain studies in mineralogy in which he took a transient interest. It is not idle to use in this connection the words *instinct* and *presentiment*. A vague notion of the specific distinctive qualities of the German genius was abroad; every one associated it with mysticism and this in itself was sufficient to attract Carlyle. He bent all his energy to his task, employed his remarkable processes of assimilation and was very soon able to read and write German. Later on, by the same method, he acquired, although less adequately, Italian and Spanish. Very quickly his knowledge of German, his contact with the contemporary works of the German genius, began to take a very important part in his life. Indeed, in a letter that every critic quotes, he wrote in August, 1820, of "a new heaven

GERMAN INFLUENCE

and a new earth" revealed to him in his hasty study of German literature.

In 1820 Carlyle had not yet a close enough knowledge of the German language for a methodical study of the literature; and his expression must be taken as the excited report of a discoverer who looks over virgin lands and divines their extent and their fertility. Even when he was engaged in his translations from Goethe he had not, as he admits in his *Reminiscences*, a perfect knowledge of the language. He was to achieve that much later. Several phases may be distinguished in Carlyle's intercourse with the German writers. In spite of his immediate enthusiasm, he required some years to adapt himself to a foreign genius, to initiate himself into the complex thought of Kant or of *Wilhelm Meister* or the altogether alien spirit of the mature Goethe. In his letters and the other records of his intellectual life between 1820 and 1826, we can follow the stages of his awakening, or the ripening of his admiration which is not the less sincere for the gradual nature of its development.

At his advice, Jane Welsh undertook to learn German, and their correspondence was soon studded with German idioms. And Carlyle became sensible of the practical value of his rare talent. The romantic movement as it changed the intellectual and emotional atmosphere of the nation, had brought out artistic harmonies between English and German literature, harmonies which had long lain unregarded; the craving for works of fancy and imagination was equally strong in the two countries; and the English public was very curious to know what was being written in Germany. This curiosity was not at first very discriminating: the work of Goethe and Schiller was less valued than that of the popular novelists with their ruined castles, their ghosts and ghouls, and all the apparatus of melodrama. Later however the favor won by these latter works was shared by the more serious writers. Carlyle's struggle to make his name in literature, long and painful as it was, was relieved by the opportunities offered him by the new taste for German things: for several years he subsisted almost entirely on what he earned by his translations and adaptations of German works.

In January, 1821, he proposed to a publisher that he should translate Schiller's *Thirty Years' War*. In April, 1822, he wrote, for the *New Edinburgh Review*, an article on *Faust*. His first important work was his *Life of Schiller*, which appeared first in the *London Magazine* (1823-4) and was published in book form in 1825. His translation of *Wilhelm Meister*, with an introduction, was published in 1824; and a letter from Goethe brought him at the end of 1824 an unexpected consecration, opening a correspondence in which Carlyle plays the part of a disciple. In 1827 he brought out his *Specimens of the German Novel* in which he included extracts, with prefatory notices, from Richter, Tieck, Lamotte-Fouqué and Hoffmann, as well as the entire second part of *Wilhelm Meister*. In 1830 he was meditating a translation of *Faust*. Further, among his critical essays, a very great number relate to German literature; among these the most notable are the studies of *Richter* (1827) and *The State of German Literature* (1827), *Goethe* (1828), *Novalis* (1829), a second essay on Richter (1830), *Schiller* (1831), *The Nibelungen* (1831), *Goethe's Works* (1832). He even projected a general history of German

GERMAN INFLUENCE 35

literature, and wrote certain fragments of it which he used as periodical articles.

II

It was primarily through her philosophy that Germany influenced Carlyle. That philosophy provided his exacting conscience with the theoretical justifications it required; and through its transcendental idealism it invested his Christian morals with a metaphysical halo. His imagination clothed with life the abstract conclusions of Kant, developing from the doctrine of the subjectivity of sensory images a poetic vision of the universe. The writer as well as the thinker in Carlyle was nourished and excited by the intellectual intoxication in Schelling's mystical dreamings.

It is established that Carlyle read Kant; but he does not seem to have achieved an exact understanding of the various parts or of the logical continuity of Kant's system. It was his custom to speak with respect of the Königsberg philosopher, although he could not always conceal a certain distrust; and there is no doubt that Kant was the model for many of the traits of the strange and wonderful Teufelsdröckh. But even if we make allowances for the popular intention of his exposition of Kant's doctrine in *The State of German Literature,* we cannot but discern in it a false perspective. The emphasis falls not upon the critical and destructive work of Kant, but on his efforts at a positive reconstruction. What Carlyle finds in Kant is neither the proof of the relativity of all knowledge nor the condemnation of metaphysics: he finds in him a new and bolder metaphysic. Like so many of Kant's

German disciples he relates the teaching of the master to its religious inspiration, which was indeed the secret principle of Kant's thought; but in so doing, and in allowing that thought to be refracted by his own dogmatic temperament, he overstressed certain of its tendencies and missed what was most fruitful in Kant. The complicated mechanism of perception and judgment, the theory of the categories, and the analysis of the forms which condition the substance of thought—all of these are neglected. What comes out most clearly from Carlyle's exposition is the distinction between reason and understanding: and, the distinction made, Carlyle proceeds to attribute to reason an unlimited power of immediate intuitive knowledge. The moral mysticism of Kant, cautious and austere, the mysticism which is merely implicit in the postulates of practical reason, colors Carlyle's whole presentation of his thought and transforms it to the prophecy of an heroic seer.

Two themes fundamental to his thought Carlyle took either from Kant himself or from the school he founded. The first is the subjectivity of space and time. Clearer than many of the other elements in Kant's system, the doctrine of subjective forms captured Carlyle's imagination, and the immateriality of the real became an article of his creed. With such a belief to start from, he fell an easy victim to the intellectual intoxication of Schelling and Fichte, so different from the severe sobriety of Kant. An inevitable fusion occurred in his mind between the transcendental negation of matter, and the passionate preference of Christianity for the things of the spirit and the mind. Puritanism, more than other forms of Christianity, had stressed the distinction between mind and body; an

GERMAN INFLUENCE 37

austere and savage idealism had replaced the discreet spirituality to which more elaborate religions still held; and now what a wonderful thing it was for so great a natural Puritan as Carlyle to find in the speculations of the deepest thinker of the age the justification of his distrust and contempt for the body and its desires. Now, of a sudden, all bodily things faded from real existences to empty shadows; and the problems of conduct, the strength or weakness of the moral will, became, as never before, the supreme, the unique preoccupation of men. It was no longer admissible that the intellect should hesitate between the physical world, the seat of the great tempter, and the realm of ends, the realm of Providence. In that decisive moment in his moral development, *The Everlasting No*, the moment in which his heroic courage routed all his physical terrors, Carlyle had the help of the new heaven and the new earth revealed to him in German thought. The Devil and his tyranny, all suffering and doubt, were dissipated with the dissipation of matter; and the soul of Carlyle, released from a crushing burden, bounded with a delicious sense of freedom.

Meanwhile his imagination was enthralled by the grandiose and tragic visions to which idealism opened the way. The abstract conception of the unreality of space and time dizzied him with a sense of the infinite; but Carlyle's imagination set to work at once to clothe this conception with concrete images, images of a singular magnificence and intensity. Over a dark and fathomless abyss, in a series of flashes, our ephemeral human life developed; from the abyss it came, to the abyss it must return, and the immense and dazzling scene in which it exists is but a delusion and a lie; at each single moment, to some one of the created souls, the dazzling scene would vanish, and extension and duration sink into eternal night. "Thus, like some wild-flaming, wild-thundering train of Heaven's Artillery, does this mysterious MANKIND thunder and flame in long-drawn, quick-succeeding grandeur, through the unknown Deep. Thus, like a God-created, fire-breathing Spirit-host, we emerge from the Inane; haste stormfully across the astonished Earth; then plunge again into the Inane" (*Sartor Resartus*). More than any other, it was the enigma of time which haunted Carlyle. His most frequent and most emphatic images are those which are inspired by the mystery of that which for our human senses is not, suddenly comes into being, and as suddenly is not again, while past, present and future are nevertheless all comprehended and consumed by a single eternity. As Carlyle watches the dissolution under the rays of reason of all the forms and colors in the tranquillising reality of the sensible world, as he watches the shadows of the past, the dreams of the future and the living familiar appearances of the present, all fused in a single inconceivable and dizzying ideality, terror falls upon his imagination. It was inevitable that the register of his emotions, the planes of his thought, the tones of his brush, should be unified in a simple and indeed monotonous opposition, in an essential unescapable contrast. For his hallucinated vision, nature was always dissolving, under a strong light, to vanish into the dark background of nothing; the truth of appearances was but a spectral illusion and the sensible world but a dance of phantoms. An imagination of Rembrandt's sort, the play of lights and shadows, sudden swift resurrections of the past, irruptions into homely certitude of a devastating metaphysical irony,—these are the artistic and literary traits of Carlyle, and they are as much the fruit of his study of German philosophy as of his own temperament. His most poignant moments are those in which he is tortured by a regret for that which has been and is not, and yet in some fashion continues, and must always continue, to be. He seems to have anticipated that modern theory of the memory which represents it as the very reality of things and not their faded copy.

The second Kantian theme in Carlyle is that of the categorical imperative. Duty was for him the most immediately evident, the most certain, of the data of intuition and experience; every fibre of his being was clamoring for an active obedience to some higher command. His Puritan conscience might have been sufficient without the great corroboration of Kant; the law of work might have implied the law of duty. But the corroboration of Kant was far too authoritative, far too solemn, not to be eagerly welcomed and adopted. By its help the basis of morality was placed beyond all contingencies, above all criticism. The weight of Kant's arguments can be divined in the lifelong immovable certainty with which Carlyle affirmed the law of duty; if the influence of the Kantian argument cannot be isolated, it can be felt.

More obvious is Carlyle's debt to Fichte; for in Fichte he found in happy conjunction the doctrine of Kant and an original philosophic personality with whom he spontaneously felt himself in accord. He quotes Fichte more often than Kant, and for the loftiness of his genius he professes the most pious respect. "So robust an intellect, a soul so calm, so lofty, massive and immovable, has not mingled in philosophical discussion since the time of

Luther." From Fichte Carlyle received the explicit revelation of idealism, in particular of the idealistic theory of the proper relation between the divine spirit, the natural world and the spirit of man. The vast stage of space and time, unreal as Kant had seen it to be, was upheld in the devouring void and incessantly renewed, by the hidden presence of the Divine. For Fichte the sensible world, instinct with the emanation of God, took on a new value as an emblem. With formulae which were forever changing, the generations of men had sought to interpret the secret sense of life; and the explanation of its mystery was the specific task of great men, priests, philosophers, or writers.

"According to Fichte, there is a 'Divine Idea' pervading the visible Universe; which visible Universe is indeed but its symbol and sensible manifestation, having in itself no meaning, or even true existence independent of it. To the mass of men this Divine Idea of the world lies hidden: yet to discern it, to seize it, and live wholly in it, is the condition of all genuine virtue, knowledge, freedom; and the end, therefore, of all spiritual effort in every age. Literary Men are the appointed interpreters of this Divine Idea; a perpetual priesthood, we might say, standing forth generation after generation, as the dispensers and living types of God's everlasting wisdom, to show it in their writings and actions, in such particular form as their own particular times require it in. For each age, by the law of its nature, is different from every other age, and demands a different representation of the Divine Idea, the essence of which is the same in all; so that the literary man of one century is only by mediation and reinterpretation applicable to the wants of another. But in

GERMAN INFLUENCE

every century, every man who labors, be it in what province he may, to teach others, must first have possessed himself of the Divine Idea, or, at least, be with his whole heart and his whole soul striving after it."

In this celebrated passage, and elsewhere, it is less the esoteric teaching of Fichte, the proud and rigorous individualism of his early works, it is rather the more popular ideas of the philosopher that Carlyle expounds. When he became the counsellor and advocate of the regenerated German nation, Fichte oriented his system in the practical direction of moral teaching; in his ideas nature had the dignity of a matter in which the divine spirit worked through men; and the sequence of the ages and of mystical revelations in time was presented as offering to the Fatherland a future so grand as to compensate for the mediocrity of its past. The practical idealism of this doctrine, so nerving and stimulating, brought to Carlyle just the nourishment that his soul required; he assimilated it and it became the substance of his thought. The entire metaphisic of Carlyle, the whole of the "natural supernaturalism" of *Sartor Resartus* is contained in germ in the passage quoted above. The spiritual quality in all that is, the immanence of the divine, the value of nature as a symbol of reality, the flow of forms, the necessary succession of beliefs and dogmas, the mystical rôle of the men of thought—all these essentials in Carlyle's general philosophy, he summarises here and ascribes to Fichte. He is right, on the whole, and we must admit the extent of the debt which by implication he acknowledges here. *Sartor Resartus* is the enthusiastic elaboration of a metaphysic grafted upon the idea of universal symbolism.

Further, in revealing the prophetic mission of the inspired man of thought, charged with the perpetual readjustment of formulae to the changing forms of the real, Fichte had prepared the way for the theory of the hero. Between the man who seizes upon the "Divine Idea" and his fellows, an abyss exists; a supernatural baptism consecrates every genius king of the realm of mind. As it has been pointed out, the natural movement of Fichte's doctrine tended to make of it an apology for the principle of authority, as well as for the specific authority of the state. Starting from a pure individualism he arrives at conclusions almost perfectly collectivist.

"To compel men to obedience to law, to bring them by sheer force into this obedience, is not merely the right but the sacred duty of whoever has the necessary knowledge and power. In case of need a single individual has the right and the duty so to compel the whole of mankind; for mankind has no right at all, no liberty whatever, to act against right."

Such is the language of Fichte in his *Staatslehre*, a book which we know to have been read by Carlyle. The importance of such teaching in confirming his temperamental inclination to authority, is great: it brings once again to the instinctive tendencies of Carlyle the high sanction of transcendental thought. To Fichte Carlyle owed not only the core of his speculative philosophy, but the encouragement of his political and social philosophy in its natural trend toward the dogma of might.

III

Broader still and more penetrating was Goethe's influence upon Carlyle, an influence which affected his entire personality. Goethe stood out in Carlyle's mind as the greatest prophet and man of letters in modern times, a model for the life of the mind and for the life of men in society. Goethe's first letter opened a lively correspondence and an exchange of presents; and although the two men never saw each other, they rapidly developed a friendly relation. Carlyle was perfectly sincere in his expression of reverent admiration for Goethe; and Goethe was quick to appreciate the effectiveness of that moral power which was the essential element of Carlyle's genius. Patriarch and Levite established an intercourse marked by reciprocal respect. There was no abjection in Carlyle's rôle; if he was disposed to reverence, he was incapable of servility: for all his sense of what he owed to Goethe he never forgot what he owed to his own personality.

Besides, the vigor of his temperament forbade any abjection: the only influences it allowed him to undergo were those consonant with itself. He could refract the ideas of others but not when they were inconsistent with his own instincts. He did not enter at once, and he never entered completely, into the spirit of Goethe: his criticisms of the author when he was engaged in the translation of *Wilhelm Meister* are there to prove the resistance of Carlyle; and if he went out to meet the mind of Goethe and to adapt himself to its modes, at the same time he adapted that mind to tally with his deepest instincts. His distortion of Goethe's teachings and even of Goethe's personality was no less remarkable than his distortions of Kant. It is true that Carlyle was not impervious to Goethe the poet and the artist; many a time he applauded the careful and exquisite music of his verse, the grandeur and the beauty of his imagination, but he preferred to quote from Goethe's prose, and it was to Goethe the thinker that he stood in debt. Whether in prose or poetry it was to moral values that Carlyle was always most alert; and it was the moral value of Goethe's doctrine, as he interpreted it, which won his heart. It cannot be denied that Carlyle took pleasure in Goethe's representations of contemporary life, in his elevation of humdrum reality to the pure air of ideal art; but the source of his pleasure was moral, it was a pleasure in the reminder to a materialised humanity that a divine splendor lay hidden behind the veil of appearances. It was not that he liked Goethe's realism: what he liked was Goethe's idealisation of the real. At no stage did Carlyle attain to an independent and disinterested perception of the values of art.

Carlyle was acutely aware of Goethe's easy eclecticism, and the boundless tolerance of his mind; and he has found just and beautiful words to celebrate the serenity of that soul which had known so many tumults and known how to quiet them. But what he respected in Goethe's tolerance was, if one may so express it, its moral value, its implicit counsel of patience and resignation. In no other way could Carlyle's genius, so triumphant in its intolerance, so savage in its hatred, have found itself in sympathy with the perfect liberalism of Goethe. As one might foresee, he colors with Christian asceticism Goethe's favorite precept of renunciation: instead of a sacrifice of the inferior to the superior possibilities in life, he interprets it as a mutilation, an amputation from the spirit of a number of its faculties. Culture he assimilates to the old Puritan concept of discipline, and Goethe's central idea of a complete and harmonious development of the self, an idea without which his moral system is travestied beyond recognition, is thrust from sight with the whole pagan naturalistic aspect of his thought. Carlyle writes in his journal, in 1831: "Which is to stand higher, the Beautiful or the Good? Schiller and Goethe seem to say the former, as if it included the latter and might supersede it: how truly I can never well see." Later on, he was to be disconcerted by Sterling's thesis that Goethe was a pagan, a dispassionate artist; and on this point the two friends never could agree. It was natural and indeed inevitable that Carlyle should always and everywhere force the element of Hebraism, as Arnold was to say, to predominate over that of Hellenism.

The influence of Goethe on Carlyle was, then, canalised by the temper of the disciple; and in the canalisation it gained in force. It was far from Carlyle's way to insert into his mind or his work any of Goethe's elegant epicureanism; but from Goethe's delight in action and from his insistence on the mastery and subjugation of the instincts Carlyle drew heavily. Goethe (or these elements in Goethe) was a living embodiment of his ideal, and, as such, a priceless encouragement to his moral energy. Carlyle's consciousness of his own personality and mission was wonderfully intensified by his intellectual communion with so admirable and noble a being, and this communion was the closer because Carlyle was among the first in England to hail the preeminence of his master.

Carlyle was Goethe's disciple in a moral sense. The article on Goethe written in 1828 defines Goethe's rôle as the offering to the whole of Europe of the proof that a literary career might shine with the brightest idealism from beginning to end. Goethe appears as the priest of a new religion, an optimism which induces men to moral activity, and through this activity conducts them to a new confidence in the values of life, a confidence which will make faith and hope flower on the ruins of older faiths. Goethe is the healer of suffering souls, the exorcist of romanticism. Tumult and rebellion were the temptations of his youth, but their barren melancholy and negations could not satisfy that great mind; and from his maturity Europe can learn how to cure itself of the *Weltschmerz*. After the tempestuous insurrection of *Werther* came the broad tolerant humanity of *Wilhelm Meister* and of *Faust*. "Close thy Byron, open thy Goethe," Carlyle was to write a little later in *Sartor Resartus*. To Goethe he owed not only his escape from the "Satanic school," but his grasp upon the value of affirmation: Goethe is no small agent in *The Everlasting Yea*. And Carlyle voices his gratitude in touching and eloquent words; Goethe has taught him, helped him "out of spiritual obstruction, into peace and light." To Goethe he owes "a change from inward imprisonment, doubt and discontent, into freedom, belief and clear activity." Of such a triumph, Goethe himself is a supreme example; one could almost say, the only example. Forty years later, when he wrote his reminiscences, Carlyle was as prompt as in his youth to proclaim his discipleship: and this was but just, for to Goethe he owed more for his marvelous measure of strength and peace and renunciation than to any other being.

In other fields besides the moral, Goethe's mind left its impress upon Carlyle's. His general thought is an element in the metaphysic of *Sartor Resartus*. His pantheism was a richer, warmer, more imaginative and poetic thing than Fichte's, revealing more surely the symbolic value of nature as a garment of the deity. There is more than an echo of this pantheism in the images Carlyle chooses to illustrate the relation between appearance and reality. It is impossible, too, not to be struck by the passage in which Carlyle describes the mind of Goethe as "singularly emblematic"; and comments upon his constant tendency "to transform into *shape*, into *life*, the opinion, the feeling that may dwell in him." This is nothing short of a description of the poetic faculty, not as a matter of metaphors and tropes but as an activity which is the quintessence of mind. "Everything has form, everything has visual existence; the poet's imagination *bodies forth* the forms of things unseen, his pen turns them to *shape*." These methods of thought are Carlyle's at least as eminently as Goethe's. His whole work is studded with their expression: his philosophic originality is not in the discovery of ideas, but in their imaginative transposition. Doubtless he became more keenly aware of his gift and the necessary way of his nature, as he analysed their analogues in Goethe. In the same way Carlyle sharpened his sense of a universal becoming by his contact with the common fund of German idealism. The method of Fichte and Schelling and later of Hegel also showed him systematic applications of this sense; but Goethe had already given him a vague notion—for it was implicit in the process of Goethe's thought—of the evolution of forms in time, and of the necessary transformation of beings. Even the theory of heroism owes something to Goethe, to his ideas on individual genius and on the prophetic rôle of the man of letters.

Second only to the influence of Goethe was that of Jean Paul Richter. Here Carlyle was aware of a peculiarly close affinity—but an affinity of a fairly narrow range.

Much as Carlyle owed to Richter's thought, his greater debt was to his art and temperament. Through Richter's example, Carlyle became more conscious of the purport of his humor; and by Richter, too, he was helped to the formation of a highly artificial style, which later became his natural form of expression and indeed his authentic manner.

In spite of their superficial differences, the moral natures of Goethe and Richter seemed to Carlyle of a piece. In his first essay on Richter (1827) Carlyle does not say as much as this; he seems to be caught by an impression of Richter's broad free humanism and his vast originality. This is the transitory stage in his intellectual life when Carlyle seemed to succeed in capturing Goethe's tolerance, and realising his notion of culture: "Let each become all that he was created capable of being; expand, if possible, to his full growth; . . . and show himself at length in his own shape and stature, be these what they may." The supreme end of all true culture, is "a harmonious development of being." But by 1830, in a more detailed study, Carlyle's sympathies modify the figure of Richter to bring it into line with an ideal in his own mind. Richter, too, had wrestled with the question of questions; Richter had built upon pain and the experience of evil and the disquiet of heart and soul, a philosophy of life which assured him a quiet spirit, self-controlled, happy, compassionate. Richter, as well as Goethe, had revealed a cure for romanticism. With Goethe only moral pain had been really acute; but in Richter Carlyle found a range of anguish and struggle much more like his own. Richter too had battled with society and with life, and had a youth clouded by poverty and self-mistrust. An involuntary

GERMAN INFLUENCE

affection operated in Carlyle's mind to emphasise less striking affinities with Richter.

Richter seemed to him to be the most perfect example of intuitive intelligence; of that habit of mind which to discover the kernel of truth in things will violently shatter the husk, never pausing to lay siege to them by logic, but preferring to take them by force. There could be no truer formula for the instinctive methods of Carlyle's own intelligence. To the gradual prudent approach, to the effort to see things clearly, to the analysis of rational reflection, Carlyle was to oppose instantaneous victories, the invincible certitude of intuitive knowledge. He was all his life to be one of the most contemptuous opponents that rationalism has ever had. Richter, along with Fichte and Goethe, offered for Carlyle the very material of idealism. The idea of a spiritual essence at the very heart of the world, and susceptible of a thousand appearances, this is everywhere in Richter and it is everywhere in Carlyle's study of Richter. The theme of the "philosophy of clothes," in the year 1830, the year in which *Sartor Resartus* was conceived, crops up at every point in this study.

Humor was native to Carlyle: in his moral being and in his temperament it had those deep roots which make it, in popular estimation, a characteristic of the Scottish mind. Fresh sharp observation of the picturesque and comic elements in mind and body, the curt sententious expression of what is observed, all the more effective because of a natural gravity, these elements of humor Carlyle shared with the rest of his family and his race. He himself has clearly proved their existence in his father. But the humor of Richter is something far more rare,—the individual fusion of a very rich sensibility with a conscious genius: the spontaneous exercising of a faculty for comic observation, a taste for the raciness of the soil, are here combined with the countless caprices of an art in which every incoherence, every fantasy, is deliberate. Even Carlyle fails, as so many others have failed before or since, to define the humor of Richter: he contents himself with relating it to Richter's playful sympathy with all forms of reality. But if he fails to define it, he has a lively enthusiastic enjoyment of it, as well as an eager perception of its presence; and the fragmentary traits in the picture he draws of it are of the greatest value, revealing and elaborating as they do the attitude of mind and the methods of expression which were to characterise his own later works.

In a later chapter an effort will be made to describe the original traits of Carlyle's style as that style takes form in *Sartor Resartus*. Here it will be sufficient to say that in this style the influence of Richter is subtly combined with spontaneous tendencies. Carlyle's indebtedness to Richter in this respect must not be exaggerated: there are other influences of no less importance, and Carlyle himself liked to think that the chief source of his own style, was the vivid rapid idiom of his father's home. Nevertheless in 1827 and 1830 his analyses of Richter's language are too penetrating not to be indicative of an uncommonly deep interest. Among the first instances of Carlyle's later manner, the very clearest are in these papers on Richter. The always unpredictable evolution of Richter's writings, their sudden stops, their digressions always with some hidden design, their combination of lyricism and humor, their golden moments, their flashes of tenderness, their ironic tone, their mock gravity,—all these qualities Carlyle praises, and all these qualities are in as large a measure his own. He divines in Richter the complete development of a highly individual and original art, because the elements of Richter's art, its moral and elemental germs, are natural to him as well. Force, independence, tragic violence, lyrical intensity, intuitive thinking, imaginative exuberant writing, impotence in regular balanced expression, —this last accepted as a virtue—the eloquent energy of sudden breaks and emphatic discords, these, Carlyle feels to be the very materials of his own intellectual and literary genius. Later on, when his nature is fully aware of itself, Carlyle will be able to write as in 1830 he can but think. Deeper than the influence of Swift or of Sterne, Richter's contagion was the deciding factor in the transformation of Carlyle's style. His primitive impulses, the suggestions of his individual temperament, the spontaneous rhythms of his sensibility, under the influence of his German model took shape and form in a collection of mental and verbal traits which were so true to his personality that they cannot be detached from it.

IV

A less incomplete study of the German influence on Carlyle would notice other writers: Schiller, for example, who was the first of the Germans to win Carlyle's admiration, and whose life he was later to write; Novalis as well, whose mysticism captured his imagination, and to whom he devoted an essay of more eloquence than true perspicacity. Novalis," he writes in his journal, "is an anti-mechanist,—a deep man,—the most perfect of modern spirit seers." To Herder, too, Carlyle is in debt. As

early as 1826 he was impressed, if a little disconcerted, by the audacity of Herder's philosophy of history, and that philosophy may well have favored the growth of Carlyle's own ideas of development in religion. The rich apparel of poetry and pantheism in which Schelling clothed the transcendental philosophy must also have had its appeal and influence. Were it not that in speaking to Sterling—in 1826 it is true, when his intellectual horizon was already beginning to narrow—he had expressed mistrust of, and even hostility to, Schleiermacher, we could wish to add the name of that preeminent apostle of spiritual liberal Christianity. With each of these writers as with Goethe, Richter and Fichte, there are specific points of contact, but it is impossible here to study the details of Carlyle's intellectual parentage. It is possible, however, and necessary, to sketch the corporate influence of German thought, as distinct from that of particular German thinkers.

At the time when Carlyle came of age, romanticism was already in possession of most European literatures. These had drawn new life from a return to the national past, and from a discovery and practice of new emotions. Whatever unity or resemblance the romantic literatures had by their parallel innovations, sets them in strong contrast to the classical spirit which one century earlier was stamped on all literary works, and in whose diffusion the culture and prestige of France had been the chief agency. The literature of reason, analysis and order had been displaced by that of emotion and intensity; and in so far as the Northern nations had given the models of the latter, its victory may be conceived as the victory of the Germanic spirit. In its triumph are involved that of intuition

GERMAN INFLUENCE

and melancholy, that of the tragic, that of the clouded and the sentimental. The love of these qualities, already latent in other nations, was roused from a slumber of centuries by a breath blown across the frontiers, so that the revival did not seem rooted in the soil. An international, a continental culture came into being, and a Frenchwoman like Madame de Staël could say that Germany seemed to her the land of her birth. In England two generations of poets had, by an unflagging creative force, revived the national poetry; and one of the greatest of these poets had found in the doctrines of German idealism a deep congruity with his own idealistic theology. But the wayward spirit of Coleridge, the instability and versatility of his character, the fragmentary quality of his work, its reputed obscurity, too, had restricted the number of his disciples and the growth of his fame; and he was quite unable, in the realm of thought, even to check the amazing progress of a movement contrary and hostile to his ideas.

In the years when romanticism was winning a hold upon the literature of England, political and moral thought was dominated by utilitarian doctrines, doctrines which still reflected the temper and tendency of the eighteenth century. The Utilitarians called for the resolution of reality into its simplest elements. By their immediate sources, the Utilitarians can be called a native English school; but their ultimate sources are in that continental rationalism which was already defeated in the countries across the Channel: for there is an evident harmony between Utilitarianism and the doctrines of the Encyclopaedists, between the sceptical and anti-religious temper of the Utilitarians and that of Condillac. It was inevitable that Utilitarianism should succeed, for it was but a formulation of the vast interests and the great social needs of the industrial middle class, just rising to its full stature. About the year 1825, it may be said, Utilitarianism made up in ethics and psychology, in politics and metaphysics, a system of ideas bold, new, irresistible, destined to a success which seemed likely to be lasting. Men of theory like Bentham and James Mill, combined with men of practice like the group of philosophical radicals to assure its success. In Carlyle's own generation the chief agent in this success was John Stuart Mill. It is to be remembered that during the first quarter of the century, the deep-laid incompatibility between the utilitarian and the romantic had not been detected; and in many of the poets there was a very complex intercalation of elements taken from these two.

Against Utilitarianism and all its works, Carlyle was to lead a crusade, a lifelong fight; and for his crusade he was to find his weapons in the armoury of German idealism. His whole life's work may be regarded as an effort to free the nation from the popression of Utilitarianism; and more than any other agency, Carlyle was to be the force which would displace that doctrine by a system or a spirit opposed to it. Through his efforts and the subsequent efforts of his disciples he was to bring a new atmosphere into England. Certain theses which were already victorious in literature, Carlyle victoriously upheld in the realms of thought and action; and opponent that he was of the egotism of Byron, he was an unconscious continuator of Wordsworth and Coleridge. His achievement thus was twofold; from an English point of view he is a great force in the defeat of romanticism; from a continental point of view, he is greater as a force opposing and destroying a temper which had lasted longer in England than elsewhere, and which was retarding the spiritual and intellectual development of that country. Consciously hostile to rationalism, a gift of France, or a bent of mind which France seemed to have made her own, he proclaimed the necessity for the moral and intellectual life of the nation to model itself upon Germany; and, affirming that the English were fundamentally a Germanic race, he called upon them to be loyal to their national origins. To mechanism in thought and materialism in research, he opposed dynamism and idealism, a sense, that is to say, of the internal organic growth of things, and a sense of spiritual activities incapable of transposition in terms of matter. The Germany of Kant, Fichte and Goethe was the home of these saving methods of thought; and the mighty stream of philosophical doctrine upon which these masters launched him, in giving a new depth to his ideas, gave a new depth to the intellectual life of England, and brought about one of the principal transitions in the history of English thought.

CHAPTER III

CRAIGENPUTTOCK

I

It is not without reason that recent biographers of Carlyle have stressed his many strokes of good luck. It is true that he had to fight his way to success, and that the bitter tone of his *Reminiscences* has its warrant in the events of his life; nevertheless it is important to note that had he had to fight much harder, his lot would have been no exception to the common lot of prophets. The fact is that the temperament of Carlyle, magnificent in its unremitting struggle with pain and grief, was not capable of the supreme heroism which is to be unaware of pain or to concede its presence only with desperate reluctance. Carlyle conquered the romantic promptings of his youth; but, like the nineteenth century, in his freedom he kept the indelible stamp of his early slavery. In spite of the ascetic formulae which he coined to express the vigor of his will, he was very human in his desire for happiness and in his confidence that he would find it. The years of his blackest despair are 1819 and 1820; in 1821 the sky begins to clear. Eighteen twenty-one is the year of his meeting with Miss Welsh; and 1822, according to the most plausible conjecture, is the year of that most decisive episode in his moral development—*The Everlasting No*. Thereafter, although he was to know many fluctuations, many relapses, the equilibrium of his life tends to become more and more

CRAIGENPUTTOCK

stable. Carlyle is nearing his thirtieth year; and with his maturity the normal temper of his life develops. It is a temper of constitutional melancholy, strengthened by a remorseless introspection, and leading to a slow corrosion of the soul. But in this temper there are redeeming elements, there are movements toward health and happiness, movements often cut short by distrust and reluctance to confess them, a reluctance and a distrust which increase with the passing of the years.

The difficulty of material subsistence was solved for the time through the good offices of Edward Irving, who by 1822 was established in London as the minister of a Scottish congregation. Irving's recommendation secured for Carlyle a post as tutor in a family of liberal ideas, the Bullers. The two boys who were to be Carlyle's pupils came to Edinburgh to follow the lectures at the university under the guidance of their tutor. The elder of them, Charles Buller, was destined to play a brilliant part in English politics, a part tragically interrupted by his untimely death; ironically enough he was to be among those philosophical radicals whom Carlyle was so bitterly to attack! Carlyle fulfilled his duties to the satisfaction of every one concerned. He spent part of the year 1823 in the country, in Perthshire, directing the studies of his charges. Then, after paying a visit to his parents, he went to London with the Bullers in 1824. In spite of the consideration shown him by the family, his independent spirit was not at ease in the situation, and in 1824 he gave it up. He had managed to save a small sum during his two years as tutor; but part of this he generously handed over to his brothers. More important, the immensity, the furious activity, of London had made an indelible impression upon him; his circle of friends had widened; and he decided to remain in the city for some time. Irving was now married and the father of several children; and in spite of his friend's fashionable success as a preacher, Carlyle could divine a crash in the near future. This is the time when Carlyle met Coleridge—as well as other men of fame—and gathered the materials for his severe judgment upon that greatest of his precursors.

These are Carlyle's wandering years; and his travels here and there with no determining goal to guide him are the material expression of his spiritual uncertainty. In London he had met the Stracheys, friends of the Bullers; he caught up with them at Dover; and in the company of Mr. Strachey and his cousin Kitty Kirkpatrick he spent a fortnight in Paris (1824). Soon after his return to London, he was off to Birmingham, following a "physician," a mere casual acquaintance of his, who held out the promise of curing his dyspepsia. The physician was unable to keep his promise; but Carlyle, after this episode, was always sensible of his need for exercise and careful habits of life. In and about Birmingham, as before at Glasgow, he had seen with his own eyes a vast laboring population, plunged into a hopeless poverty. In March, 1825, again in Scotland, he rented the farm of Hoddam Hill, adjoining his father's farm; and while his brother Alexander undertook the actual farming, Thomas began to make his translations from German novelists. His months at Hoddam were serene and almost happy. In this serenity the most powerful factor was a new influence, that of the final stage in his moral formation—his engagement to Jane Welsh, which occurred in the first weeks of 1825.

CRAIGENPUTTOCK 59

Jane Baillie Welsh was the only child of a Haddington doctor, whose death in 1819 of a fever contracted from a patient had given him a posthumous local fame. This moral title to pride was coupled in the mind of his widow and daughter with the claims of long descent. The social status of the family placed them on the footing of the comfortable middle class; they had no money besides the revenue from an estate, Craigenputtock, surrounded by moors, in a wild gloomy part of Scotland. All the more did Jane and her mother strive to preserve their status. Jane was born in 1801; with her fiery eyes, jet-black hair and dark complexion, she must have been very attractive. As a child, she gave proof of a quick and spirited temper, brilliant abilities and original ambitions. She insisted upon a boy's education, learned Latin, wrote verses, dreamed of a literary career. As a mere child, she had had Irving for her tutor; and had fallen in love with him. When he met Jane again in 1815, he was already engaged to Miss Martin, daughter of the minister at Kirkcaldy. Jane's love was still warm and Irving's quickly revived; but, when the parents of his fiancée claimed his promise, he kept it. His attitude in this episode, the tone of his letters, the progress of his noisy empty career disillusioned Jane; and when the attachment to Carlyle began to clamor for the first place in her heart—(whatever some critics may have said)—it found no serious rival to block it.

Fate willed that Irving once again should be the architect of Carlyle's destiny. In May, 1821, when they happened to be in Haddington, he introduced Carlyle to Mrs. Welsh and her daughter. The history of Carlyle's emotions at this first encounter with Jane is told in *Sartor*

Resartus under certain disguises; we can follow there the rapidity of his passion, the intoxication of love breaking down all the reserves in his nature and making him eloquent, expansive and eager. Jane's studies formed a common interest for them; Carlyle became her adviser; and this "post" was the pretext for their correspondence. The letters they wrote during the following five years, letters now accessible to us, are the most significant documents we have for the understanding of the relations between the two. They light up, for us, the painful enigma of the imperfect lifelong marriage between two persons whose respective share of the blame for its imperfection has been the subject of stormy controversies. However unpleasant this problem may be, it has given rise to so much inquiry, and led to solutions so contradictory to one another, that it is now impossible to omit it in writing the life of Carlyle. For the judgment one passes on the personality of Carlyle is deeply involved in one's interpretation of his relations with Jane.

II

There are two clearly distinct phases in the psychological drama recorded in the letters which passed between Carlyle and Jane. The first phase precedes and the second follows Carlyle's victory, the engagement. To any observer, the drama seems to develop on lines quite obvious, to an inevitable end. There is a flagrant disparity between the two minds, a disparity due partly to the inferiority of Jane, and partly to certain unconscious automatic habits which make the superiority of Thomas more oppressive; so that the future of their common life is only too ominous.

CRAIGENPUTTOCK 61

In the first phase the two young people appear in the attitudes which civilisation claims to be natural. Carlyle urges his suit and Jane Welsh stands on guard. There was never a suitor more affectionate, more patient, more humble; there was never a conquest undertaken with greater nobility. All the fire of Carlyle's genius, all the ecstasy of a mind which has just discovered its abilities, all the heroic firmness of a will which has been purged by suffering and which is elastic now and not yet rigid, lend their force, grace and animation to Carlyle's passion. And it is the passion of a man who is certain of himself and of his beloved. Carlyle directs Jane's studies; he spends, without stint, the best of his time and his thought in suggestions and counsels, and he never fails to clothe them with the rich splendor of his vigorous and ardent imagination. Above all else, he encourages and rouses an energy which is failing and a vocation which is slipping away. He believes in Jane's abilities and in her future with an unqualified faith; and he finds persuasive words to urge her on,—she will be famous among women, her talents assure her glory, she has only to adopt the means he proposes—to apply her efforts to the cultivation of self, as Goethe understood it, the cultivation which prepares one for achievement in literature and science. He directed her reading in English, French and German; and with the most scrupulous and unrelaxing care he mapped out for her courses of study and programmes for her day's work. He did not neglect to advise her against the excesses of application which had broken down his own health, and to counsel daily exercise and recreation. Beyond the narrow world of books he revealed to her life and manners as a vast domain awaiting her observation and capable of supplying her inexhaustibly with matter for reflection.

This master, however, so affectionately authoritative, was also a model suitor, deferential, humble almost, resigned to the misfortunes which fell upon him in goodly numbers. His first declaration was very ill received: he bowed to his fate. Contrary to Jane's warning, he ventured once again to Haddington—to encounter such coldness that for a whole year he dared not repeat his audacity. A rupture was narrowly escaped; but already Jane was recognising the power of a mind and a heart so rare; circumstances were favorable, and Carlyle was restored to her good graces. "As it is," she writes at this time, "every new day shows more forcibly what a treasure I possess in your friendship, every new character I study but reveals some new superiority in yours." Carlyle without the least complaint accepted Jane's coquetries, the procession of her suitors, suitors now noble, handsome and wealthy, and now obscure and absurd—and Jane would with a certain complacence describe their virtues and their defects. Carlyle was tolerant, and so tolerant indeed that to one's great surprise he found formulae for compromise. He wrote, for example: "The truth is, everything has two faces; both these sentiments are correct in their proper season, both erroneous out of it." The moment that Jane inadvertently pronounced a word which seemed to promise more than friendship, Carlyle went into transports; but only to be rebuffed a second time and to accept this rebuff as gallantly as the one before. Carlyle gave up his independence and his authority, laying them at her feet, recognising her absolute sway in all things and declaring himself an altogether obedient subject.

CRAIGENPUTTOCK

At last a day came when before the ardor and zeal of Carlyle's genius, Jane could no longer repress a cry of admiration. "It *will* burst 'as the bolt bursts on high from the black cloud that bound it!' . . . oh! that I heard a nation repeat your name." Carlyle replied with a hymn of joy which was checked by the chilly admonition: "My Friend, I love you. . . . But were you my Brother I would love you the same." Carlyle begged forgiveness and agreed that he should be her guide, philosopher and friend, and nothing further. A new quarrel arose in which Jane admitted her guilt and besought him to pardon the suffering she had caused: and Carlyle forgave. Quite indifferent to his *amour propre*, she rallied him on his "infamous" accent: "My poor ears are in a fever every time they hear it." But the reader of their correspondence can perceive that Jane is almost won: so much energy, so much passionate will, so much love, were beyond resistance. Once again Carlyle asked for her hand and once again he was rejected; but the terms in which Jane rejected him betray her genuine feeling and foretell their engagement. She wrote: "Not many months ago, I would have said it was impossible that I should ever be your Wife; at present I consider this the most probable destiny for me. And in a year or so perhaps, I shall consider it the only one."

What figure does Jane cut in this first stage? Her spirit is not quite on the level of Carlyle's. Charm and vivacity and wit, delicacy and dignity, she has, and she is capable of tenderness. But she is younger than he, less aware of the conditions of life and suffering; her ardent enthusiasms have not the depth which promises continuity; there is something romantic in her emotions, and in her ambitions an alloy of worldliness. The first great obstacle to Carlyle's passion—and it was an obstacle which long remained—was the discrepancy between her social position and his; on this point Jane is more than a little in agreement with her mother. She will never be able to forget the peasant origin of her husband. Once she has conceded the essential nobility of genius, their problem becomes more precise—how could the young couple live? The simplest prudence would have suggested that they wait; but Jane's way of recalling to Carlyle that he has no fixed position, no certain income, her way of specifying the minimum of "elegant comfort" without which the marriage would not seem to her desirable, this way shows a practical sense somewhat more calculating than we should have expected from a person of her intellect and tastes. Her conception of success has no mark of idealism in it. She is eager for fame, for flattering praise, for the noise of applause: she wishes to live upon the lips of men, to multiply her life in their interest. She requires of Carlyle that he achieve glory as a condition necessary to merit. It is not at all enough for her that he should conceal in his mind treasures of intelligence, that he should hold commerce with eternal realities and, indifferent to a neglectful present, should work for some possible future fame: Jane will give him her full esteem only if he can succeed in impressing himself upon the world.

Meanwhile she can take pleasure in describing the high social rank, the handsome presence, of those smitten with her charms; and while she can see through such gifts, there is in her manner of toying with them more than a suspicion of frivolity and coquetry. Should Carlyle pro-

CRAIGENPUTTOCK

pose for the future, life at Craigenputtock, the hereditary domain of the Welshes, with its implications of frugal farm life, Jane protests. "For my part," she exclaims, "I would not spend a month at it with an Angel." Feminine as these attitudes of hers appear, she never wearies of expressing horror of the traditional woman, limited by the circle of domestic duties. To cultivate her mind, to exchange ideas, to read and to write, these are the tasks for which she yearns. She would have liked to be a man; domestic tasks are intolerable to her; she begs heaven for a happier and higher destiny than to "marry and make puddings."

Unfortunately her literary ambitions are threatened by a strange sterility. Her projects crumble one after another; perhaps it is fatigue, perhaps disgust, perhaps it is her very versatility, which leads her to give up the labor she has undertaken. Or perhaps it is just impotence and a confused sense of a creative incapacity. In vain Carlyle proposes to her a collaboration which would have given him deep happiness; whether it were poetry or fiction or the translation of German stories, the same destiny thwarted his suggestions. The inventive power of her friend, his literary fertility so laborious but so copious, do not appear to have stimulated her; rather, in the shadow of his genius, hers appears to have drooped and died.

There are men so great that their proximity is devastating to lesser mortals, and Carlyle was probably one of them. But it is amazing that even at the outset Jane made no effort to react against the effects Carlyle produced. She was incapable of moderating her ambitions to suit her talents—she craved all or nothing. If she might not have the glory of which she had dreamed she would be barren rather than effective in a modest way. And as she became more and more of a pessimist concerning her own abilities, Carlyle won more and more of her heart. A year and a half after the third rejection, her pride had subsided so far as to pay him this magnificent homage and testimony of gratitude: "Our meeting forms a memorable epoch in my history, for my acquaintance with you has from its very commencement powerfully influenced my character and my life." Slowly, very slowly her pride was softened as gratitude became confidence and confidence became love. Soon she was able to admit she loved him: "I owe you so much! feelings and sentiments that ennoble my character, that give dignity, interest and enjoyment to my life. In return I can only love you and *that* I do, from the bottom of my heart." In the earlier days of their courtship she had taken an impish delight in exciting Carlyle's jealousy; now she does not trouble to conceal her own. Has Kitty Kirkpatrick, the Eastern beauty, won his heart;—certainly she has every quality a man desires. The affection of Jane was becoming warmer and warmer. Words, she wrote, could never tell Carlyle the fullness of her love. Her beloved books lie unused. What are books to her? She can afford to go without them; the greatest pleasure they have in store is the delight which she would find in a new proof of his affection; and that she has already enjoyed. Nevertheless, in her fidelity to her romantic ideals and to her spirit of independence, even in the letter in which she accepted Carlyle, she was cruelly precise in marking just how deep her feeling went: "I love you," she wrote, "I have told you so a hundred times; and I should be the most ungrateful and injudicious of mortals if I did not; but I am not *in love* with you; that is to say, my love for you is not a passion which overclouds my judgment and absorbs all my regard for myself and others."

No sooner had the die been cast, and their engagement become a fact, than a remarkable change came over the pair and the relation between them. In this second phase, their positions are reversed. Carlyle received the marvelous tidings with a simple serious and delicate pleasure; and to the very end his letters remained affectionate and even romantically chivalrous. Nevertheless the tone of his affection was now quite different. It is possible that his affection had been slowly undermined by Jane's persistence in distinguishing between the quality of her feeling for him and that of the passion of which she believed herself capable. It is possible too that the many jars in which the less pleasing sides of Jane's character had been revealed may have brushed from his love a little of the first bloom. He had certainly perceived defects in his beloved. An unconscious irritation had now and then shown itself in his words, and two or three times his will had revolted. In his letters a new note was beginning to be audible; he had distinguished in Jane the development of the woman from the development of the scholar; she was no longer his collaborator, an equal, bent over her own task, but now just his inspirer, the adornment and the reward of *his* labors. In the very moment of his victory, just when Jane was about to concede his conquest, he was no longer certain that in their union he would find his happiness. Together, he writes, we may not find happiness; if parted, we must be unhappy. . . . All such symptoms are now growing more pronounced. It is as if the heredity, the instincts, of Carlyle had just pressed into the foreground, as if the sense of success and its perilous excitement were replacing the docility of the suitor by the authority of the fiancé. Now that he was face to face with the long distant desire to found a home and a family as the men of his race had done in the past, the spirit of Carlyle fell into harmony with the conservative wisdom of his people; and he began to conceive the economy of the home and the relations between husband and wife in the old traditional ways of his family.

Henceforward his tone was that of the master, respectful still, but thoroughly firm. There is still affection, but not so vividly expressed—disciplined affection. No longer was Jane flattered with the prospect of an intellectual career with glory as its goal; Carlyle now denounced the sham of letters and proclaimed the superiority of real living. He wished that Jane should be a model wife, that she should learn the arts of housekeeping. In his projects for their life together, his rôle is the writing of an "allotted number of pages," and hers an occupation with household duties: the division of labor is in the old tradition. He frankly claims the undivided supreme authority: "The man should bear rule in the house and not the woman. This is an eternal axiom, the law of Nature herself which no mortal departs from unpunished." The definite prescription of the Bible reinforced here the natural direction of his temperament. And soon he began to voice the familiar commonplaces on the nature of woman "which is essentially passive and not active." The romantic phase, the phase of fancies and whims, is past; there has been enough thinking, action is the healthy ideal, as it is the imperative need, of the present time. All his life Carlyle was to repeat and elaborate this theory: it marks the prin-

CRAIGENPUTTOCK 69

cipal transition between his youth and his maturity. Of all the various teaching of his great master Goethe, all he was to retain was the worship of action; the authority of German speculation and German wisdom was now no more than a corroboration of his own Puritanism.

The moment for action had arrived; and Carlyle made his will known and felt. He had determined to live in the country, and fixed upon Craigenputtock. To begin with he rented a farm at Hoddam Hill and told Jane, only after he had done it, of his design. He offered the most energetic opposition to the presence of Mrs. Welsh in their household, and Jane, whose relations with her mother had never been too easy, did not care to insist. Then came the project of selling the Welshes' house at Haddington, a project with which Carlyle found a thousand faults. Meanwhile his indefatigable quest of better health was more and more giving to his character a bent of stubbornness, and his temper was becoming more and more uncertain. It was natural that after five years of intimacy Jane should suppose that the soul of her fiancé was quite intelligible to her, but Carlyle found it necessary to warn her of surprises in store, and to give the warning in disturbing form: By degrees, he says, you will learn what man I am; at present, I hardly know myself. . . . From his home education he had acquired a taste, a craving, indeed, for reciprocal sincerity and frank sermonizing. That he meant to spend a fortnight, lecturing and being lectured, he had let her know at the time of their engagement; and he kept his word. He was clearly aware of his character, he had even a theory about it; its defects he ascribed to "a disordered nervous system"; and he hoped to avoid if not to subdue "the influences of disease." As the date of his marriage approached, his tortured soul became more and more susceptible, impatient, timorous of the future; he underwent a crisis of hypochondria; and the spirit which ruled him during the last weeks before the marriage is explicit in these sad words in which one cannot but discern a prophecy: "I swear it will break my heart if I make thee unhappy. And yet I am a perverse mortal to deal with, and the best resolutions make shipwreck in the sea of practice."

As the personality of Carlyle was becoming more decided, exhibiting all its angles, Jane's personality was in compensation acquiring a quite new docility and sweetness. She too appears to have been conquered by her heredity, and to be veering toward the ideal of a wife as it has been developed in England by the wise tradition of centuries. Once again she ventured to complain, almost to threaten, Carlyle when, shortly after their engagement, he had failed, during a month's holiday in London and Birmingham, to write her even once. But now she was no longer a mistress of irony; and the anxiety of a heart freely and entirely given to him was too deep for concealment. With a sincerity that is very touching and indeed very simple, she admitted how deeply her feelings had become involved, and how strenuously she was trying to achieve a love in which there should be no reserve. It was not long indeed before her letters became more affectionate, more passionate, than his. The inadvertence of a certain Mrs. Montagu informed Carlyle that Jane had once been in love with Edward Irving; whereupon Jane admitted that she had done wrong in concealing this from Carlyle, revealed a quite new humility in imploring his pardon, and accepted the form that pardon took;—generous and tender as it was, it was superior, supercilious almost, and sermonising. His proposal to give her back her freedom stirred in her heart a terrible storm of grief and terror. She wrote: "Had I but strength, I would come to you this very day; and when I held you in my arms and you saw my tears, you would forget everything but the love I bear you. O, I do love you, my own Friend, above the whole earth: no human being was ever half so dear to me,—none, none; and will you break my heart?" Her attitude toward the discrepancy between their social positions and their pecuniary resources was henceforward that of a woman deeply in love. "Dearest," Jane wrote, "speak not another word about your *poverty*. Every such word comes home to me with the force of a reproach." Absolutely, feverishly, even, she threw herself upon the intelligence, discretion and strength of the man who had won her; her only wish was to be his beloved slave exulting in the happiness of admiring and ministering to him. "I am tractable and submissive towards you"; she wrote, "I hearken to your voice as to the dictates of a second conscience." In announcing her marriage to a relative, she expressed her joy that her husband had "a towering intellect to command me." In the last letter before her marriage she made a formulated homage of her obedience: "not my will be done but thine." And yet, one may wonder whether such a gift of herself was really a simple, happy, complete act. A year before, she used an expression in which there seems to have been a quiver of regret, an expression which if it was half in jest was also half in earnest: "I have nothing for it but to submit in this as in all things else: 'my whole will,' Mrs. Montagu says, 'must be thrown into *fusion* and *cast* according to another mould.' A barbarous process really! I wonder that the bare mention of it did not terrify me into the resolution of remaining single all the days of my life."

Miss Welsh visited Carlyle's parents in September, 1825, as his avowed fiancée. Certain critics have found in this step a result of the revelation to Carlyle of her former love for Irving. However this may be, her visit was the realisation of a dream Carlyle had expressed a score of times; it cannot be said that she was responsible for their actual union.

For a full year more, circumstances appeared to be against that union. In June, 1826, Carlyle gave up the farm at Hoddam Hill to go to Scotsbrig where his father had transplanted himself. His plan of living there with his wife did not appear feasible. Neither the farm at Craigenputtock nor the house at Haddington could give them at the time the quiet shelter in which he had hoped to found his home. The young couple finally decided to rent in Edinburgh a little villa which Mrs. Welsh agreed to furnish. Their marriage was celebrated the 17th of October, 1826.

The slow and difficult adaptation of their two natures had come at last to the end which had long been certain. They had given five feverish years to this adaptation, and one might at first imagine that the harmony of their hearts, being the work of a perfect sincerity, might withstand the shock of time. But if the lines of moral development that we have traced are not fantastic, their harmony was in reality far from complete and, indeed, had the seed of grave disagreements. At the very moment when their souls had seemed to touch, secret changes had come to modify the two souls, and in so doing to shake the very bases of their reciprocal understanding. The present and the past, the true and the seeming, the deep instincts of their temperaments and qualities which they had hastily acquired, all were confusedly mixed in a deceptive sense of a perfect moral union. Carlyle, despite the savage severity of his love for truth, had been a suitor of the common sort; he had unconsciously softened his character in his desire to please, and he had not revealed himself in his entirety for the man he was. Jane Welsh, incapable of realising her ideal of what she should be, had relapsed into the typical reality of the woman of her race; her own personality, as yet but half-defined, had not had the strength necessary to flower out, and therefore had given way before the advance of impersonal hereditary tendencies. Nevertheless there did remain with her the memory of what she had hoped to become and the dissatisfaction with what in fact she was, and this condemned her to the hidden bitterness of those who know themselves to be weak.

These two persons, so large of heart, so fine in soul, both capable of love, were not to find happiness in their marriage. For this sad misfortune, Jane was certainly the chief offender; she had become Carlyle's wife only at the cost of an intellectual regression which she had not willed with enough clearness, with enough awareness of what she was about, to be able to accept joyously and definitely. She had not developed according to the law of her being, as Carlyle with his inflexible energy had done. However it was precisely in this energy that Carlyle went astray. He was too exclusively preoccupied with action, with the total realisation of his potentialities, to criticise the modes of his activity, the conditions of his success, with a clear enough sense of what they implied for his wife. And in his very quest for health he was an unconscious egotist. He did wrong in bringing Jane to the lonely moor of Craigenputtock, for which she had so frankly expressed her aversion. He did wrong to shut himself up with her, and force upon her on the very morrow of his marriage, and in a rather brutal form, the traditional rôle of housewife. He ought to have understood that Jane was the victim of a transition, a divided spirit, that if she did not possess the strength and the lucidity of the woman of the future, neither did she possess the strength and the simplicity of the woman of the past. He might have guessed how weak she really was, have pitied that weakness, and have adapted himself to it. He might have thought more about her and for her when he was organising his life—had he not asked her to marry him? And if no duty appeared to him to rank as high as his prophetic mission, if he wished to sacrifice all else in its fulfilment, why did he bind another's destiny to his own, why did he not seek the austere solitude in which a hero is strong and free? He might have spent some of the invincible untiring courage with which he came to dominate the world, to change the spirit of his age, in dominating himself, in controlling the vagaries of his temper. Only at this cost, could he have prevented "the songbird" he had tamed from suffering as a caged bird suffers.

III

From October, 1826, to the spring of 1828, the young couple lived in Edinburgh at 21 Comley Bank. Their home was simply and comfortably furnished and it was in a pleasant bracing quarter of the city. It was under really happy auspices that their life together began. Nevertheless their future was terribly uncertain. Although Miss Welsh had always had the tastes and demands of an heiress, her inheritance was largely on paper. Her father had bequeathed to her what was most solid in his property, the farm of Craigenputtock; but Jane had transferred its revenue to her mother and only kept the title to the land. Carlyle thoroughly approved her generosity when—somewhat late—he was told of it. His independent spirit was not sorry to have the complete responsibility of his household. Mrs. Welsh offered to make the couple an allowance but he declined to accept it. It was necessary to discover a means of livelihood. His literary work had brought him in a relatively substantial sum; but it had come at irregular intervals and it became necessary to increase it. The reading public had not been very eager to buy Carlyle's latest translations from the German. Very opportune it was, then, that Carlyle was put in touch with the powerful editor of the great Whig periodical, the *Edinburgh Review*. Such a favorable impression did he make upon Jeffrey that that accomplished but sensible sceptic freely welcomed him as a contributor. There was something paradoxical in Carlyle's writing for the *Edinburgh Review*. To readers who were absorbed in the political conflicts of the time, Carlyle hoped to communicate the treasures of German mysticism. It was in this anomalous medium that Carlyle's first critical articles came out, and even in them he revealed a fully mature thought. So forceful were they that they immediately attracted notice and Carlyle was never again ignored by the cultivated minds of Scotland. The high society of Edinburgh sought him out: brilliant connections opened before him; other letters from Goethe, more flattering even than the first, added to his prestige. But, to the favor of society Carlyle opposed a severe reserved front, and shut himself up in a life of hard work, interrupted solely by the visits of a few chosen friends. Meanwhile Jane, worried already by the solitude upon which he insisted, might still believe her life a happy one.

Carlyle continued to be haunted by a fear of the morrow. He wished for a fixed situation; but there were very few compatible with his temperament. Twice he applied for a professor's chair. First at the University of London, which had just been organised, and later at the University of St. Andrews; but in spite of the support of the highest authorities, twice he failed. The promise of his genius had not yet had a sufficiently academic ring. It was after these failures that an old project came once more to haunt him. Since the struggle for health had become with him a conscious systematic effort, he had hoped to find what he sought in a mode of life in which intellectual work and open-air exercise should be harmoniously balanced under the quieting influence of the country. At Hoddam Hill he had found what he needed; and during his engagement he had dreamed of setting up a household at Craigenputtock. This solution of his financial worries was certainly the simplest he could find; day-to-day expenses, which at Edinburgh were too heavy for his purse, would at Craigenputtock be cut in half. In 1827 his brother Alexander had settled there to work the farm and get things ready for him. For still another year Carlyle deferred going there, aware of his wife's aversion to it. Indeed he seems to have done everything he could to avoid it. Probably when he did go he was yielding to an

CRAIGENPUTTOCK

unconscious desire, for he whose will was at every other point invincible was here conquered. In March, 1828, rejecting Jeffrey's advice, he established himself in that desolate place, and began the critical period both in his literary career and in his married life.

Craigenputtock is not the wretched farm that legend has painted. Beside the tenant's house is a gentleman's residence which quite deserves the name of manor. Solidly built to resist the wind and rain which beat down endlessly upon these heights, the stone walls of the manor have the protection, exceptional in the neighborhood, of a clump of trees. It is true that life at Craigenputtock must needs be frugal and lonely; but the poetry of the open spaces, of the wild moors, of the changing skies and the pure air, appealed deeply to the heart of Carlyle. At Craigenputtock he was once more in the kind of place where he had grown up; indeed Annandale, where his parents now lived, was not far, and neither was Templand to which Mrs. Welsh had retired. In this out-of-the-way place, five miles from the nearest village, there was nothing to disturb the concentration of Carlyle's thought. He had no bores to fear, and his suffering nerves found a sweet reprieve in the silence. Carlyle adapted himself without effort to his new environment; he felt it to be in blessed harmony with the imperious needs of his genius, now drawing in upon itself to prepare a masterpiece of meditation. His long mornings and evenings at work, his daily wanderings over hill and dale, skirting the little streams and the gloomy marshes, his rides on horseback, all this was exactly what his vital instinct clamored for. He could now write the book which for so long had been obscurely fermenting inside him.

Beside him, however his wife's happiness was silently perishing. There is nothing more perplexing than to find the true road through the confusion of arguments and theses which have grown up about the domestic tragedy of the Carlyles. The details are sordid and saddening. But if one limits one's attention to the essentials, some few conclusions are inevitable; and the light thrown upon their two souls by the implicit avowals of their love letters projects upon their early married life a guiding gleam. There are two distinct orders in Mrs. Carlyle's grievances; and the order which seems more important is really less. She complained, not to her husband, but to her friends, in letters which public malignity was later to exploit, of the tiring and humiliating tasks she had to perform. The exact nature and magnitude of these tasks does not very much matter. Whether it was regularly or only exceptionally that she baked the bread and milked the cows; whether making her clothes and keeping the household running took much or little of her time; such questions are far from the central point. Domestic service, easy to get at Edinburgh, must naturally have been insufficient at Craigenputtock; it was natural and necessary that Jane should there have more work upon her hands. Her education as a young lady and her tastes had held her far away from practical training; and so late an apprenticeship doubled the difficulty of what she had to learn. Pride in her social position, some little worldly vanity, a mind only too ready to exaggerate its troubles and to be embittered by them—these qualities in Jane suffice to explain her complaints and in some measure disprove their importance. But it remains to ask whether if her heart had found what it sought it would have occurred to her to complain? The other order of her sufferings, immensely more difficult to detect, scarcely formulated even to herself, is the more real, the more exacerbating. Carlyle may be charged with the failure to hold his wife's love. Her affection for him was sorely tried and damaged in the trial; and for this their two natures were responsible, along with the secret misunderstanding on which their union was based. Mrs. Carlyle was later to write that she had married for ambition. This cynical admission reflects the bitterness of a long trial; for at the moment of their marriage, as her letters show, she had for Carlyle a lively tender affection if not a great passion.

Jane was suffering because she found herself in a condition where courage and sacrifice were needed, and because she had nothing of the spirit of heroism for which courage and sacrifice are a joy. All she could feel was a bitterness in the exercise of prosaic unappreciated virtues, and against this the rebellion of all her instincts was too sharp to be suppressed. In a half-hearted way she attempted to combine the duties of the household with the pursuit of literature. In Edinburgh Carlyle had seemed to favor this effort; and often through later years he urged and encouraged her in it; she did continue to write even if she published nothing. Jane had lost all faith in herself; to restore it would have required a deliberate art on his part; and he had set other goals for his life. He accepted without any sorrow or anxiety the change in her ideals and horizon which seemed to imply a transformation of his wife's character; indeed he was only too ready to find such a change the natural thing. Conscientiously she set about being the inferior, and indeed humble, assistant which the expansion of his genius required. She kept up a brave and even a smiling front; and exaggerating, in her wounded pride, the duty of bearing pain without recrimination, she went so far as to reach the point where by the repeated violation of the duty of frankness and confidence in marriage, her affection began to stray and fade away. For her bitterness she found in her letters to others a satisfaction almost mean; and the daily burden that she was trying to lift from her shoulders only fell back with a more painful shock. She had thought that she was equal to the trials of poverty; but she had nothing of the instinctive passive endurance of the women whom in her youth she had scorned; she had nothing either of the passionate love which might have unified her soul, and struck from the rock of her devotion a flashing stream of joy. She resented her slavery and the injustice of her fate just because her love was no longer strong enough; and it was the sense of her slavery which hastened the disintegration of her love.

His every energy strained in the struggle, absorbed by an anxiety about their material future and by the painful labor of his thought, Carlyle pressed on through pain toward victory, blindly and with no fear that he might be vanquished. Their projects of close collaboration and of close moral solidarity, their projects of spiritual communion and confidence, had not been realised; and Jane was more and more retiring into the fastness of her own soul. It is true that he continued to keep her informed of his work; subtle and skilful as she always was, she gave him her best advice, and helped him by her social tact and by her prestige with his admiring friends. He showed her his manuscripts and she found encouraging words: "It is a work of genius," she said of *Sartor Resartus*. But henceforward he was fascinated by the flame that burnt on the altar of his own mind; all his energies were devoted to tending that flame; as a result he was no longer capable of radiating affection. He had become accustomed to working alone; and if Jane sat with him by the fire, it was merely to busy herself silently with her needle work. He praises her in his letters and thanks her for her gift of silence. Her rather fragile health prevented her from accompanying him on long walks: he went out without her. Now and then they rode on horseback together; sometimes too they took an excursion or a trip; but their intimacy was broken by frequent separations. Always very devoted to his relatives, Carlyle often invited one or another of them to stay with him; and often too he visited his parents. In his letters to his mother he expressed the most absolute, the most expansive affection: and Jane knew only too well that in his mother she had a rival already victorious, and likely to become stronger and stronger with the flight of time.

If they had had children, her life would certainly have been different; but children they were never to have. In her loneliness she longed to be spoiled, to be surrounded with a vigilant affection. Prone to insomnia and to headaches, she was in need of constant attention; but at Craigenputtock they were far from any doctor; and since Carlyle suffered from the same ailments, he had as much sympathy for himself as he had for her. He had his woes, too, and in overcoming them his sense of pity had become hardened. And his constitutional gloom was further darkened by recurring crises of indigestion. Irritable and imperious, he could not but hurt even those who were dearest to him. Sustained by his own vivid faith in himself, he had no need to look for moral comfort to his wife; she was able to give him nothing very deep, and the charm and merriment for which he came to her, she could refuse him, as she bitterly reflected, without his making any complaint. There was, then, a deep chasm between them, although they continued to live side by side. Carlyle was not unhappy, and he had never hoped for a positive happiness: but Jane found that without happiness, her life was a calamity. It was a calamity for Carlyle too when after her death he found out that she had been unhappy; but in these years he did not know this, and he made no effort to learn it. The great spirit of Carlyle, shot through and through with the most penetrating genius, capable of grasping the significance of the world, deeply tender behind its rugged visage, was narrowing and thinning to egotism as his tyrannical will, pressing all his potentialities to their full realisation, forced love to be nothing more than a useful element in life.

The days went by, each with its mixture of pleasure and pain: the Carlyles met them together and no doubt, in a way, loved each other. In the tranquillity of his heart Carlyle wrote his most ardent pages. His years at Craigenputtock were decisive; it was then and there that his spirit came to its full stature. While continuing his contributions to the *Edinburgh Review,* he wrote articles for other periodicals, *Fraser's Magazine,* for instance, and *The Westminster Review,* the centre of young radical thought. For many years he had been looking for the form in which he could best express himself. His self was not the plaintive ego of the romantic, for that he had firmly shut up in a deep unbroken silence; it was the tormented aspiration, the mystic ferment, all the churning of ideas and impressions in which more and more he came to discover what was most real and profound in himself. His attempts at poetry and fiction had been failures; in spite of the poetic vigor of his imagination, he had no sense of rhythm or of rhyme or of harmony. He was no less lacking in gifts essential for fiction—the objective sense, dramatic invention, and the mysterious power of developing character. In his critical studies of men and books he had revealed himself only in rapid puzzling flashes; only a handful of men of great perceptive power had divined in Carlyle the greatness of genius. He was aware, nevertheless, that he had a book to write which should, in its naked simplicity and ardor and sincerity, be of the very substance of his moral life. In a sort of semiconscious automatism he began the composition of *Sartor Resartus*. It was to be a short fantasy; but page followed page; and Carlyle in astonishment watched the birth of a strange and powerful philosophical allegory.

The work was finished in July, 1831. Would it bring success and glory? Carlyle took his precious manuscript to London the following month. All the publishers to whom he offered it rejected it. This was a cruel disappointment which cast its shadow over many years to come. In response to his tender letters his wife met him in London, and there they enjoyed together a more active and stimulating life than they had known for many a year; the exile at Craigenputtock seemed all the more onerous when, all hope abandoned, the chief stake of his literary future lost, Carlyle decided to return in March, 1832. In January he had received the news of his father's death, and in the most pious and intimate of eulogies he has voiced the depth of his sorrow. Soon after his return he heard of Goethe's death, the death of his spiritual father.

The horizon had never been darker; Carlyle was about to enter upon the second phase of his trials, less severe than the first, despite the sense of responsibility for the life he had joined to his, less severe because he had found himself. His wish had been to earn an honest living for his wife and himself by conscientious toil; the event had been unfavorable. A post as astronomer was vacant in Edinburgh; Carlyle applied for it and failed. He continued his stoical perseverance. Fraser agreed to publish fragments of *Sartor Resartus* in his magazine; but the effect was calamitous—he was showered with protests by the subscribers. Carlyle had exhausted the best German subjects and besides, the vogue of German things was waning. He turned to another field. For years he had been fascinated by the French Revolution; in it he saw the most terrifying lesson the Divinity had ever given mankind. He undertook to write its history. He was able out of his preparatory studies to develop his papers on *Cagliostro* and *The Diamond Necklace*. But the necessary books and documents were not to be had at Craigenputtock; most of the winter of 1833-34 the Carlyles spent in Edinburgh; and Carlyle at this time was tempted by his desire to try his fortune a second time in London. He had had some auspicious signs—the visit of Emerson, attracted even to the desolation of Craigenputtock by the impression Carlyle's articles had made upon him, Emerson whose loyal active friendship was in the following years to be of precious value. In May, 1834, Carlyle left for London; and a few weeks later his wife joined him.

There, in the suburb of Chelsea, on the bank of the Thames, they set up their home.

Carlyle was to find in London a dazzling triumphant success, and he was to find it soon. His days of trial were very nearly over. But the seed from which the grief of his old age was to grow had already sprouted and rooted. Carlyle was not responsible for it as an individual: he had been dominated by the energy he had inherited from his race, eager and stubborn to conquer the world of the flesh and the spirit, the heavens and the earth. It was this energy which had sustained him, nourished his heroism and his resistance through the long years of combat; without it, he would not have been himself. To achieve a yet greater conquest of himself, to soften that fierce wish of his to realise the fullness of his powers, to give himself the anxious solicitude, the perilous prodigality of emotion, which an omnipotent love requires, he would have had to draw upon the very source of his strength and—beyond doubt—to lessen that strength; weakened in that way he would no longer have been Carlyle. But the life he had taken in his charge would have been happier. Later he was sorry that he had not seen more clearly what his wife was undergoing; but he was never sorry for the essential decision of his temperament; he never abjured his doctrine. The fragile weight of one human being's happiness would not have been enough to persuade him to do so: had he ever been summoned to decide, he would have affirmed, as superior to all else, as the primordial duty of man, to act and to endure.

CHAPTER IV

EARLY ESSAYS

I

In Carlyle's earliest essays there is no suggestion of genius. How suddenly, in the series of review articles beginning with the essay for the *Edinburgh* on Richter, does the flash of genius appear, and what a brilliant flash it is! A very few years separate his *Life of Schiller* from these articles. But during the interval the major influences in the formation of his character have had their full effect. His moral crisis has ended in victory; a serene balance has succeeded to the paralysing anguish of his youth; strong in its spiritual certitude, ripened with a richer consciousness of its specific quality, the mind of Carlyle has turned to action. German thought and German literature have classified and systematised his gospel; what they have done for him he will do for others; and the pride he takes in his initiation into their secrets, the pride of a discoverer, has redoubled his consciousness of his powers. In this interval has come also the experience of love—desire, struggle and victory, with the pride of possession and the intoxication of a life shared with the beloved. Not yet has he sunk back into himself; not yet has he felt the first sharp wounds of disillusion. The masterpiece, the definitive and complete expression of his youth, is still far ahead; but in the years which precede it, Carlyle could give the measure of his greatness in his essays.

EARLY ESSAYS

The articles that he wrote between 1819 and 1822 for the *Edinburgh Encyclopaedia* are merely the work of an able student. The *Life of Schiller* (1823-1824) leaves, by its mechanical correctness, an impression of youth and diffidence in the writer. Its regular flowing style has the symmetry of traditional prose, the mark of the eighteenth century. Under the flowing folds of this commonplace dress, one catches the sight of limbs vigorous far beyond the common, and the narrative has a remarkable vivacity and animation; a bold and original imagination appears in it, and is allied with a warm eloquence. An unusual familiarity with philosophy, a faculty for welding ideas into systems and travelling over vast prospects of speculation, show themselves in the easy mastery with which Carlyle expounds Schiller's ideas. Most important of all, the bias of Carlyle's mind is revealed: his interest is fixed on the man; in the man's work, the moral basis attracts him most; and man and work alike he judges by their practical and human value. For him literature is a religion; and the noble figure of Schiller easily changes in his reverent hands into that of a priest. The glorious example of his life, and the fortifying lessons in his tragedies are his best titles to glory. Schiller's technique, his theory of art, his achievement of effects in which the senses take pleasure, these are, for Carlyle, but trifles and to them he gives only half his mind. In his conception of a poet, mastery of a poet's craft is unimportant. The value of Carlyle's interpretation of Schiller is in its sympathetic quality: swiftly and surely he seizes upon the most spiritual elements in Schiller's work, upon the pure idealism of the creative mind which gave birth to a *Wallenstein* and a *William Tell*. The justness of Carlyle's sense of the whole makes all his criticism of detail acute. The sympathetic quality is distinctly personal; it is no exercise of a supple mind but the direct expression of a spiritual affinity. Carlyle loves and understands Schiller because he resembles Schiller. A covert preoccupation with himself can be detected in these pages: the struggles and trials of Schiller, his victory and his career as a thinker and a prophet, seem to excite in Carlyle a secret but intense delight that his own ambitions and agonies are like those of his subject. Unwittingly, in the distribution of emphasis and the passing of judgment, he reveals the traits of his own moral personality, his conception of himself and his apprenticeship to life.

The preface to his translation of *Wilhelm Meister* (1823) and the notices prefixed to his *Specimens of the German Novel* (1827) are written in an idiom more vigorous and more concise than Carlyle had elsewhere mastered. It is in the year 1827, with his study of Jean Paul Richter, that he begins his series of review articles which, later collected in the volumes of his *Miscellanies*, make the most substantial part of Carlyle's critical essays. It is possible to examine as a distinct unit the earlier and more interesting half of this collection—the essays written up to the end of 1832. From the very first they have the stamp of maturity. The style expresses a fully conscious originality, although it has not as yet all of the audacities of *Sartor Resartus*. Carlyle is not able in these articles to give free rein to his fancy; writing here under a review editor, it will take him a longer time to arrive at perfect freedom of form.

In the article on the *Life of Heyne* (1828) Carlyle gibes at the regular monotonous cadence of the academic style: "Every sentence bears a family likeness to its precursor; most probably it has a set number of clauses (three is a favorite number, as in Gibbon, for 'the Muses delight in odds'); has also a given rhythm, a known and foreseen music, simple but limited enough, like that of ill-bred fingers drumming on a table." Carlyle opposes to this style the style of Richter, describing with a remarkable precision the strange disorder of an idiom thoroughly independent and original. His admiration appears in his critical description; and the descriptive passage is no mean example of the style it describes: "Not that he is ignorant of grammar, or disdains the sciences of spelling and parsing; but he exercises both in a certain latitudinarian spirit; deals with astonishing liberality in parenthesis, dashes, and subsidiary clauses; invents hundreds of new words, alters old ones, or by hyphen chains and pairs and packs them together into most jarring combination; in short produces sentences of the most heterogeneous, lumbering, interminable kind. Figures without limit; indeed the whole is one tissue of metaphors, and similes, and allusions to all the provinces of Earth, Sea and Air; interlaced with epigrammatic breaks, vehement bursts, or sardonic turns, interjections, quips, puns, and even oaths! A perfect Indian jungle it seems; a boundless, unparalleled imbroglio; nothing on all sides but darkness, dissonance, confusion worse confounded."

The whole article is written in the style Carlyle exemplifies here; and, indeed, this freedom of construction, these inversions, these aposiopeses, this marvelous exuberance of expressive and picturesque words, these rhythms flowing directly from a headlong vigorous mind, all these will remain in Carlyle's prose, and be the instruments with which his imagination will realise and communicate its vivid visions.

Although in these studies Carlyle does not attain complete freedom of form, in them he contrives a solidity of structure, an economy of expression, that we miss in the luxuriant verbosity of his later works. These studies have a remarkable compactness, going directly to the point and affecting no repetition. Repetition as an aspect of expression, a means of eloquence and persuasion, a result of an eager dogmatic way of thinking, will before long be a constant trait in the work of Carlyle; but here it is absent.

Most of these articles are purely critical; in none of them is Carlyle's doctrine expressed; it is at most implicit. Throughout he keeps the attitude he took in the *Life of Schiller:* he judges, and in his judgment he mixes literary with moral values. The genius of the writer and of the thinker is a unit, his artistic and his moral consciousness are but one—united in their reverent intuition of spiritual reality. Sympathy presides over these studies; and the sympathy rings true because of the extraordinary intensity of Carlyle's loves—as well as of his hates. A glow of enthusiasm suffuses them as Carlyle celebrates the depth and the beauty and the nobility of the German genius. Scotland and England are also represented. Scotland by Burns and England by Dr. Johnson. With these two, and more particularly with Burns, the character of Carlyle has a deep affinity; and in his studies of them, so spirited and so discerning, he seems to be re-creating personalities and not merely analysing works. So robust, so sincere, and beneath an uncouth exterior, so essentially fine and fastidious were they, that Carlyle succeeds in giving them the honors of "heroism" in all but name.

Voltaire, on the contrary, who represents France, comes out badly, although Carlyle makes an estimable effort to be just toward him. The lesson of his career, according to Carlyle, is that mere "cleverness," the particular gift of the French nation, is capable of nothing but destruction, and can serve only the negative ends of God.

The philosophic position of Carlyle is not sufficiently articulate in these studies to claim examination. The names of Kant and Fichte occur more than once; the transcendental metaphysic is often in question. When he speaks of Goethe or Schiller or Richter or Novalis, Carlyle points out the fund of ideas these men had in common; and he praises in all of them the idealistic spirit of inquiry and belief. These are but the themes of which *Sartor Resartus* will be the mighty orchestration. But there is in these studies one idea which will recede into the background in Carlyle's later works and indeed finally disappear: the idea of culture in the acceptation of Goethe. Carlyle's mind was never again so liberal as when he wrote these essays; at this happy period, allied with his rugged independence was a plasticity of mind, a tolerance, that age and fame gravely weakened. The weakening begins indeed as early as 1825; but the intensity of Carlyle's intellectual activity combats his moral fanaticism, and up to 1830 holds it in check. *Sartor Resartus* marks the point in his development when the balance between the two forces was perfect.

On the whole, it has been seen, Carlyle twists Goethe's teaching toward the Puritan austerity of his own instincts; during a few years, by close intimacy with his master, he appears to have possessed genuinely intellectual freedom, a disinterested love of truth and a wide curiosity. Writing to Jane Welsh, he had enjoined upon her as a duty the free and full development of all one's faculties; in many of his formulae he had been directly inspired by the great man of Weimar, and he had even said that to be freely one's self is the individual's most binding duty. Through these expressions of lofty individualism, Carlyle takes his place in that line of moral thinkers which begins with Goethe and culminates in Nietzsche. The Calvinist's obsession with conduct and the instinctive need for activity in Carlyle lay in wait for this alien individualism, and succeeded in scotching if not killing it.

II

In three studies Carlyle speaks in his own name; and those studies have a remarkable wealth of ideas and interest.

In the article "On History" (1830) Carlyle inveighs against the pretensions of history so-called, a mere mechanical knowledge of certain aspects of the past. The essential question for true history, for the philosophy of history, is a question it has always neglected: "What the aim and significance of that wondrous changeful life it investigates and paints may be?" The rationalist historians of the eighteenth century were bent upon simplifying the immense complexity of the past. Carlyle with a clear sense of the vulnerable points in their method, attacks them by stressing how inextricable are the connections of things: "The old story of Sir Walter Raleigh's looking from his prison-window, on some street tumult, which afterwards three witnesses reported in three different ways, himself differing from them all, is still a true lesson for us." The determining causes are always collective causes. Political history has set too much store by "battles and war-tumults," and by laws and constitutions; it has made too little of the silent enigmatic crowd which maintains the life of society: "Of Phœnician mariners, of Italian masons and Saxon metallurgists, of philosophers, alchemists, prophets and all the long-forgotten train of artists and artisans." What could be more delicate than the sifting of evidence? Witnesses are often incapable of seeing or understanding what they see; and witnesses rarely agree among themselves. "It is, in no case, the real historical Transaction, but only some more or less plausible scheme and theory of the Transaction, or the harmonised result of many such schemes, each varying from the other and all varying from truth, that we can ever hope to behold." It can never be otherwise; the vast becoming of humanity prevents it—events happen merely in a series, not in related groups. "Narrative is linear, Action is solid."

The philosopher of history (unless he subscribes to the conclusions of faith and is content to meditate with reverence upon "the mysterious vestiges of Him whose path is in the great deep of time") must have a sense of the relativity of things, and a healthy humility to check the audacities to which his science is prone. Moral forces must no longer be treated as simple calculable quantities. Rather "a growing feeling of the infinite nature of History" will issue in a division of labor: in history there must be artists and artisans. The artist will attain a vision of the whole and will interpret details in the light of that vision; and the artisan will be a specialist, exploring a single province of the immense empire of history. Beside political history, regenerated by the fruitful conception that causes are social, other branches will develop to supply the present deficiencies of the subject. There will be the history of institutions, the history of the sciences and the arts and above all there will be the history of religions, the vast inquiry into the spiritual development of humanity, stressing not so much councils and schisms as the secret movements in minds and souls: "nay, in its highest degree, it were a sort of continued Holy Writ; our Sacred Books being, indeed, only a History of the primæval Church, as it first arose in man's soul, and symbolically embodied itself in his external life." In these ideas, which were to sway Carlyle's own practice, he gives a powerful echo to earlier German thinkers and notably to Herder. Hereafter he went out of his way to ridicule the philosophy of history; he contrasted with the rationalism of a Gibbon or a Macaulay, who would coldly and lucidly pick apart a past assumed to be perfectly intelligible and in no way marvelous, his own sense of the impenetrable mystery of the past, the fervor of his religious idealism, his imaginative grasp of the substance of life. But one must not exaggerate Carlyle's renovation of history: he merely substituted for the creed of the rationalists another creed equally dogmatic, if more comprehensive.

Signs of the Times (1829) and *Characteristics* (1831) are also polemics. They may be considered as the overture to that far-ranging criticism of his own age which was soon to occupy Carlyle to the exclusion of all things else. The tendencies in these two studies are in appearance contradictory. In *Signs of the Times* Carlyle inveighs against the universal mechanism of the age, finding in it the scourge of civilisation and the root of moral and social disquiet. In *Characteristics* he finds the root of this disquiet in a new consciousness, a new moral attitude. If one wishes to consider consciousness and mechanism as exclusive of each other, then there is a clash here; but on closer inspection this contradiction disappears. Mechanism, in Carlyle's idiom, is that form of intelligence which arranges—arranges ideas, arranges materials. The rational philosopher and the man of affairs are both mechanists. The whole activity of the age is, he says, directed to the adaptation of means to ends. In these words Carlyle reveals the convergence between the two great movements of the time—the economic and social movement of the industrial revolution and the political and intellectual movement of utilitarian liberalism. Carlyle's intuitive perception of the unity of these two trends is perfectly sound. The progress of England at that time was entirely a progress toward a rational deliberate adaptation of the national life to a doctrinaire mechanism. By such an adaptation, the sovereign promptings of instinct are endangered; and in Carlyle they find their defender. To the mechanism which would dominate England in body and soul, in religion and industry, in morals and in methods, Carlyle opposes dynamism—the irrational forces of life. These are the most fruitful forces, the only fruitful forces. All the great movements of history are of their making, for all these movements begin in the secret activities of souls. These silent forces are about to regain their power; Carlyle prophesies their resurrection; and finds, for his inspired words, an echo in Emerson and in the followers of Saint-Simon.

In the study *Characteristics* Carlyle arraigns consciousness, by which he understands not the simple awareness of life on the part of men, but the effort to understand the nature of human being, the effort of the reflective mind to reduce and if possible to eliminate the rule of the unconscious: "The healthy know not of their health, but only the sick: this is the Physician's Aphorism; and applicable in a far wider sense than he gives it. We may say, it holds no less in moral, intellectual, political, poetical, than in merely corporeal therapeutics; that wherever, or in what shape soever, powers of the sort which can be named *vital* are at work, herein lies the test of their working right or working wrong. . . . All Science, if we consider well, as it must have originated in the feeling of something being wrong, so it is and continues to be but Division, Dismemberment, and partial healing of the wrong." Primitive innocence was not conscious of its state of being: "The memory of that first state of Freedom and paradisaic Unconsciousness has faded away into an ideal poetic dream. We stand here too conscious of many things." The relation between the concept of mechanism and the concept of clear consciousness is a very intimate one.

This axiom applies as much to the life of societies as to the life of individuals; for society is definable as the vital organisation of a number of individuals in a new and collective individuality, and the life of this organism is healthy as it is unconscious. The highest mode of being is mystery; to know one's self, to express one's self is to decline from that mode; and silence is the distinguishing attribute of the divine. "Well might the Ancients make Silence a god; for it is the element of all godhood, infinitude, or transcendental greatness; at once the source and the ocean wherein all such begins and ends." Action and not Thought is the true end of man; action alone can give him certitude, curing the disease of reflection and the otherwise insatiable disquiet of the mind. This principle of moral hygiene is a fruitful one: it illuminates and judges the age. The political fever of 1830, the revolutionary disturbances which had been at work for a century, these are marks of a deep-seated malady. The prevalence of analytic doctrines is another symptom of the malady: Benthamism and Utilitarianism are tending to destroy spontaneous organic activity, and born of a weakening in men's faith. Romanticism also is a symptom of a corrupted sensibility: it flourishes in its sentimental luxuriance only where the lofty and generous affections of the soul have withered and died. The love of nature is a conscious deformation of a normal healthy instinct: it is only in modern times that a lover of nature becoming "entirely aware that he was worshipping, much to his own credit, . . . thinks of saying to himself, 'Come let us make a description.'" Pessimism flows from the modern consciousness. The consciousness of one's existence has two phases: a phase of pride followed by a phase of pain. Humanity is now in the second phase: "Our whole relations to the Universe and to our fellow-men have become an inquiry, a doubt."

Consciousness is, then, an effect of weakened vitality; but consciousness may also be a means to salvation. Wisely controlled, subject to a sincere desire to attain the best, it is capable of planning out the difficult road that leads men back to primitive health. "Self contemplation is infallibly the symptom of disease, be it or be it not the sign of cure." Humanity is not likely to perish; from the very excess of its suffering, its cure will come. And Carlyle announces the regeneration of man in words that are vivid and resplendent. Scepticism will devour itself and the impurities of which it was generated. "The principle of life, which now struggles painfully, in the outer, thin and barren domain of the Conscious or Mechanical, may then withdraw into its inner sanctuaries, its abysses of mystery and miracle; withdraw deeper than ever into that domain of the Unconscious, by nature infinite and inexhaustible; and creatively work there. From that mystic region, and from that alone, all wonders, all Poesies, and Religions, and Social Systems have proceeded: the like wonders, and greater and higher lie slumbering there; and, brooded on by the spirit of the waters, will evolve themselves, and rise like exhalations from the Deep."

Carlyle's mind never worked with greater force or better order than in this passionate attack upon lucid and systematic thinking; nowhere do his ideas leap forth more copiously or more easily. This was his period of full and spontaneous intellectual activity and creation, the period when his genius, fertilised by German thought, had a sense of its endless fertility and gave itself up to the new excitement of harmonising with the bent of his own temperament the rich stock of ideas adopted from others. The bursts of anger and bitterness, the claims of the art of controversy with a view to immediate results have not yet come to impede and impoverish the play of his mind. Nowhere has Carlyle grasped more firmly the essential thesis which his life and work were to illustrate a thousand times. Burke is his precursor: Burke found in this thesis the very principle of his mortal hostility to the rationalisation of political justice. Carlyle extends its application far beyond the realm of politics. He denies and destroys the whole effort of the modern mind: in his glorification of the unconscious he seizes at one move upon all the formulae and programmes of reaction, political, religious or purely mystical. With an unfailing intuition he perceives the deepest line in the social and psychological transition of England in the nineteenth century, the transition which gave new bases to the thought and the civilisation of the people. It was by a broadening consciousness of herself that England threw away the fetters and the weapons of her past, threw away her strength. All his life Carlyle will deny that the transition was necessary; he will also deny that it was useful, and thus discharge at it his strongest volley. He will be aware of the peril that comes from diminishing force, and he will refuse to see any nobility in the destruction of limitations. Finally he will denounce as a danger and as a disease every conquest that clear thinking and clear consciousness have made over the activities which are instinctive, and as such subject to the blind but infallible orders of life itself.

CHAPTER V

SARTOR RESARTUS

I

FROM the time when his mind had come to maturity, Carlyle had been tormented by a desire to write the book in which he should find full expression. In 1830 he had an obscure feeling that the hour had come. In April he wrote in his *Journal:* "I have now almost done with the Germans. . . . After all, one needs an intellectual scheme (or ground plan of the universe) drawn with one's own instruments." He had been charmed by many projects: a life of Luther, for instance, and a history of German literature. The former he had quickly rejected, but the latter had held his interest for a good part of a year. He wearied however of this work and sought to divide his material into periodical articles. "I could write, and will write, something infinitely better, ere long," he says in a letter to his mother, in August of the same year. About the same time he said in his famous letter to Goethe: "When I look at the wonderful Chaos within me, full of natural Supernaturalism, and all manner of Antediluvian fragments; and how the Universe is daily growing more mysterious as well as more august, and the influences from without more heterogeneous and perplexing; I see not well what is to come of it all, and only conjecture from the violence of the fermentation that something strange may come."

To his brother Dr. Carlyle, in a letter of the following 19th of October, he announced that he was working at "the strangest of all things, begun as an article for *Fraser's;* then found to be too long (except it were divided into two); now sometimes looking almost as if it would swell into a Book. A very singular piece, I assure you! It glances from Heaven to Earth and back again in a strange satirical frenzy, whether fine or not remains to be seen." In November he decided to do two articles rather than a book; but his decision is accompanied by lasting regret. He sent off the manuscript to Fraser; but in January, 1831, he changed his mind—it is to be a book, it must be a book. For six months he worked away at it. On the 4th of August he left for London in quest of a publisher. In spite of his failure he continued to believe in his work. It was, he wrote, the best he had in him; "what God had given, and the Devil shall not take back."

In the very conception of the book, then, there was a vein of conscious strangeness, expressing itself in the enigmatic title, reminiscent of Richter. A new and symbolical meaning comes to dignify in an unexpected degree the trade of tailor; as in the 18th century Montesquieu had written the *Spirit of Laws,* Carlyle in the 19th wrote the *Philosophy of Clothes.* There was nothing original in the theme about which his ideas on life and nature had crystallised. It is not of much importance that he did not consciously derive from his predecessors, that he believed the germ of his allegory to have sprouted in a virgin soil. The truth is that his thought had been fertilised by the reflection of centuries. His theme is as old as the Oriental imagination, as the Biblical saying: "As a vesture shalt thou change them, and they shall be changed." Swift had likened the universe to a complete outfit of clothes: "Look on this globe of earth, you will find it to be a very complete and fashionable dress. What is that which some call land but a fine coat faced with green? or the sea, but a waist-coat of water-tabby?"

Goethe had revealed the Earth-Spirit weaving on the loom of time the garment that makes God visible. Language itself bears the traces of a reflection purely traditional and anonymous in which a representative value, pregnant with philosophical possibilities, is affixed to all that clothes. It was left for the genius of Carlyle to give an immense expansion to the scope of the ancient allegory, to make it the very soul of a powerful troubled book, rich in humor, satire and lyricism, arranging the most abstruse meditations in the guise of brilliant fancies.

From the very first, the book is on the ironical plane of a transparent fiction; it adopts disguises and seeks to mystify the reader in the manner of Richter. The editor—who remains anonymous—presents to English readers an original and mysterious being, the German Teufelsdröckh (the devil's excrement), professor of Allerleiwissenschaft (things in general) at the University of Weissnichtwo (nowhere). The editor draws a humorous picture of this personage, the principal elements of which are derived from the legendary figure of Kant, the personality of Richter and the normal traits of jovial, scholarly, idealistic Germany—metaphysical discussions, beer gardens, simplicity of manners and so forth. The singular professor has just written a book which has caused a sensation: *Die Kleider, ihr Werden und Wirken (Clothes, Their History and Influence)*. In this marvelous chaos of ideas, where the most dazzling flashes traverse the obscurity,

SARTOR RESARTUS

the kindly editor attempts to introduce enough order to reveal the hidden treasures. He is unable, however, to follow a systematic plan and gropes about in the confusion. A guiding line is given him by the Aulic Councillor, Heuschrecke, friend, boon companion and admirer of the great philosopher. The editor receives from Germany, sealed and stamped with the signs of the Zodiac, the sacks containing the materials which Teufelsdröckh himself had collected to illuminate the development of his thought. What a disappointment to the editor: the materials are a chaos of detached reflections, recollections, anecdotes, quotations, notes and figures. Twice the humorous theme of disorder so dear to Richter is brought before us. But this is not mere imitation on the part of Carlyle; in ascribing the discontinuous progression of his book to a necessity imposed upon him from without, he is attempting to translate into a virtue what is really an inherent defect. *Sartor Resartus* is the first of his books in which he finds complete expression; his intuitive and discontinuous method achieves here the effects natural to Carlyle's genius; his inability to produce organised works or to manage clear developments of ideas was thereafter manifest. All vestige of the mathematical mind once so dominant in him was thereafter effaced by the fierce ardor of his passion. His theory of the superiority of instinct to reason, confirming the natural bias of his temperament, left the logic of feeling undisputed mistress of his work, free to develop in his writings a vital if confused order.

From Teufelsdröckh's book however and from the complementary documents, the editor succeeds in piecing together an account of the strange scholar, his philosophy and his life. Teufelsdröckh's book is in two parts—the history of clothes and the influence of clothes; and the second of these is much the more important. *Sartor Resartus* follows the division of its original. In the first four chapters of the first book, the subject is defined, the personality of the writer is limned, and the nature and sense of what is to come is indicated. The space from the fifth to the eighth chapter is taken by a *résumé* of the first part of the German treatise, that which describes the history of clothes. In the eighth chapter the study of their influence begins; but in the eleventh chapter, which is the last in this book, the philosophical analysis abruptly breaks off: the mysterious sacks arrive from Germany. . . . The whole of the second book is devoted to a development from the new materials of a moral biography of Teufelsdröckh. In the third book Carlyle begins to analyse the influence of clothes, making his own commentary; and in the final chapter of the work he draws his conclusions. The plan is patently a complicated one; but the material is so much more complicated that Carlyle is forever departing from his plan. By references to what is to come and allusions to what has already been said and by unexpected digressions, Carlyle achieves here such an inextricable entanglement that the only unity is the unity of the whole. It is impossible thus to give a clear account of the content of this book without adopting a simpler order than Carlyle's. *Sartor Resartus* contains his complete teaching. In it there is a metaphysic, an ethic, and a theory of social relations, the last in germ rather than in full flower. Each of these we must examine separately.

II

In *Sartor Resartus* Carlyle's most comprehensive ideas about the universe come out, in terms of the dualism of

SARTOR RESARTUS

reality and appearance. In the symbolism here adopted this dualism is expressed through the central ubiquitous image of that which is clothed and that which clothes. It is not only Carlyle's metaphysic that turns upon this image; his ethic and his theory of society do so as well. In the three domains he preaches one doctrine—that of revolutionary frankness, of the stripping away of all veils. While showing the necessity of appearances, he degrades them to the level of mere shams. Beneath the spurious dignity of the garment, he reveals and reestablishes the superior, the substantial, dignity of the thing clothed.

The central idea is as old as human thought. It is the deepest principle of all idealism, ancient or modern: things are not what they seem, but quite different. The mainspring of his thought and the whole force of his temperament impelled Carlyle to this age-old affirmation. His Puritan inheritance left in him a profound, an insatiable need of a spiritualist philosophy; to his distinction between body and mind, the influence of religion naturally coupled a passionate preference of the mind to the body; and from this preference it was but a step to the denial of the reality of the body. The German idealists corroborated and accentuated this sovereign tendency in Carlyle. Like Emerson, he always conceived of them primarily as transcendentalists, as men whose reflection bore upon the supreme realities, transcending the field of sensible appearances. The transcendental movement, the ascent toward what is above, toward what is beyond, was to be the constant rhythm of his thinking, the scheme of his doctrine. It made no difference to him that the founder of German idealism had affirmed the transcendental realm of the noumena only in a few digressions, brief and obscure: his temperamental craving for a religion which should satisfy his reason became more conscious and more audacious, from his contact with the idealism of Kant. It was at this contact that he determined, for the expression of his confident and ardent faith in the universe, upon the age-old subject of men's doubt, the falsehood of appearances; it was at this contact that his moral personality issued its confession of belief, that the central book of his life took shape.

The true, the transcendent reality, according to Carlyle, is spirit. This is an old teaching—spirit is the noble, the central reality immediately known, as it is the only mode of existence, matter excepted, under which we can conceive of absolute being. Spirit is the divine. There is here a fusion, inevitable in Carlyle, between religious consciousness and philosophical belief. Carlyle felt no need to follow Kant's circuitous path, positing the necessity of practical reason; for him as for Schelling, there was an ecstasy, a direct intuition of the infinite irradiation of the Divine. He habitually refers to the supreme reality as God. In his later books he prefers to call it by vague, more prudent names—the Eternities, the Immensities, or the Superior Powers. And he will link it very intimately with the Universal Will. But his conception of the Divine will never stray far from that old Hebrew God, so much of a personal being in his definite inexorable interventions in human life. The spirit of Carlyle's conception will always keep just as narrow a watch upon conduct as the old Hebrew God. The sanctions according to which the doing of evil will be punished and the doing of good rewarded, will, in Carlyle's doctrine, remain perfectly clear and the recompense will be rapid if not immediate.

Carlyle leaves with the Divine, in a certain measure at least, the attributes of personality. The demands of his strict conscience halt his doctrine long before it approaches pantheism. Certainly he conceives of the universe as the "city of God," filled with His spirit: in every blade of grass, in every living soul "shines the splendor of a present God." Some of his expressions recall the ecstatic ravishment of the great mystics. When John Sterling accused him, upon reading *Sartor Resartus*, of professing pantheism, his rejoinder was half-hearted at best. The insistence of his friend upon the personal character of God stirred in Carlyle at least a doubt and a passive dissent. All we can say is that upon this essential point of the personal or impersonal nature of God, he did not formulate his belief with perfect clarity; such a formulation his sense of intellectual obligation did not require of him. God was; God was even the supreme being. His nature was either unknowable or but partly knowable by men; our finite modes of knowledge failed to comprehend him. Only one aspect of his being impressed itself strongly upon us: He is Good, He is not Evil. The moral responsibility of man delimits the immanence of God. Upon one point Carlyle departed from the old Calvinistic teaching which had given his soul its shape: he did not accept in fact the dogma of predestination. The doctrine of Kant had nourished in him an ineradicable sense of moral autonomy. The force of action which Calvinism took from a doctrine of fate, Carlyle found in a doctrine of freedom.

Another limit to the crushing omnipotence of God is in the personal existence of the principle of evil. The Demon, the Puritan devil, is everywhere in *Sartor Resartus*. No one is more often mentioned in the writings of Carlyle or in his familiar letters. By the circumstances of his education and by the atmosphere of his father's home and the habits of speech in the circle where he had lived, as well as by the authority of the Bible, the Evil Spirit came to take in his thought the part of an obsessing reality. In spite of the philosophic vagueness of the terms in which Carlyle sometimes refers to him, he exists clearly and completely and acts continuously and definitely. If Carlyle's conception of God is somewhat vague, his conception of the Devil is much plainer, and indeed his belief in the Devil appears to have been more definite.

From the divine reality, by an obscure processus, the created spirits of men emanate; and these spirits are centres of representation and action, endowed with a mysterious power. From Fichte, perhaps, Carlyle takes his insistence upon the primordial rôle, the essential actuality, of the ego. He was brought face to face with the riddle of a personality which questions itself; of those hours "when in wonder and fear you ask yourself that unanswerable question: Who am *I*; the thing that can say 'I'?" Humanity, that cortège of spirits, is an emanation from God, sent forth into the infinite; in its mad career it creates nature and the whole of the stage upon which its ephemeral life flashes and fades. Faith alone can penetrate the dark abyss from which humanity comes and to which it goes. The brief evocation for every spirit of a universe flashing with light is regulated by the interior innate laws of spirit. Carlyle takes over the Kantian doctrine of forms. He does not say, with Berkeley, that the sensible world is a complex of images and ideas suggested incessantly to created spirits by the divine spirit; he says that the general modes of perception, entirely subjective, fashion a reality which is itself inaccessible and clothe it in the garments of appearance. These general modes are time and space. Carlyle does not venture into the more difficult world of the forms of judgment: he merely alludes vaguely to the power of custom, mother of our axioms and reflections. All the categories he includes in a comprehensive denunciation of "systems" and "aphorisms." It is the unreality of space and time which seizes most strongly upon his mind and obsesses his imagination. "These, as spun and woven for us from before Birth itself, to clothe our celestial ME for dwelling here, and yet to blind it,—lie all embracing, as the universal canvas, or warp and woof, whereby all minor Illusions, in this Phantasm Existence, weave and paint themselves. In vain, while here on Earth, shall you endeavour to strip them off; you can, at best, but rend them asunder for moments and look through."

Transcendental intuition is within our powers; it is even among our duties. The door which Kant merely left open leaves the way clear for the impatient dash of the mystic. Reason can pass beyond the bounds imposed upon understanding. "Admit Space and Time to their due rank as Forms of Thought; nay, even, if thou wilt, to their quite undue rank of Realities: and consider, then, with thyself how their thin disguises hide us from the brightest God-Effulgences!" The traditional metaphysic, no doubt, is sterile and inane. "Which of your Philosophical Systems is other than a dream-theorem; a net quotient, confidently given out, where divisor and dividend are both unknown?" There is something of Kant's own spirit of bitter criticism in Carlyle: even Kant himself is not spared his own dose of irony. Carlyle was not naturally inclined toward the more abstract sort of thinking; whatever his intellectual vigor, he was conscious of the robust practical instinct of his race. He rallied the divagations of Coleridge the philosopher. His thinking always had the solid Earth underfoot, and the closer it was to earth the stronger it was. But what spurred Carlyle to yearn for knowledge of the suprasensible being was his preoccupation with conduct and his tormented curiosity about the destiny of man; where metaphysics had failed he would have religion risk its chance. Beyond space and time the gaze of the seer can penetrate to the eternity and the infinity of the Divine. "Nevertheless, has not a deeper meditation taught certain of every climate and age, that the WHERE and WHEN, so mysteriously inseparable from all our thoughts, are but superficial terrestrial adhesions to thought; that the Seer may discern them where they mount up out of the celestial EVERYWHERE and FOREVER: have not all nations conceived their God as Omnipresent and Eternal? . . . There *is* no Space and no Time: WE are—we know not what;—light sparkles floating in the ether of Deity!"

In such words as these, the philosophical enthusiasm of Carlyle which exalts every part of this strange book and concentrates its force in some magnificent effusions, culminates in adoration. Religion is the point of conclusion as unconsciously it was the point of departure. The irradiation of the Divine pierces with its swift burning darts the dull clouds with which German criticism smothered human knowledge. There are pages of ecstasy in *Sartor Resartus;* and in its ecstasy, in its intellectual intoxication, is the great strength and the great beauty of the book. The ideas Carlyle expresses about the secret nature of reality and the dualism of reality and appearance are not original. They are but an incomplete, popular and sometimes naïve transposition of Kant under the species of Fichte and Schelling. The most original element is in the fusion of transcendental idealism with Puritan mysticism. Such a fusion was nothing very audacious, if recent critics are correct in their ascription of pietist influences to the formation of Kant, and in their relation of his doctrine of practical reason to the genius of German Protestantism.

Carlyle is not a creator in the philosophic field. What is original with him is the intensity of his imaginative vision, and the marvelous ardor with which he seizes and re-creates the idealistic conception of the world. Into ideas which are in themselves cold and colorless he breathes the life of a supernatural revelation; he animates them, warms them, vitalises them. His voice is the voice of a prophet; he reveals the secrets of the universe with a religious emotion. He perhaps goes too far in preparing us to expect the marvelous; we catch him wondering at his own power to bear the strain of revelation. But this is, in some sense at least, an element of his humor. Fundamentally sincere, he is intellectually entitled to his moments of exaltation. No one has expressed in more striking fashion the effort of the spirit to penetrate beyond the realm of appearances, to dissolve them and to fathom the dark enigma that they screen. To the very end, through the whole body of his work, the visionary power of Carlyle, the power to strip off the sheath of things, to reveal in one dazzling moment their mysterious heart, will be his supreme excellence as an artist and as a thinker.

III

Ethics relates to the world fashioned by time and space: the problem of conduct has to do with the spirit in its contact with the world. The seminal idea of *Sartor Resartus* appears in this connection as a symbol of the relation between that which clothes and that which is clothed. The physical experiences which operate to destroy our sense of spiritual life are to that life as the garment is to the body. All the grandeurs, all the events, of the world are significant only in the measure that they express the inner reality or react upon it. Just as all the fabrics woven by man wear away and perish, the concrete objectifications of his beliefs, churches and rituals, are subject to the law of change. Hence the conception of a necessary evolution dominates Carlyle's doctrine concerning the birth and rôle of the moral and religious consciousness.

Carlyle owed to German literature and thought the sense of a universal becoming. Herder's doctrine of the movement of humanity; Goethe's conception of the progression of vegetable forms and of living species, and his other doctrine of the moral development of the individual soul through certain phases; the metaphysical rhythm which Fichte set at the very base and source of the world; the Hegelian dialectic unrolling its combat of thesis and antithesis—all of these Carlyle knew in their original statements or by their refraction in other writers. The whole of German thought, as he dimly perceived, had developed by opposing to the static analyses and reconstructions of the French a mystical sense of becoming. In Novalis as in Richter Carlyle had breathed the pantheist's intoxication with life, his sympathy with "the vegetable universe" by which our internal lives are related with the organic development of nature, with the progressive ramifications through which tree or plant germinates, grows and flourishes. This will explain the infinite number of images in *Sartor*, in which Carlyle affirms the deep similarity between the moral and social expressions of the soul and the forms of life we behold in nature, with their infinite flux and reflux. One might have the illusion in reading the book that one felt the flowing of the sap in a forest of eternal youth, where the new bark was perpetually forcing the old to crack and fall away.

Carlyle's ethic rests, in this book, upon the idea of personal evolution. Morality is a conquest and its necessary preliminary is conversion. Therefore the account of an ethic that we may find in *Sartor Resartus* takes the form of a psychological biography. In the second book we learn the history of a spirit. As in *Wilhelm Meister*, we look on at the youth of Teufelsdröckh, at his years of apprenticeship and of travel. The first chapters describe the childhood and intellectual formation of the hero. Many of the episodes are heavy with memories and reminiscences under a foreign name, transposed to the plane and the tones of German manners. The village here described is Carlyle's birthplace, these are the familiar rural scenes that had been about him, this is the awakening of Carlyle's senses and his mind. These pages of tender or caustic narrative or of humorous description are more than mere episodes; they are fraught with metaphysical meaning. In them Carlyle defends an idealistic thesis concerning the nature and the evolution of thought. The history of this young soul recalls the *Prelude* of Wordsworth; there is in the two cases the same hostility to the narrow dry formal method of associationist psychology; there is, too, the same intuition of the secret processes and silent lessons by which experience and the contact of things shape the soul; and finally there is the same insistence upon the emotions and the imagination as the vital sources of the obscure development of consciousness. Carlyle reaches the deepest grounds of his own moral being when he exhibits young Teufelsdröckh receiving the germ of religious life in his father's home, and with it the reverence for the infinite which is the highest virtue of man.

Adolescence and youth test the young personality still in the making. Carlyle is still quivering with his own spiritual crisis as he traces the stages and reveals the meaning of Teufelsdröckh's; but his maturity enables him to broaden his own history, and to give it the scope of a rich humanity. In this book which is at once his *Werther* and his *Wilhelm Meister*, he shows a suffering generation how a great mind suffers and then how it recovers. His tale is a confession of the most gripping psychological truth: only the circumstances are fiction. The cause of Teufelsdröckh's sorrows is an unfortunate love; and this is to be taken as a concession to a literary tradition too despotic for Carlyle to evade it. Teufelsdröckh is deeply in love with "Blumine," a symbol of feminine beauty in which it is not wise to find too much either of Jane Welsh or of Margaret Gordon; parting from her after a moving scene, he sinks into despair. But if the relation here established between a sentimental disappointment and a chronic melancholy is a license of imagination, other traits are very close to reality. Teufelsdröckh, like Carlyle, adds to his wounded heart, a mind tormented by doubt, tortured by the loss of his religious faith. The torments which he undergoes comprehend all the aspects of the *mal du siècle;* he may be said to traverse in his own person the romantic movement. In fact to the reader who scans the book with a really critical eye, the love affair sinks to a mere pretext; it is nothing but the palpable stroke of fate upon a soul already on the point of despair. Half a century had passed since *Werther,* and meanwhile the pangs of passion had lost their freshness and their power to move. There is no suicide here; the hero makes up his mind with amazing celerity; his disappointment becomes material for philosophic reflection. And with this essential transition Carlyle feels himself to be on firm familiar ground.

A romantic pilgrim, Teufelsdröckh carries through the world "the pageant of his bleeding heart." He visits the capitals, the ruins, the deserts. In Paris, in Rue Saint Thomas de l'Enfer he undergoes the devastating spiritual rebellion which is the first stage in his regeneration. We have already examined the relation between this "moment" and the biography of Carlyle. In this present context it takes on its full significance. The first principle of moral life is sacrifice and renunciation. Once this principle is fixed the trivial pitiful problem of happiness, the insanity of the age, dissolves; Byron is succeeded by Goethe, the prophet of a newer time. This is the deep meaning of *The Everlasting No.*

Thus does the soul restored by one heroic measure to the possession of itself, but tortured still by many a wound, find an impregnable fortress in its essential freedom. From this fortress it will sally forth to take, after bitter battles, the realms of faith and action. Henceforward Teufelsdröckh can count upon having "a fixed centre to revolve round." Henceforward he gnaws his heart out only at rare moments "and clutches round him outwardly on the NOT-ME for wholesomer food." He is outside himself. He interests himself in all labor, in all the various modes of social action. He travels and traverses cities as the spectator to whom nothing human can be alien. He is occupied with history and with the scenes of great events. In this transient phase, in this passing from self-obsession to altruistic curiosity he is in *The Centre of Indifference*. Its distinctive trait is the torpor, or at least the partial torpor, of sensibility; the soul can find in it repose if not peace. Despite the quietude of its spiritual temper, there is a sadness here, the sadness of resignation, and the vision of the nothingness of individuals and the littleness of man. "Pshaw! what is this paltry little Dogcage of an Earth; what art thou that sittest whining there? Thou art still Nothing, Nobody: true; but who, then, is Something, Somebody? For thee the Family of Man has no use; it rejects thee; thou art wholly as a dissevered limb: so be it; perhaps it is better so!" *The Centre of Indifference*, so conceived, well expresses the temper of Carlyle's moral life between 1822 and 1825. In these years he could feel the resurrection of his long latent energies; he acted, he embarked on various enterprises; he travelled, visited London and Paris, met men of mark, stood on the scenes of great events; he felt that he was enriching his mind, and yet he could not lift the melancholy which lay upon him; he was feeling his way, uncertain whither it led, and seemed to be as far as ever from the serenity he desired.

The final stage is *The Everlasting Yea*. This is the culminating point, the positive pole, of moral life, the moment when the affirmations of practice meet those of faith and metaphysics. The soul which has renounced itself moves slowly but surely toward belief, guided by a secret instinct. The rays of spiritual truth filter through the twilit realm of *The Centre of Indifference;* the presence of the Divine shines through nature. "Or what is Nature? Ha! why do I not name thee God? Art not thou the 'Living Garment of God'? O Heavens, is it, in very deed, HE, then, that ever speaks through thee; that lives and loves in thee, that lives and loves in me?" The perception of a divine essence latent in the merely relative gives a new and infinite value to the weakness of humanity; pity and love are stirred in the soul. "O my Brother, my Brother, why cannot I shelter thee in my bosom, and wipe away all tears from thy eyes? . . . Man, with his so mad Wants and so mean Endeavors, had become the dearer to me; and even for his sufferings and his sins, I now first named him Brother." There is tenderness here for all the scorn, all the bitterness, which it cannot hide, tenderness so rare in Carlyle that one comes upon it with a sense of relief and solace.

The supreme command of the divine will, a command that we can read on the tables of our heart, is the gospel of labor—the law of action without which there is no true conquest of self. "For the God-given mandate, *Work thou in Welldoing,* lies mysteriously written, in Promethean Prophetic Characters, in our hearts; and leaves us no rest, night or day, till it be deciphered and obeyed; till it burn forth, in our conduct, a visible, acted Gospel of Freedom." "Up, up! Whatsoever thy hand findeth to do, do it with thy whole might. Work while it is called To-day; for the Night cometh, wherein no man can work." Thus did Faust, having exhausted all the possibilities of life, reveal his wisdom in his generous activities; thus did Lothario in *Wilhelm Meister* discover that his "America is here or nowhere." "Yes here, in this poor, miserable, hampered, despicable Actual, wherein thou even now standest, here or nowhere is thy Ideal: work it out therefrom; and working, believe, live, be free."

In truth it is in the duty of love and action that the soul finds its joy, and finds because it no longer seeks for joy. This is the crown of the spiritual conquest of self. "There is in man a HIGHER than Love of Happiness: he can do without Happiness, and instead thereof find Blessedness! . . . Love not Pleasure; love God. This is *The Everlasting Yea*, wherein all contradiction is solved: wherein whoso walks and works, it is well with him." At Hoddam Hill, in 1825 and 1826, Carlyle experienced times of peace and even of joy; it was then and there that his new moral equilibrium was fixed. His visit to Birmingham and the influence of his friend Badams, in 1824, had directed his religious doubts toward a faith more active than any he had previously known; in the quiet of the country, in the tranquillity of his heart after his engagement to Jane Welsh, he came to know that he possessed the indispensable nucleus for a faith that would endure as long as he lived. "This year," he says in his *Reminiscences*, "I found that I had conquered all my scepticisms, agonising doubtings . . . and was emerging free in spirit into the eternal blue of ether, where, blessed be Heaven! I have for the spiritual part ever since lived." This is certainly a decided movement toward the certitudes that action requires, but alas, it is also a movement toward the certitudes that develop into dogmas and prejudices. The Carlyle of *The Everlasting Yea* often makes us regret the extinction of the Carlyle of *The Centre of Indifference*.

The ethic of Carlyle scarcely seems to differ from the

ethic of Christianity. Have we not come to the threshold of a Christian sanctuary, come before the temple in which sorrow is enthroned? "By strange, steep ways had I too been guided thither, and ere long its sacred gates would open, and the *'Divine Depth of Sorrow'* lie disclosed to me." Carlyle's ethic is certainly not an unqualified duplication of Christian doctrine. He could in no sense be called an orthodox Christian. Each time he met Irving—and was not Irving himself suspected of heresy?—he felt the chasm which separated them to have grown wider. His belief was the belief of a philosophic mind. According to him, religion like morality appears in this world of appearance under the guise of forms and formulae: religion is not excepted from the operation of the universal law of becoming. Not only are cassocks and surplices, the insignia of ecclesiastical dignity, subject like all other garments to dilapidation; but churches themselves, and their forms of doctrine and discipline, are but the vestments of the pure divine idea. Necessary vestments, indeed, for without them, worship, a social and collective act, could not exist; society is indispensable to religion as religion is the soul of society; or rather, from Carlyle's more perceptive point of view, religion is a spiritual tissue, the nervous system, as it were, of the body politic. Like all other fabrics, this wears out and dies; the Churches are none of them eternal. Some of them outlive their natural life and survive, mere horrible masks with unseeing eyes; while elsewhere, in unsuspected places of life, a new faith is born, and new tissues form. Among modern religions none is exclusively true; Christianity itself cannot be squeezed into the form of any sect whatever. Christianity is as broad as human culture to which all who have thought, and all who have been inspired, have made their contribution. Christianity comprehends among its means of expression the literature of the world, and the writers of the world are its true priests.

Despite his impatience of sects, Carlyle remains Protestant and even Puritan. His criticism of empty forms and outworn vestments is primarily a criticism of the pomps and hierarchy of the Catholic Church. It is true that he jeers at the 39 articles of the Church of England, but he is passionately loyal to the individualism which was the principle of the Reformation of religion. For him the personal contact of the soul with God is the indispensable sufficient essence of religious life. His sympathy is always with the mystics; and in his eyes heroism itself, the source of all great actions, derives from spiritual contact with the transcendent energy. The most solemn day in modern history was the day when the poor cobbler Fox made with his own hands a leathern garment, and breaking with the shams which surrounded him sought in solitude and meditation to achieve a life which should be really divine. A symbolical gesture it was: to solve once and for all the problem of vesture, the problem of religious organization, by reducing it to the minimum of complexity. This is to turn religion away from the pomps of worship to the ecstasies of the soul. George Fox was not only the founder of the Quakers; he was a perfect example of sincerity, the very type of religious truth. He was a heretic; he is still a lonely figure. Social necessities, at almost all times and in almost all places, have degraded the essence of religion with mortal shams. Christianity has not been able to evade the law of time; but the living centre of Christian faith is the idea of morality. "Knowest thou that '*Worship of Sorrow*'? The Temple thereof, founded some eighteen centuries ago, now lies in ruins, overgrown with jungle, the habitation of doleful creatures: nevertheless, venture forward; in a low crypt, arched out of falling fragments, thou findest the Altar still there, and its sacred Lamp perennially burning."

It was in this way that Carlyle discovered by the rough road of doubt the essential certitudes of faith, which, to be perfectly exact, he had never really lost. The morality of renunciation, pity and love—and also, in certain respects, the morality of action—this is indeed the traditional teaching of Christian morals. Carlyle discovers it within himself and raises it to a law binding upon us as well. Refracted by his robust personality, by his instinctive Puritanism, this morality was destined to develop much less in the direction of love than in that of action.

It is through love and action that we come in contact with our fellows. The social teaching of Carlyle emerges from his moral doctrine; and a first sketch of this social doctrine is given in *Sartor Resartus*.

IV

In the very movement and development of the book there is a wealth of significance. In its fancy and humor there is a social purport. The philosophy of clothes is by definition a philosophy of society, a philosophy of social relations. Our clothes modify our physical relations with the external world and especially our intercourse with other persons, regulated as this is by the countless exigencies of convention—decency, fashion, position, hierarchy. Passing lightly over the first of these, Carlyle explores the possibilities of the other three very fully, and gives copious illustrations of the part symbolism plays in human society. His idealistic conception of law, regnant throughout the book, is specially developed in some of its chapters—in those where Carlyle touches upon social justice and the war between the classes.

Professor Teufelsdröckh's great book opens with a picturesque study of the variety of garments in which at the several points of his history man has clothed himself. This beginning is the pretext for a comic catalogue of the strange and varied fashions in clothes to which men have always been prone. But there is a serious philosophic essence in these opening pages—their irresistible suggestion of the relativity of things. Moreover they dissociate the idea of man from the several artificial envelopes in which it is enclosed, and from which it is to be extracted only with great difficulty: by these pages we become capable of conceiving a world out of clothes. It is not merely the bodies of individuals that clothes cover, adorn, protect and conceal; the bodies of groups and institutions and the body politic and social itself are clothed. Literally clothed by the various uniforms and insignias they adopt; metaphorically clothed too—are not the police and the army like a leathern apron, tough and protective? All garments, however, are by some mysterious power, the instruments, the agents even of a spiritual force—the authority of law. The red robe says to the blue jerkin, "Go and be hanged"; and the blue jerkin by a miracle submissively inclines its neck to the hangman. And so we arrive at the paradoxical conclusion that clothes are the very foundation of society.

So far the thesis of Carlyle has been presented on the plane of humor. To appear to establish that clothes are all is to put in a glaring light the fact too often forgotten that clothes are nothing. A necessary symbol, an indispensable accompaniment of law, in practice they are confused with the legal principle. If one presses the association of principle and vestment to its logical conclusion, it is only to recognise in it the indolence of mind which protects from a just accounting the hypocrite and the weakling. Beneath the soldier's mail is there always valor, beneath the bishop's purple is there always holiness, beneath the judge's wig is there always integrity? Do we in our herdlike passivity render obedience to the intangible hypothetical spiritual virtue of the man, or to the outward insignia, the braid and the epaulet? The primordial importance which, in the inadequacy, the weakness, of our perceptions, we accord to clothes, aggravates instead of remedying the evil. Substituting for the mystical order of souls a hierarchy visible to the physical eye, the reverence for clothes merely perpetuates a thoroughly mediocre moral code, and permits the survival of a universal sham. Undress society, and it is swept away in a gale of ridicule. The imagination refuses to picture a noble duke, speaking —himself entirely naked—before a House of Lords similarly stripped. Now if the bodies of men are too miserable to be exposed to the light of day, what of their souls should they once be seen entirely naked? It is to this Swiftian question, with its curious amalgam of the burlesque and the bitter, to this attempt to substitute within the realm of appearance the more genuine for the sham, that the first chapters of *Sartor Resartus* conduct us. This is the train of thought of a social philosopher at once audacious and ironical; and Teufelsdröckh, so Carlyle tells us, is one of the most uncompromising speculative radicals the world has ever had.

Toward 1830, the word "radical" was in its freshest novelty and bore a very strong meaning—it designated the opponents of the *status quo*. The political instincts of Carlyle had been shaped by two principal influences which were in clear opposition. The first of these he had met in his father's home, where there was a spirit of independence and a sense of the inherent worthiness of man; the contact with German idealism had prepared him to accept revolutionary audacities; he had himself known what poverty was and perhaps what want was too; he had become clearly aware of the economic sufferings of the age; and in the coming crisis it was unthinkable that his strongest sympathies should be with the party of privilege. His religious conception of life and his commerce with the Bible had strengthened his social conscience; the germs of Christian socialism which lie concealed in the mysticism of the English and the Scottish mind were still alive in the mind of Carlyle.

On the other hand he was at an early age disgusted by the ignoble conception of the good, and the mediocre methods of action, that he found among the reformers. Utilitarianism, in which the reformers of the age sought their intellectual sanctions, annoyed him by its methods and by its objects. Most important of all, there were other tendencies, deeply rooted in his temperament, which gave promise of a maturity in which a prudent, regulated and orthodox spirit would reign. As a child he had deferred to the undisputed authority upon which his father insisted; and in his home he had grown to love moral and social discipline. Later his instincts for discipline become more definite and were strengthened by new elements, by a respect for the imponderable soul of nations, by a vigorous sense of the continuity of history, a scorn for the decisions of the crowd and the prestige of majorities, by a belief in the power of individuals. By all these spiritual convictions he was repelled farther and farther from the prospects opened up in the triumphant development of the middle class. From 1830 to 1840 his mind was much occupied by the doctrine of heroism; and his opposition to anarchy was becoming more certain and more energetic.

His definitive social doctrine was to emerge from this complex group of reactions. At the time when *Sartor Resartus* was written, he was still most responsive to the burning enthusiasms of his youth; the social critic was still more in evidence than the prophet of order; and both for himself and for his hero he accepted the democratic term of radical. Preoccupied by the dissonance between the moral realities and the physical symbols of law, he composed here what may be called an iconoclastic satire upon social life. Teufelsdröckh strips away from things their disguises and decorations with the audacity of a *sans-culotte*, a *sans-culotte* who is also a mystic.

Society he says is not merely ailing—it is dead, for its soul, its collective faith, its religious creed is dead; and, with the death of these, what lives on is but a spectre or an illusion. Utilitarian individualism seems to provide a collective faith. But in this doctrine there is no unifying power—this doctrine is a principle of conflict, anarchy and death. Against liberalism in politics, free competition in economics, hedonism in ethics and associationism in psychology, Carlyle protests with all the passionate vehemence of an idealist. The impious Malthus had communicated to the upper class an intense and depraving fear of the fertility of humanity; and yet there were virgin forests, there were distant countries offering infinite resources to the immigrant. Why should not the degenerate aristocrats of England lead forth into the American groves and prairies peaceful armies of pioneers? This is but the first appearance of a theme which was later to be resumed and developed.

Teufelsdröckh's criticism of society is sometimes so bold as to call in question the very principle of the existing economic order; but on the whole it accepts that. In August, 1830, Carlyle had received a message from the French Saint-Simonians in whom the *Signs of the Times* had excited the fantastic hope that there might be an intellectual communion between themselves and the writer; not long after Carlyle translated a pamphlet of Saint-Simon, *The New Christianity*. Goethe however wrote to him to beware of their principles, and the warning was scarcely necessary; by all his social and religious instincts Carlyle was attached to the traditional foundations of the existing order. His social doctrine was *étatiste*, it never was and never could be socialist.

There will always be rich and poor. But it is intolerable that while the rich are perishing of a plethora, the poor should be perishing of want. The proprietary classes have forgotten their duty. They are occupied by imbecile inanities. The Dandy, that garment-made man, is a significant monstrosity, confirming by his colossal absurdity the philosophy of clothes. In Ireland, meanwhile, famine rages; in sinister contrast to the Dandies, the class of "poor slaves" take and keep the vow of poverty. "*On voit certains animaux farouches* . . ." La Bruyère had said. In the same spirit of assumed dispassion, Carlyle's humor explores the strange manners of the poor—shows up their rags, their wolfish appetite perpetually disappointed, and the darkness of their understanding. Between the two sects, the rich and the poor, the chasm is always widening; the two "nations," of which Disraeli was to speak, were already face to face; from one pole to the other, at any moment, there might flash forth the spark of a revolution.

A horror of imminent upheavals in the social order haunted Carlyle like a nightmare as he grew older; but the writer of *Sartor Resartus* was still young and elastic enough in thought not to be desperate because he was certain that there would be great changes in the near future. His imagination was fixed by the splendid vistas of German historicism; the theory of palingenesis, of the eternal repetition of things, was a refuge from too tragic a fear of the morrow. Another and vaguer element in Carlyle's optimism was the general but intangible influence upon him of Saint-Simon.

It is true, he thought, that society is dead; but like the Phœnix, it will be reborn from its ashes. Visions of the golden age come to brighten the dark horizon of the present. In a mystical chapter, one of the most substantial of the book, the chapter on *Organic Filaments*, Carlyle attempts to trace, in the corrupt mass of the present anarchy, the scheme of an order in becoming. The principal element in this scheme is the great fact of human solidarity, that love, which, far below the apparent oppositions of egotism, connects all human beings. All the generations of men are bound by the close tie of time. After a necessary destruction, reconstruction will follow. Representative government, the least bad of polities, will probably survive; political reforms, electoral or other, will be but the superficial incidents of a development which in comprehending them will exceed them. But the surest guarantee of the future of man is that admiration which nerves and elevates the soul, the worship of heroes. A new Church is in process of birth: the Church of Letters. The thinker, the writer—the priests of the new undogmatic faith—will communicate to the hearts of men a harmony of feeling which will be the soul of social life in times to come. And Carlyle's prophecy closes with this animated evocation of the future colored by religious and humanitarian feeling. It is wrong to forget, as so many of his readers do, that beside the dark raging spirit of the older Carlyle must be put the noble and perhaps more perspicacious enthusiasm of his glowing youth.

V

With *Sartor Resartus* the doctrine of Carlyle has taken its definitive shape; all its elements are there and Carlyle is already aware of their organic unity. None in fact of the great directive ideas of his later books is absent from this. Some of them were destined to develop, such as the theory of heroism and the theory of social relationships; and others, as the happy picture of the inevitable progress of human becoming, were to fade into the background. There was not, however, to be any renewal of Carlyle's thought, nor any modification of its main lines. To the end his thought was to be nourished from within, from that treasure of spiritual wisdom in which the tendencies that he inherited and those he acquired in his youth were coupled. He was to have brilliant success, to take the country by storm, to be one of the great intellectual and spiritual forces of the time; but none of his books was to have the richness of substance of the first one, ignored or ridiculed as it continued to be. For into this first book he had poured the whole torrential sap of his genius. The sense that at last he had expressed what he bore in his mind was to sustain him in all his future battles; and with an untiring energy he was to go on repeating, until people would hearken, what in *Sartor Resartus* he had completely said.

This book set for Carlyle a career as prophet. Formerly intended for the Church, he had retained the preoccupation with morals and the spiritual elevation that such a destination might promote—and he had also retained a liking for preaching. Like Irving he now meant to exercise an undogmatic ministry; more slowly but more surely than Irving, he would draw to hear him, crowds which would hang upon his words. Very soon after the writing of *Sartor* he decided that the pen was not by itself sufficient to satisfy his preacher's instinct: he wished to communicate his doctrine by word of mouth. Some months before he left for London with the manuscript of *Sartor* he wrote to his brother John: "Nay, I have half a mind (but this is in deepest secrecy) to start when I come there, if the ground promise well, and deliver a dozen of Lectures, in my own Annandale accent, with my own God-created brain and heart, to such audience as will gather round me, on some section or aspect of Life in this strange Era, on which my soul like Eliphaz the Temanite is getting fuller and fuller."

It turned out that he was to give such a series of lectures and to challenge his age in person. His book *On Heroes and Hero Worship* took shape as a series of lectures. But once he had conquered the reading public with *The*

French Revolution, the written word intended for that numberless audience became his favorite, his most effective instrument. It was a struggle to make that instrument do his bidding and carry all he meant it to carry, as it had been a struggle to discover and shape his thought. With *Sartor Resartus* Carlyle mastered his instrument. All its powers are here revealed, all its effects achieved. In the strangeness of the subject, the visionary quality of certain of its parts, in the German atmosphere in which the hero lives and which suffuses the whole development of the book, Carlyle found an authorisation and an invitation to the deliberate audacity of a created language. The influence of Richter, fusing with the instinctive suggestions of Carlyle's temperament, gave to these latter a new pungency and precision. In the brusque energy, the ellipses and inversions, the constructions which fit like a glove upon the swift unpredictable development of the idea, in all these modes in which Carlyle is striving for the effect of the most headlong sincerity, he is completely spontaneous, he is altogether himself. He is no longer imitating the model of Richter, he has assimilated Richter and gone beyond him. If he had never discovered himself, he would have continued to write in quite another way; but from *Sartor Resartus* on, his style and his thought are indiscerptible; the two, moreover, are inseparable from his temperament.

Carlyle's style, destined for exhortation and combat, is forged of the hard metal of Saxon words; and these, curt, sharp, words of sensation and action, Carlyle manipulates with an instinctive felicity; he loves them because he finds then weighted with the oldest elements of the race, and because through them he can return to the savage ancestors of England for whom he has an affectionate reverence. From Germany, England's Teutonic sister, he borrows a few turns of phrase, a few words. He follows the Germans in the freedom of their sentence structure, and on a German analogy he arranges words in new and expressive combinations; he creates compound adjectives and nouns; he attaches adverbs to verbs to achieve a more massive and concise effect. Sometimes he simply translates a German expression or models his sentence upon it. Certain critics have also found in his style a provincial vein, and dialectical forms of expression; the idiom of Annandale, the reminiscences of domestic conversation, were the essential origins of everything in Carlyle.

He also had other resources: the rough Saxon words are harmonised with the foreign but naturalised elegance and suppleness of the Latin. The long majestic learned Latin polysyllables, breathing an air of subtle abstract thought or of refined grace, are indispensable to philosophic reflection and apposite to the play of irony and humor. Carlyle melts and fuses them with the popular Saxon idiom. And are they not acclimatised to English soil, do they not bear the superscription of Shakespeare and Spenser, do they not suggest the rich colors of Elizabethan poetry? When English prose became an art, toward the end of the 16th century, was it not from Latin and French culture that it took its models, its rhythms, half of its vocabulary? The eloquent and devotional prose writers of the 17th century, all fragrant with archaism, Taylor, Sir Thomas Browne and Milton, had been restored to their proper eminence by the romantic critics;

Coleridge had vaunted them as models for the fine use of prose; and Carlyle, for a certain period at least, had taken them as his masters. He had rallied Irving for his too deliberate imitation of older masters, but the elaborate disposition of their sentences and paragraphs, and the display of their enormous erudition, had worked their effect upon him as well. For all the jaggedness and incoherence of the new idiom he had evolved, echoes of the fullness of their cadences and reminiscences of their splendor of phrase remain. The style of Carlyle is as various and composite as it is personal.

Its supreme lord, its deepest inspiration, is the imagination. The imagination animates and sustains the heavy agglomerations of words, gives them their intensity and makes them kindle with sudden flashes of light. By right of his imagination, Carlyle is a great poet. While it is powerful, its range is limited; there is a monotony in the effects it achieves, but the monotony itself is grand. Its savage contrasts and its sublimity are the qualities of the Bible and of the primitive Anglo-Saxon spirit. Carlyle's intercourse with the German mystics and idealists had left him with a magic faculty for moving in an immaterial world. He is capable either of projecting his image in all its tingling brutal reality, or of opening deep spiritual channels through material things and making these float like translucent shades upon a dream background, on which of a sudden the infinite surges up. His favorite images are those of light and shade, images in which light has a heavenly glory, and shade the darkness of the abyss. All is moving in Carlyle, moving with the most dashing impetuosity, with the cosmic amplitude of a natural force, suggestive indeed of the sky, the sea and the wind. A marvelous auxiliary to his metaphysical preoccupations, his style makes it easy for a mind to pass from one plane to another; and emphasises the force and the scope of the intellectual activity which comprehends and unifies those planes.

BOOK II
THE PROPHET AND HIS AGE

CHAPTER I

CHEYNE ROW

THE Carlyles set up house at 5 Great Cheyne Row, Chelsea. From this old and roomy house they had a view over the Thames, close at hand, and the green of suburban gardens. In the distance were the towers of the Abbey and the dome of St. Paul's; at night only the reflections of its lights revealed the nearness of the great city. There was a garden in which Carlyle could ply his spade, trim his hedges, grow jasmine and gooseberries. Tranquil as the suburb was, he found the street noises more than he could bear; and time and again the Carlyles were obliged to revise their domestic arrangements. But the house was restful and comfortable, and gay too, for Jane had taste and personal charm. When she died, her memory continued to preside over a house which Carlyle had kept at first rather from habit than from deliberate choice.

In outward seeming the story of Carlyle is from this point as placid as its beginnings were tempestuous. Its significant dates are those in the progress of his labors and his fame. His way of living will not henceforth be as lonely as it had been in Scotland: but it will remain secluded, packed with daily work usually of an arid and exacting kind. He gave all the morning to composition; and in the afternoon went afoot, now to Kensington Gardens, now, skirting the river, to Hyde Park, now, lost in thought, to the British Museum. Jane seldom accompanied him: her health was always precarious. From time to time, they had visitors or dined out; but these concessions to society left Carlyle exhausted, enervated, soured. They travelled too; one or other of them often spent some time in Scotland. Carlyle did not, however, find there the peace which London also denied him; and beneath the even tenor of his life, the struggle with the demon of disquiet went on unabated.

As years rolled by, the circle of their acquaintance was enlarged; and more intimate friends, too, grew in numbers. The oldest and dearest of these came to an untimely death in 1834, heartbroken by the tragic crumbling of his mystical dreams; a vanquished prophet, he succumbed after a day's success, just when the chum of his youth was about to conquer. Irving had been without the robust sanity, the single-mindedness, the sense of realities, the stubborn grasp upon life, which were the salvation of Carlyle. At Chelsea lived Leigh Hunt, that curious personage, Bohemian, artist, revolutionary: the households of the two men of letters were on intimate terms and a friendship grew up between them, secured by the very contrast in their natures. A friendship more tender and more nearly complete than this united Carlyle with John Sterling, an eager, tortured and aspiring man in whom Carlyle found one of his closest disciples. Carlyle had already made the acquaintance of John Stuart Mill, who already promised to outshine his father: they became more intimate, certain similarities of mind and a reciprocal esteem cloaking their essential incompatibility. Carlyle maintained an active correspondence with Emerson, who shows himself the devoutest of his admirers, the most adroit of agents: through Emerson's efforts an American edition of *Sartor Resartus* appeared in 1836, two years before the publication of the work in England. In fact, before long there was scarcely a single man of eminence in letters or politics who was not in some degree an acquaintance of Carlyle. Southey, Wordsworth, Dickens, Tennyson, Browning, Maurice, Kingsley—he met them all. Among the younger men, his ideas were deeply and broadly influential. People wrote to him, confessed to him. Little by little, an atmosphere of deferential and distant devotion surrounded the Sage of Chelsea, but was powerless to disarm his wrath against a century far-gone in frivolity and busy in the service of false gods.

It was three years after his installation in Cheyne Row that Carlyle's triumph came; and during these dragging years he was intimate with doubt and not a stranger to despair. As soon as he had set up house, Carlyle began the great work on which he was staking his last hope, the *History of the French Revolution*. John Stuart Mill was lavish with his encouragement, and even loaned to Carlyle his own collection of works on the period. With great labor, Carlyle accomplished his reading and set about composing; his first taste of the writing of history left him with a feeling of uncertainty and difficulty with which he was destined to grow familiar. He came to the end of his first 'book' and was engaged on his second when a disaster seemed to dash all his hopes: his manuscript, loaned to Mill, had been destroyed by a careless maid. He had kept no copy; all his arduous labor, all the intense activity of his mind, fusing in a tragic vision thousands of facts noted from documents, had gone on without systematic complete notes. Nothing remained; all must be done afresh. Without admitting despair, Carlyle rewrote his first book; but the task drew from him cries of anguish. In January, 1837, his martyrdom was over; six months later the work appeared in print; the reading-public, astonished, hesitant, conquered in its own despite, allowed itself to follow the warm enthusiasm of the *élite;* before the year ended Carlyle was famous and a part of the literature of England.

The tempo of his personal and domestic life knew no change. Money worries did, indeed, disappear: affluence came by degrees. Upon the death of Mrs. Welsh in 1842 the income from Craigenputtock swelled the household resources. But Carlyle was already a helpless victim of disquiet: worry over the works in process of composition, resentment at the unpleasant trivialities of the passing day, continued to provoke him to ill-temper and sadness. His health, too, was no better, or at any rate he thought it no better. His inner life was woven of two threads: one made of confidence, peace and strength, the other of anxiety and tenacious resentment. The former was firm, indeed, but hidden: it was the second which dominated his life. Since the days of Hoddam Hill he had found what belief he needed to go on with life; and the cure of his soul had been very sweet to him. "What my pious joy and gratitude then was," he exclaims in his *Reminiscences,* "let the pious soul figure in a fine and veritable sense, I, poor, obscure, without outlook, almost without worldly hope, had become independent of the world. . . . I understand well what the old Christian people meant by '*conversion,*' by God's infinite mercy to them. I had, in effect, gained an immense victory and for a number of years, had, in spite of nerves and chagrins, a constant inward happiness that was quite royal and supreme, in which all temporal evil was transient and insignificant, and which essentially remains with me still, though far oftener *eclipsed* and lying deeper *down* than then." There is the secret of the renewal of his energy, an energy no longer merely inherited and instinctive, but conscious, reflective, deliberate, an energy which was to nourish and sustain Carlyle's activity to the very end. His Christianity stripped of its dogmas, his faith in a moral universe, had driven away the nightmares of his youth; and secure upon its spiritual bases, his life was now opened to happiness. He was, indeed, by nature in possession of the spring of gladness which had quenched the thirst of many a soul less lofty than his.

But the law of his nature ruled that *he* should not be refreshed. Let us concede the rôle in his misery played by his insomnia, his physical discomforts, the weight of the nervous disorders from which he was never to be free. Let us grant also to his sensibility, wounded for so long, its right to remain unhealed. But let us confess, too, that in his being Carlyle had an inward principle of bitterness—the return upon itself of an energy drawn in close that it might fight the better. The prophet was about to denounce an impious age with a fury altogether sincere; and his finest accents, the very force of his indictment, were to be forged by the genuineness of his wrath and of his anguish; it was written that the love in Carlyle should adopt not only the language but the very characteristics of hatred. He was born to scorn men. In the very page in which he shows us the genesis of his secret peace of mind, he pictures himself rising, free of soul, into the eternal blue of the empyrean which he was never to leave, and casting a glance of haughty pity toward the countless throng of souls still mired in doubt. He was too conscious of the isolation to which he was chained by his destiny: he was incapable of putting into practice that doctrine of his which would discover and cherish in every imperfect creature a spark of the divine and spiritual splendor: in him the holy anger of the just blended with a feeling of his unicity, and an instinctive affirmation of himself. The loneliness in which he lived was the creation of his own mind and his own heart.

He suffered from this loneliness, and his complaints fill the poignant pages of his private journal. "My isolation, my feeling of loneliness," he wrote on the 1st of October, 1834, in this journal, "unlimitedness, what tongue shall tell? Alone, alone! Woes too deep, woes which cannot be written even here." Such is the burden of his daily notes in this journal, alternating with spurts of savage determination or of desperate resignation: "Complain not. Struggle, thou weakling." There is sublimity in this obstinate untiring struggle, in which his courage is whipped on by the invincible force of his soul; and it is impossible to follow the stages of the struggle without marveling at his heroism. What penetration, what touching humility, there is in the confessions in which Carlyle judges the harshness of his own character: "One of the things I need most is to subdue my polemics, my ill nature." Alas, as he had said to Jane, his best resolutions foundered in the sea of practice.

Jane, invariably devoted and courageous, shared all the pains of this life of his. The burden of the household, so heavy at Craigenputtock, had grown light: in London there was pleasure and variety of occupation to be had for the asking; but she accepted the conditions material and moral of the life—necessarily egocentric—of an anguished genius. She had however found friends; in their society she let herself go and relieved her mind of its intolerable weight of sadness. Nothing is more painful than these confidences of Jane. Despite the little disagreements which wounded their mutual affection, that affection appears to have remained unimpaired. During the times of separation Carlyle wrote her letters of supreme tenderness. In moments of sudden insight he perceived the real value of the treasure she was to him. But why, in his journal, these cries of anguish, these confessions of distress and infinite loneliness? Jane was made to be the companion of thoughts such as his, she had nobility of soul sufficient to understand him and to replace for him the thoughtless and unworthy world. But she did not fulfil her destiny, the destiny of which both had dreamed. Their love was powerless to warm their hearts. Suspected too late by Carlyle, the secret divorce of their minds was irreparable. Would Carlyle have agreed to pay the price necessary to repair it? He wrote to Jane in 1841: "Neither man nor woman, nor any kind of creature in this universe, was born for the exclusive, or even for the chief, purpose of falling in love or being fallen in love with. Good heavens! It is *one* of the purposes most living creatures are produced for; but, except the zoophytes and coral insects of the Pacific Ocean, I am acquainted with no creature for whom it is the one or grand object. That object altogether missed, thwarted and seized by the Devil, there remains for man, for woman, and all creatures (except the zoophytes) a very great number of other objects over which we will show fight against the Devil." Natural tell-tale impatience: rationalisation of a failure as well as of a preference. The gospel of action, once Carlyle's intellectual virility had been affirmed, had encroached to a frightful extent upon the gospel of love.

Soon an influence from the outer world was to aggravate their divorce, and make Carlyle's faults weigh heavier than those of his wife in the balance of their misunderstanding. The growth of his reputation had given him contact with the aristocracy of money and of birth as well as with the aristocracy of brains. He had invitations from the great, invitations which he did not always decline: and despite his hatred of society, some of his experiences brought him pleasure. Like many another man of the craft he was not indifferent to the smiles of his titled admirers. He had the maximum of pride, the minimum of vanity—but was he innocent of snobbishness? He confesses to a measure of it in his *Reminiscences;* and, despite his "independent mind," his spirit of purely intellectual idealism, he does not seem to have been free from the subtle, perilous foe which so few can repel without compromise. His *amour-propre* was pleasurably tickled. Was there anything further to explain the ascendancy over him of Mrs. Baring (later Lady Ashburton), whose acquaintance he made in 1845? Her brilliance and sweetness were certainly enough to enchant him. She was attached to her husband, she did nothing to detach Carlyle from Jane; and their friendship never aroused the least scruple in a conscience which was as pure as it was puritan. Nevertheless, although Carlyle remained literally faithful to Jane, his spiritual fidelity was imperfect; and his wife's jealousy was only too legitimate. She complained of a preference humiliating to her; and up to the very death of her rival in 1857, a misunderstanding was always smouldering in the household and now and then flaming forth. Jane's shortcomings, her biting sharpness of tongue, her severe interpretation of trifles, and, in this case, the tactlessness of her complaints, do not make an excuse for a weakness which was far too great to be set in the balance against them, and for which she cannot be made responsible with any justice. If we did not appreciate the utter dogmatism of his conscience, we should find it difficult to understand why Carlyle did not seize the simplest, most radical means of allaying the suspicions which sincerely troubled him. In his sight it would have been a falsehood, the worst indeed of petty acts, to seem to prefer peace of mind to the brute truth.

Some weeks before the publication of *The French Revolution* Carlyle had made his bow as a lecturer: on the 1st of May, 1837, he delivered the first in a series of six lectures on German literature. A biographer pictures him on this occasion as he impressed his audience, attentive and curious: tall, gaunt, with long, massive head, with undistinguished features. His intense, abrupt delivery cost him a great expense of energy; but its vigor, its novel, disconcerting beauty, the fiery play of his imagination, brought decisive success. The revenue from these lectures, joined to that from the *French Revolution*, guaranteed Carlyle freedom from want: he was never again to know the terror of the future. In 1838 he lectured on *The History of Literature* and *The Periods of European Culture;* in 1839 upon *The Revolutions of Modern Europe;* in 1841, finally, upon *Heroes, Hero-Worship and the Heroic in History*. The text of this last series, revised by Carlyle, appeared in print in the course of the year; of the three earlier series, we have only fragments.

His mind was, however, becoming more and more preoccupied with social problems. England was traversing the gravest crisis of modern times. In 1832, after a long agitation, the First Reform Bill had shaken the political structure and given the determining power to the upper middle class. But scarcely had the noise of battle died away when a new and graver danger menaced the recently established order: behind the merchants and the manufacturers, now pacified, rose the threatening proletariat, angered, disappointed by a victory to which it had contributed but the fruits of which were destined for others. The measures sponsored by the government which came in on the wave of the Reform Bill, revealed its strong conservative tendency. This government did not bestir itself to alleviate the misery brought to England by the blind expansion of the factory system. In the cities there had grown up a class without any ties, without traditions, without specific organisation, powerless to react upon the social conditions of the country, injured by the régime of free competition, forced to destructive overwork; the rate of pay, the hours of labor, the unsanitary state of the factories, overpopulation, ignorance, intemperance, all conspired to create a far-reaching and deep disquiet which broke out in strikes, riots, incendiarism. More than one factory went up in flames, and in the depopulated rural sections, where the wages of employees had fallen steadily lower and lower, the burning stacks would flare upon the night. Worse even than the misery of the English proletariat, was that in Ireland; for there the oppression of one race by another was added to the pressure of economic trends.

From this variety of ills was engendered in the employing classes a sense of uncertainty, and in the working classes, rural and urban, a desire for revolt, which grew in force and definiteness. The upper middle class had won the right to vote and profited by it: the same weapon would permit the proletariat to shake off the yoke of the oppressor. The efficacy of the political machine had once more been proved: why not make this machine work for the profit of the majority? From such bases grew the Chartist movement, a powerful but confused expression of the dream of social justice. The people's "charter," won by "moral force," aided perhaps by the force of arms, would give to the working classes a legal status which would ensure the respect of its rights.

The year 1839 appeared to foreshadow a swift and bloody crisis. In February, a Chartist National Convention met in London; in July there were serious riots in Birmingham. In November Carlyle finished "a long review article, thick pamphlet, or little volume, entitled CHARTISM." The long-repressed waves of his wrath and his prophetic indignation poured forth here like a flow of lava. "The thing has been in my head and heart these ten, some of it these twenty years." Declined by the *Quarterly Review*, the great conservative organ of the day, the "article" appeared in book form before the close of the year, to be greeted, as Carlyle observed, by the "barks" of the radicals heretofore friendly to him. Following upon this, appeared his *Miscellanies*, in which Carlyle collected his early studies in criticism, adding a sheaf of new ones. He felt himself free, then, to attack a task he had long projected, the religious history of the Puritan Republic. He was fascinated by the figure of Cromwell: this man, who seemed to possess every attribute of heroism, could not be the intriguer and impostor that he was represented by the stubborn malevolence of tradition. The work was long in taking shape in his mind; the copious materials, so difficult to organise, sterilised his efforts.

In 1843 Carlyle interrupted his labors upon Cromwell: the preceding year had brought the wretchedness of the working classes to an intolerable pitch; the economic crisis had become more acute than ever before; sympathetic simultaneous strikes, amounting almost to civil war, had disturbed the North of England. His pamphlet upon Chartism was but a preface, a first chapter, of his social doctrine: following the advice given him by Emerson, he spoke without reserve to the ailing world, and now the world heeded his speech. A book read by chance fixed the setting of his work: this was an old chronicle, dating from the twelfth century, written by a monk and telling with a touching simplicity of the virtues of an abbot of his order. The discipline, the excellence of the temporal and spiritual organisation, of the Middle Ages, struck Carlyle by their contrast with the anarchy in which contemporary England was wallowing; with not one false start, without a trace of the uncertainty and doubt with which he was usually tortured in composition, he wrote within two months *Past and Present* (1843). With a mind less harassed, he returned to Cromwell; and after spending almost an entire year in barren efforts to organise a synthetic history, he limited his plan. He decided to write

CHEYNE ROW

merely a biography of the great Puritan leader; nay, less even than that, he would give merely a collection of his letters and speeches accompanied by a commentary. The work now took shape; it was finished and published in 1845.

Past and Present had, after bitter wrangling, achieved a striking success: the reception of *Cromwell* was a triumph. This work was the means of righting a grave injustice: England, docile to Carlyle, discovered in it the greatness of one of her sons, in whom the national character was obvious. The pride of the Anglo-Saxon race was thrilled on both sides of the Atlantic. The author of *The French Revolution* had won glory, but the author of *Cromwell* won that artistic kingship which is reserved for those who express the deepest instincts of a nation or a race. New documents, unpublished letters, came in from all sides: Carlyle incorporated these novelties in a second edition published in the following year. There followed a period of inactivity, agitated, uneasy. In January, 1848, Carlyle notes in his journal projects of literary work. Among them is one which bears a bizarre title: *Exodus from Houndsditch*, that is, the necessary exodus of mankind from the forms of Judaism and the formulae of the Bible, in which apparel its religious spirit is still encased, an apparel similar to the old clothes sold in the Jewish emporia of Houndsditch. Carlyle was never to write this book which would have audaciously clarified his religious doctrine, and applied it to the specific problems of modern Europe. "That alas!" he exclaims, "is impossible as yet, though it is the gist of all writings and wise books, I sometimes think—the goal to be wisely aimed at as the first of all for us. Out of Houndsditch indeed! Ah, were we but out, and had our own along with us. But they that came out hitherto came in a state of brutal nakedness, scandalous mutilation; and impartial bystanders say sorrowfully, 'Return rather, it is better even to return.' "

The February Revolution in Paris brought Carlyle's mind back to the study of politics. He had never altogether forsaken the field: the free-trade measures of 1846 had reconciled him with Sir Robert Peel, the Conservative leader. He wondered whether a statesman might not yet be found who would have the courage really to govern England, a statesman who would spare his country the infection of the revolutionary madness which was upsetting thrones and nations on the continent. Hastily he set down in writing, in March, 1848, the plan of a new work on Democracy. But event followed upon event with disconcerting speed; victors found themselves vanquished, the riots were suppressed, law and order were reestablished; the falsehood of artificial monarchies took on, once more, the semblance of reality. Carlyle could not organise the inchoate mass of his ideas. He wrote letters to the daily papers, to the *Spectator* and the *Examiner*, but a sense of his impotence crushed him. "May I mark this as the *nadir* of my spiritual course at present?" he asked in his journal (August 10, 1848). "Never till now was I so low—utterly dumb this long while, barren, undecided, wretched in mind." The stimulus of events however finally roused him from his paralysis; he had met Peel, believed vividly in him; a trip to Ireland had given him ocular evidence of the frightful poverty, the moral anarchy, of a people without discipline. The century was ripe for a final prophetic appeal: from January to July, 1850, without respite, he threw out a series of eight articles on problems of the day. These were the *Latter-day Pamphlets*.

Henceforward Carlyle lived in retirement from the life of political and social controversy. He had always had to struggle against fatigue, but up to now he had always been victor in the struggle: now, however, he felt fatigue rising in him in deeper, irresistible waves. His mind took more pleasure in scanning the past; in October, 1848, he registers surprise in his journal at the old memories, "strange old reminiscences and secret elegiac thoughts" which possessed him.

He was no more than fifty-three and he had thirty-three years to live. But his impression of autumn's coming was sound; as the century reached its middle, the last phase of his career began. Bereavements in his immediate circle were many: in 1842 Jane had lost her mother; in 1844 his young disciple Sterling had died; the health of Carlyle's own mother had long been poor; called to her death-bed in 1853, he felt that the years of his primal strength were past. Outside of his *Life of Sterling* (1851), and some productions of secondary importance, all his activity was henceforward absorbed in the heavy task which at once attracted and frightened him, his history of *Frederick the Great*. If the truth is to be told, with *Past and Present* he had exhausted all his themes as a preacher. He had made the essential applications to morals and sociology of his general philosophy, as this had been worked out in *Sartor*. It was, of course, possible to make other and novel applications of it: but striking as they might be they added no new element—they could not—to the substance of Carlyle's doctrine. From 1835 to 1845 Carlyle elaborated and applied his prophetic creed: from *Cromwell* on, he hammered tirelessly upon the same themes, and his old age was filled with his vehement reiterations.

CHAPTER II

THE PHILOSOPHY OF HISTORY

I

THE philosophy of history is, for Carlyle, illuminated through its whole expanse by a magnificent and terrible revelation from above. The French Revolution had cast its spell upon him very early. His imagination, formed by assiduous reading of the Bible, recognised in this movement one of those catastrophes in which, amid the noise of falling empires, the voice of the Almighty speaks to mankind. His intellect, shaped by German influence to believe in a universal becoming, perceived in the departure of one dispensation the necessary arrival of another. His deepest and most urgent feeling, that of the retributions meted by Providence, drew from it a redoubled confidence. The laws of conduct, inherent in the very being of things, as he had learned, as he felt with an intimate conviction, as in his turn he had preached, drew, nevertheless, from their development in time, an infallible sanction. Like a prophet of Israel, he reminded his age of the bitter fruit that the tree of evil bears. The old faith, meanwhile, was losing its hold upon hearts; impious, frivolous generations, proud of their progress, of their increasing wealth, merely gave lip-service to the denunciations of the Divine writings; they had ceased to believe in Divine vengeance: success, wealth, unprecedented prosperity were the sufficient recompense of their labors, labors devoted entirely to the conquest of matter. The great drama which had drenched France in blood had given such generations a momentary tremor of remorse and terror; but very quickly this impression was effaced, and the crowd jostled even more eagerly about the altars of Mammon. Must one despair of converting these generations? Was God abandoning history, and was the course of events inflicting on the prophet a cruel, ironic discomfiture? Not at all; to-morrow might be as yesterday was; the force of example and instruction in the French Revolution cast far into the future an admonitory glow. Hence, in Carlyle's view, its inestimable value, its unique attraction. It was one of the pillars of his doctrine, and his conviction. He went even so far as to ask what would have become of him without it.

Such is the spirit in which he undertook to recount its progress. He had a high, and scrupulous conception of his task. Contemporary scholarship requires a stricter preparation, a more rigorous critical method, an expositor less heated and partial. But in an age when our contemporary conception of history had scarcely become intelligible, when the romantic spirit still tyrannised over all evocations of the past, Carlyle exhibited a very proper sense of the rules of knowledge. He had an intuition—incomplete it is true, but strong and active—of the impartiality necessary to the historian. Documents in archives were not within his reach; even had they been so, his was not the mind to profit by them; for he had neither the leisure nor the austere courage which go with the slow building, block by block, of the edifice of truth. Besides, he had the vision of a synthesis too vast to permit his verification of all the materials it involved. The moment was favorable: the French Revolution, a subject of controversy during the half-century which had elapsed since its outbreak, retained the reality of an event still fairly recent and was already, nevertheless, passing through the mists of legend. Time was developing its lights and shadows, bringing out in relief its ruling features: its visage was already sculptured in its eternal form, although the laborious criticism, the belated revisions, which were to correct and revise the details, were not yet under way. The last actors in the drama were on the point of disappearing; memoirs, diaries, pamphlets, letters, and all kinds of documents were at the disposal of the imagination which prized in life its tragic and picturesque qualities; but the prudent and substantial monographs were not yet there to encumber with their aid the bold, synthetic spirit of Carlyle. His reading was comparatively extensive and copious: he compared conflicting evidences and weighed them with genuine care. Above all, he was anxious to achieve perfect, adequate expression: despite the epic movement which carries him away, we can detect the historian's conscience, his desire to be just and to be impartial. Need we add that these barriers are again and again broken down by the impetuous flood of his mystical enthusiasm, or his hate, or his admiration, or his wrath? The violent spirit of Carlyle allied itself in vain with a pious respect for fact; the religion of divine retribution was stronger yet; Carlyle interprets, judges, and condemns even as he narrates; the lofty sense of his mission is the source of his bold ardor which claims to fathom the souls of men, and make up at times for deficient knowledge by the exercise of divination.

To write history was, for Carlyle, in the first place to

prophesy in the past tense. But it was also to illuminate continually the concept of time. If the *French Revolution* is, as it is, his artistic masterpiece, this is because its irresistible rhythm, the strict logic of its events, the very balance of its massings throughout the action which continues without break from the 14th of July to Vendémiaire, bound Carlyle to obedience to the principles of order and unity. His task was merely to group scattered lines of action, to complete the spontaneous organisation with which the phenomenon presented him; for once he was capable of construction—for the plan was there to aid him. The matter which he was to elaborate, was marvelously apt for the exercise of his visionary gift. The supreme greatness of the crisis, the infinite stakes of the game, the boundless prospects which prolonged and amplified every circumstance, not only permitted but abetted the favorite play of his hallucinated fancy. Behind every personage, every moment, of the drama, the destinies of humanity are visible, in a mystical fog; filled by a more than earthly quality, the Revolution illuminated the entire process of time, explaining the past, foretelling the future. Carlyle was, therefore, able to magnify his recital of the daily details by the transcendental views it opened upon eternal things: he was able to give to a thousand facts, precious or prosaic, all the touching value of what is unique and irrecoverably past, and the mysterious dignity of what remains, translated to a superior level of being. He was finally at liberty to give free rein to the innate law of his genius, to throw over the vanished years the glory of a resurrection, to plunge them anew in the shadows of death, to construct once more the æsthetics of his thought upon the antithesis and the succession of day and night, truth and fantasy. This is the interest, the gripping strength, of the work. Its philosophic contribution is not considerable: its directive ideas come straight from *Sartor Resartus*. France is, for Carlyle, the nation chosen by the divine Will to make evident to the ages, in a sinister and prodigious manner, the laws of conduct and of life. These laws are confirmed and exemplified by the French Revolution; but a single maxim of Teufelsdröckh would have contained all the significance, all the substance of this history. The sage would have said that the old monarchy of France was a body parted from its soul, a worn-out garment; the garment then was rent, the body died—while a new soul was slowly and painfully weaving for society a new garment.

II

Carlyle finds in the great drama three acts. His first book, "The Bastille," examines the causes of the revolutionary explosion, and follows its course as far as the ultimate collapse of the monarchy. The second book, "The Constitution," describes the evolution of the political situation thus created, the unsuccessful efforts of the Revolution to organise itself, the emigration of the gentry, the outbreak of the schisms between the various parties of the movement, under the Constituent and the Legislative Assemblies. The third book, "The Guillotine," narrates the climax and the dénouement of the tragedy: it begins with the events of September, 1792, with the proclamation of the Republic, and goes on through the Reign of Terror to Thermidor and Vendémiaire (October,

1795): in this book Carlyle evokes the final effects of the cataclysm and, bringing his work to a close with the first symptoms of returning peace, he elicits the moral of the upheaval. His history is at once a drama and a sermon: Book I—How the French Revolution came about and how it got under way; Book II—How it brought to light and realisation the forces of destruction and anarchy latent within it; Book III—How, with its mission performed, it came to an end; this is the scheme that Carlyle proposed to illustrate. Its mission: *there* is, beyond a doubt, the generating idea of the book; an idea that pious consciences, frightened by the course of events, and yet incapable of rejecting the notion of a Providence, had watched rising before their eyes. Carlyle made of this idea a great and dazzling historical thesis. When given its place in the divine plan of the universe, the Revolution is not merely explained, it is justified. *Sartor* had rung the changes on the doctrine that only the spiritual reality exists, it alone has the right to exist. Semblances which are not rooted in it are but spectral deceptive things: it is the business of every upright conscience to banish these phantoms, to shatter the hollow masks behind which there is no living face. In the becoming, the perpetual becoming, of time, social and political forms, the garments of the collectivity, are replaced, even as worn-out clothes: governments, institutions, usages, last so long as they express a deep truth, a spiritual reality. If the constitution of a nation survives the soul which produced it, if it is not incessantly revised by pious prudent labor, that it may coincide with the changing soul, it becomes a tyrannous lie; and if the longanimity of fate, the frivolous heedlessness of mankind, prolong this constitution, aggravate its

PHILOSOPHY OF HISTORY 159

discrepancy from the soul it once embodied, a catastrophe, a revolution, must supervene to rend the dead trappings from the body politic.

Such a phantom was the French monarchy in the later years of the eighteenth century: the hollowest of semblances, the aridest of fictions. Once it had been a reality: in its feudal—even in its barbaric—beginnings it had roots in a fact and a law—in might. What was then the King, but the man who can (King, koenning, can-ning, according to the fanciful etymology of Carlyle), the strongest and hence the best? In this was his divine right: he was the vessel of true authority, the object of genuine obedience. His power derived mysteriously from his right, and as mysteriously it grew. But the monarchic ideal, like all ideals which pass into reality, degenerates. Louis the Well-Beloved is the laughable, foppish, degraded heir of Clovis and of Charlemagne, and of their successor Louis the Great. The rule of the King's mistresses is a caricature of royal rule. Faith in the sovereign, the Lord's anointed, the son of Saint Louis, is dead: Versailles is the cynical temple of an unbelieving, grotesque worship. The derivative authorities about the King are likewise smitten by decadence or by death; all have been severed from their vital roots in the spirit. The Church, terribly declining from its former greatness, has let slip from her unworthy hands the cure of souls, and the charge has been undertaken by unbelieving men, *philosophes*. The nobility, since the Fronde, have replaced the sword of battle by the courtier's rapier. On close inspection, the business of the nobles appears as no more than dressing with elegance and eating in luxury. The common people, meanwhile, huddled in poverty and ignorance, are exposed to every tax and every *corvée*. Their outcries find no echo. But the wrath of heaven is rising and the heavenly vengeance will be terrible.

In the essential corruption of former powers, new energies grew, fostered by their reality and their right. Classes, intensely alive, rose in the social scale: new guides for the spirit appeared, men of thought, men of letters. In this advent of thought, is a principle of social fertility and salvation. The men of letters, heroes of the modern day, might have saved the older order from the bloody upheaval which threatened. Instead, they hurried it on to its doom, they precipitated the Revolution; this was because their doctrine was not creative or religious, was the nefarious theory of the sovereign reason. They were engrossed in the denial of falsehoods: they were unable to affirm the necessary truths. Like England in 1830, under the thumb of the Utilitarians, France in 1780, led by the Encyclopædists, was ripe for every anarchy. Along such lines as these Carlyle's judgment takes shape, and his other preoccupation, his penchant for criticism and condemnation, becomes definite. The divine mission of the Revolution was performed by human hands: human wills led astray introduced into its performance elements of error and crime. The political doctrines elaborated by 18th-century thought are but a monument of pride and falsehood. They are grounded on reason, or logic—arid, prosaic bases: edifices built on such foundations are regular and symmetrical but woefully fragile. In the nature of facts, in their stupid obstinacy, there is a higher kind of reason; and our highest, surest wisdom is in confiding ourselves blindly to this. When our logical reason renounces its rule, as it inconsistently does, it does so to the profit of a morbid sentimentalism; humanitarianism is the caricature of the love of man; the effusions of a weeping heart are no more than an inane and perverse sensuality; there is no genuine love without strength; the true lover of man is he who loves the austere law of duty better yet, he who has conquered his moral freedom by the painful sacrifice of a part of his being. For the notion that man is naturally good, that the instincts should be left unbridled, that the golden age should be restored by universal emotivity, for all of these fantastic dreams, Carlyle has nothing but castigation. For the Gospel according to Jean Jacques, for the Social Contract, his contempt is absolute.

Does he retain any of the democratic spirit which animated so many pages of *Sartor*? The study of the Revolution hastened the natural movement of Carlyle's ideas: the spectacle of such a tragic upheaval sharpened in him a passionate craving for order: his chief preoccupation— for a healthy authority—completed the suppression of his passing flirtations with equality and justice. His doctrine is taking in this work its bitter imperious accent. To be sure he quivers yet at the sight of starving crowds, he still grasps the profound reality of the savage despair which moves them; the sincerity of the revolutionary mind, the justice of its revolt, still convey to him a sympathetic shock. He is with the oppressed, without any aristocratic reserve or conservative superstition. But he fears and hates oppression by the many—mob riots— just as he fears and hates the tyranny of a degenerate upper class.

From the day in which the republican principle became the principle and guide of the Revolution, Carlyle exhibits the movement as on its way toward the abyss. He explains the Reign of Terror less by the provocation given by foreign governments, the fear of a people menaced on all its borders, the persistence of intrigue and treason at home, than by the fatal dizziness of an anarchy delivered absolutely to its own impulses. Individualism founds nothing, destroys everything. From the incoherent play of appetites and unchecked forces, violence alone can come forth. Nowhere does Carlyle accept the Revolution, nowhere does he welcome it as the arrival of equality and justice, or the establishment in France of representative government. For the errors and failures of parliaments he has already an absolute severity. His social doctrine will henceforth be more conscious of its several components: its chief component is the passionate worship of fruitful authority. If Carlyle has any honor for the French Revolution, this is because it was exceptional, and so confirmed the rule; it was an inevitable upheaval, legitimate only because inevitable; it destroyed an order which had ceased to be real and to accord with the occult will of things, an order against which disorder had, for once, authority.

It was in this way that Carlyle perceived the philosophy of the Revolution. As a spectator held by a sort of religious terror, he followed its phases during those breathless years from 1789 to 1795. Great artist that he was, he endued the great scenes and events of the drama with a tragic intensity: the capture of the Bastille, for example, the riots at Versailles, the festival of the Federation, the flight to Varennes, the 10th of August, the September massacres, the execution of the King; the clash of the Girondins with the Mountain, the Reign of Terror, the

PHILOSOPHY OF HISTORY 163

fall of Robespierre, and the symbolic volley, the whiff of grapeshot, with which Citizen Bonaparte, artillery-major, reestablished in their reign the principles of might and right. One must surrender one's self fully to Carlyle to appreciate to the full how his intensity of narration can seize upon the mind as effectively as the very events narrated. The book is a genuine epic, the greatest modern epic, as has often been said, embracing as well as Paris—the volcano of the Revolution—the rumbling, provinces, the frontiers, centres of loyalist conspiracies. It is a frank and ardent book, the product of an inspiration rising from heroic deeds, in which truth and a legendary value are inseparable. The book is more than just an epic: the poet's feeling spurts forth in apostrophes, in lyrical cries, and his ardent and serious intelligence expresses itself in meditations which are sublime. Never was a more stirring text accompanied by a more vibrant commentary.

But the interest of the work is not solely artistic. If it adds nothing substantial to the fund of Carlyle's ideas, it nevertheless marks the development of certain principles in his thought, and their increased emphasis. It is a commonplace that the author of the *French Revolution* was able to breathe life into the crowds that he manipulates, to reveal their importance in the great convulsions of history; and it is equally a commonplace that the folk of France, and especially of Paris, are the chief actors in the drama that Carlyle presents to us. Carlyle owed his sense of collective action to a powerful imagination, to an intuition of natural and primitive forces which was native in him, and which had been fortified, not weakened, by his study of German philosophy. In his book, he often appears to be a precursor of the contemporary science of "crowd-psychology." Nevertheless, it must be noted that as his imagination gives substantial reality to the movements of crowds, it also endows these movements with an additional symbolic value; it personifies them and merges them in enormous entities, real and mythical as well. Carlyle's vision is not the expression of a scientific rational mind, it is not an attempt at the explanation of reality: it is a poetic creation, a synthesis as spontaneous as its object—he had a lively perception of the momentary simplifications by which instincts converge in one direction. These collective entities—"philosophism"—the party of the free-thinkers, "patriotism"—the patriots, "patrollotism"—the armed citizens—the national guard—"rascality"—the dregs of society—and above all "sans-culottism"—the insurgent fourth and fifth estates bent upon equalitarian anarchy and the rule of force. These mythical entities live and move over the pages of Carlyle: they jostle, they conspire: they are among the principal springs of the action—in its whirlwind the individual wills impotently bestir themselves.

This brilliant vision of collective causes reveals the genuine bent of Carlyle's mind: not in anonymous and abstract forces as much as in individual energies is his belief: the human personality, autonomous, infectious, strong, this is the source of influence, this is the centre of movement, the absolute beginning of things. His mind is always passing farther and farther under the domination of a mystical belief in superior men: and he clothes in a robe of glory the heroes of the French Revolution. In an age fruitful of heroes, Carlyle finds but two—men of a manly, forthright vigor, accentuated by a certain ruggedness and violence. These men are examples of the moral type that he sought everywhere and venerated wherever he came upon it—why not?—it was the type to which his own temperament belonged. La Fayette is not a hero: there is a strain of Sir Charles Grandison in him, Carlyle discovers; his chivalrous impetuosity, his dignity err on the side of frigid elegance. Camille Desmoulins has a claim upon our sympathy: but his personality is, after all, a slight one. Saint-Just is no better than a sinister logician, Robespierre but a traitor taken from melodrama, sly, venomous and vile. Carlyle's choice falls upon the thundering tribunes of the mobs: he permits them a certain moral laxity, provided he finds evidence of a sincerity at the bottom of their souls. Danton is Carlyle's man, and more even than Danton, Mirabeau. "Conspicuous among all parties, raised above and beyond them all, this man rises more and more. As we often say, this man has an *eye*, he is a reality; while others are formulas and eye-*glasses*."

At the close of the work, a third hero is presented, meditative, intense: a man of taut energy, functioning with the support of a supreme sense of reality; a man who conforms better than the others to the definition of heroism, for his language is action: Napoleon Bonaparte.

The French Revolution, says Carlyle, was a failure: it failed to give men the absolute liberty, that in their madness they craved. It was the gory herald of a new order: capable of destruction, indeed; but able merely to substitute for the tyranny of one class, that of another—the tyranny of the middle class, the business people.

Written constitutions, ridiculous structures, run up by the stupidity of pure reason, crumbled to pieces; from the profound necessities of life, from the eternal requisites of authority and order, a social and political organisation, merely provisional and mediocre, slowly arose. How far it is from the youthful hopes, the glow of enthusiasm which gilded the first day of the States-General meeting at Versailles, the dawn of a painful progress! The coming of democracy is an inevitable thing: but two centuries more will pass before democracy finds its balance, the proper interconnections of civic rights and civic duties. May the example of France serve as a lesson to Europe and the world! The England of the time when Carlyle was writing his history was stirred by the spirit of social revolt; and if she was to avoid the abyss, she must put an end to injustice, that is to shams and simulacra. Even "Sans-culottism," terrifying monster, murderous hydra-headed anarch, had its divine mission; a brutal reality, it rose up in an infernal, sulphurous splendor; at its fiery breath, the empty formulae, the deceptive appearances, the cloaks and masks of a society in which there was no truth or substance, were consumed, rent to pieces, scattered afar. So, Carlyle says, will it be, one day or another, with all phantasms, and happy the nations who will exorcise them in good time, armed with a savage loyalty to truth. His doctrine, so grave with its social wisdom, has its natural conclusion in a religious and mystical meditation:

"Fear not Sans-culottism; recognise it for what it is, the portentous inevitable end of much, the miraculous beginning of much. One thing thou mayest understand of it: that it too came from God; for has it not *been?* From of old, as it is written, are His goings forth; in the great Deep of things; fearful and wonderful now as in the beginning: in the whirlwind also He speaks; and the wrath of men is made to praise Him."

Did Carlyle understand the French Revolution? Many of its causes escaped him, there is no doubt; on many points his knowledge of men and events is inadequate, erroneous or *simpliste*. Most important of all, he could not embrace the whole of the moral forces in conflict with an intuition sufficiently penetrating and understanding; he had not an adequate belief in the deep seriousness, in the pure and noble flame, of the spirit of France; he often misinterpreted and calumniated the hours in which an entire nation rose to heroism; his prejudices, his doubts, his partialities, limited his field of vision. He fails to do justice to the constructive and creative achievement of the Revolution, to the immense effort of its assemblies, the lasting value of so many parts of the social structure it prescribed. His failure to attend to the play of economic causes prevented his noticing the quiet changes in the ownership of property. Nevertheless, the picture of the Revolution as he saw it, and as he gives it, has the elemental grandeur of natural forces, the better represented that they appealed so strongly to the sublimity of his Hebraic imagination, and associated themselves so profoundly with the activity of Providence. So dramatic, so magnificent is this poignant nightmare-piece, this modern apocalypse, that England was possessed by it, as it were; and that, even to-day, the Anglo-Saxon world sees the French Revolution through the medium of Carlyle's genius.

III

In the lectures on *Heroes and Hero-Worship*, Carlyle makes a further application to human history of his doctrine. And in these lectures the doctrine is presented in a didactic form. For the philosophy of Carlyle was to become more and more a philosophy of action; its principal object was to be the regulation of individual and social life. His thought was to descend from the shining citadels of metaphysics to which it had risen in *Sartor*, and was to stand upon the solid ground of practical life. Here is another of the victories of the instinctive tendencies of the English mind, tendencies to which Carlyle gave himself up without reserve. In a letter written to Emerson in October, 1840, he expresses his strengthening desire for objective activity. He is thanking his friend for the first number of *The Dial*, the transcendentalist periodical, and in so doing, his congratulations seem perfunctory beside the reservation he makes. "And yet you know me—for me it is *too* ethereal, speculative, theoretical: all theory becomes more and more confessedly inadequate, untrue, unsatisfactory, almost a kind of mockery to me! I will have all things condense themselves, take shape and body, if they are to have my sympathy." The fever of intellectual life with which his German studies had inoculated him was henceforward a memory; what it left with him was nothing more substantial than a fundamental idealism in his character and conduct, and a warm appreciation of spiritual values. In his later years his prophetic zeal fastened with an ever-tightening grip upon the world of experience which, illusory though it might be, had at least the definitive and irresistible authority of fact.

He was now inflecting his doctrine of inspired supermen, a doctrine which he had taken from Fichte, toward a philosophy of action. He was ready to recognise his debt to Fichte whom, in the first lines of his lecture on *The Hero as Man of Letters*, he celebrates in terms scarcely different from those he had used in his article on

PHILOSOPHY OF HISTORY 169

The State of German Literature: "Fichte, in conformity with the Transcendental Philosophy, of which he was a distinguished teacher, declares first: That all things which we see or work with in this Earth, especially we ourselves and all persons, are as a kind of vesture or sensuous Appearance: that under all there lies, as the essence of them, what he calls the 'Divine Idea of the World'; . . . To the mass of men no such Divine Idea is recognisable in the world; they live merely, says Fichte, among the superficialities, practicalities and shows of the world, not dreaming that there is anything divine under them. But the Man of Letters is sent hither specially that he may discern for himself, and make manifest to us, this same Divine Idea: in every new generation it will manifest itself in a new dialect; and he is there for the purpose of doing that." Moreover in Fichte's teaching Carlyle could find a justification of all authority exercised upon the fiat of a spiritual certitude of truth; in this doctrine the man who has an intuitive certainty of supernatural origin is assigned the right to compel others, and the duty even of tyrannous sovereignty.

Carlyle's theory of heroism is really the refraction by his own temperament of ideas taken from Fichte. So deeply was he impressed by a belief in the primacy of will, that his very conception of inspiration is tinged with it; and among the modes of mystical revelation he inclined to accord the first place to pure energy—to action. In his mind, the seeds of an authoritative politic sown by Fichte grow apace; and with a boldness far beyond the position of the German thinker he equates the manifestation of might, creative or destructive, with the inspired perception of the divine idea. Throughout his work, beginning with his very earliest essays, this current of thought may be traced; it makes its appearance in the *Essay on Burns* (1828) in *Sartor*, in the studies of Schiller (1831) and of Johnson (1832); it broadens out in the *History of the French Revolution;* and in *Heroes and Hero-Worship,* isolated by a spirited effort of his intelligence, it becomes Carlyle's principal theme and the nucleus of a new formulation of his teaching.

In his first lecture Carlyle lays down his principle with a dogmatism which sweeps aside all qualifications. History, he affirms, is but a sequence of acts flowing from individual causes, the history of man is but the history of heroes: "They were the leaders of men, these great ones; the modellers, patterns, and in a wide sense creators, of whatsoever the general mass of men contrived to do or to attain; all things that we see standing accomplished in the world are properly the outer material result, the practical realisation and embodiment, of Thoughts that dwelt in the Great Men sent into the world: the soul of the whole world's history, it may justly be considered, were the history of these." To illustrate his thesis Carlyle chooses from points in time and space far removed from one another, six categories of heroes "in mere external figure differing altogether." Beneath the diversity of appearances, Carlyle reveals a fundamental unity; and the qualities of heroism in all the categories are about the same.

The deepest element in human life, says Carlyle, is religion. The beliefs of men determine all the qualities of their being. The hero is first studied as a source of religious inspiration. Carlyle does not, however, come at once to the class of the hero-prophets; these he reserves

PHILOSOPHY OF HISTORY 171

for his second lecture. In his first he ventures back to the common source of religion and heroism, to that form of belief in which the heroic person is invested with the prestige of a god, to that form in which the god and his prophet are one. This form is paganism and the principal representative chosen is Odin. The error of paganism has within it a mite of truth, for paganism discovers a divine quality in nature and in man. Paying to the creature the worship which is proper only to the creator, paganism at least pays homage to the most worthy object of which it is aware, for is not man the image, the very temple, of the Divine? There is a spark of truth shining in the darkness of the Norse past; it shines in every religion; it is at the heart of the great illumination of Christianity: it is the obedient respect for what is truly great. Every human organisation is founded upon the principle of respect. Every hierarchical society which has any validity in its organisation is an approximation to a real order of values, determined according to the scale of heroism; if the hierarchy is not valid, revolutions supervene and democracy springs up, democracy which is a necessary revolt against sham, but which is itself but a sham, whenever it is not founded on the principles of hierarchy and respect of which God is the source.

In vain are the labors of impious reason bent upon breaking down these essential principles of subordination and command. Science like democracy has denied the superiority of the individual factor in the life of nations. The modern method is to explain the great man as the product of his age, rather than the age as the product of its great men. Carlyle is inexhaustibly ironical at the expense of such a method. Circumstances and conditions are but the great man's fuel; only the hero, the heavenly fire, can set it alight. The worship of the hero will survive all the mad attacks now proceeding against it. It is sanctioned by the general consent of peoples and ages. No century, no nation, has been without some form of "hero-worship." By instinctive eternal ties a submissive respect of what is greatest is rooted in the hearts of all men, even the lowest. In the modern shipwreck of convictions, in the upheaval of societies and of souls, this faculty of admiration and of obedience is an indestructible foundation on which we can build a hope and a faith in the future of man.

Carlyle dare not go so far as to affirm the existence of Odin; he is too familiar with the negative conclusions of German exegesis; he mentions the work of Grimm, and raises no protest against his findings. By a circuitous path, however, he does arrive at a dogmatic affirmation; some Odin, some superior, inspired and heroic man did exist. With pride Carlyle depicts the religion of the Northmen; his Germanic patriotism connects with it the spiritual and intellectual development of his race, and from these Northern origins Carlyle derives its mysticism, its faith, its quiet stubborn valor. The supreme virtue of the Anglo-Saxon soul reveals itself here in its purest nobility—its sincerity. The Valkyries are symbols of another and no less crucial virtue—valor—the denial of fear, the contempt of pain which had emerged in *The Everlasting No* as an essential stage to salvation. It is of little moment to Carlyle whether Odin was a chieftain in the labors of war and peace, whether he really revealed to his companions the hidden mystery of nature or the contempt for death, or even whether he himself attained an obscure consciousness of a divinity in the universe. What is of moment is the existence of a tie which unites in the vast procession of the ages the Puritan energy of Cromwell to the rugged valor of his Scandinavian ancestors. Modern religion, broad and tolerant, will not reject the support that Scandinavian paganism brings to some of its major contentions.

In the subsequent lectures Carlyle reviews the several forms which heroism took in adapting itself to the successive phases of human history; and here as in so many parts of his work Carlyle follows the guidance of Fichte. After the God comes the prophet: Mahomet and Islam. Then come lectures on *The Hero as Poet* (Dante and Shakespeare), *The Hero as Priest* (Luther and Knox), *The Hero as Man of Letters* (Johnson, Rousseau and Burns) and *The Hero as King* (Cromwell and Napoleon). Cromwell and Napoleon are represented with the background of the two great revolutions of the preceding age; and it is their relation with this background which explains their somewhat surprising sequence—in a roughly chronological order—to the literary heroes. The sovereigns of the future are in Carlyle's eyes the men of letters; but a type of sovereign newer still and yet more necessary is that of the restorer of order, the offspring of great social upheavals, upheavals which he is capable of quelling. There is a certain arbitrariness in Carlyle's choice of typical heroes; there were, for example, more brilliant literary heroes than Dr. Johnson available to Carlyle's pen and it is, at the least, extraordinary that, simply because the English reading public was unfamiliar with his works, Goethe, who for fifteen years had been Carlyle's spiritual guide, was omitted. The tendencies and preferences of Carlyle's very rigid temperament are everywhere present; and indeed his very conception of heroism was merely an unconscious imposition upon the development of human history of his consciousness of himself, as a personality of rugged energy and sincerity. "Rugged" is his favorite adjective of praise—and there is a deep significance in his regard for the rough unpolished might it suggests. Ruggedness in body or in spirit, ruggedness in virtue as in thought, all of them arouse Carlyle's instinctive sympathy. The qualities which this word suggests are for him the signs and conditions of all worth.

Carlyle's mode of demonstrating that his chosen individuals are heroic never varies; he repeats without ever wearying a few simple energetic statements, as curt as dogmas and as rigid; he never fails to reveal the same penetrating insight into a few of the profound connections between the energy of individuals and the course of history. There is no doubt that by his intuitive method he arrives at certain divinations of truth which go deeper than the superficial regard of an unintelligent rationalism. An example of his success is to be found in his revelation by the vividness and completeness of his sympathy, of the profound sincerity in the religious life of Islam and Mahomet. It was Carlyle who destroyed the old theory of the imposture of Mahomet and the deception of his successors. Carlyle can reveal in flashes of light the unsuspected depths in individual souls, and into the dark night of the past and the future he can project as far as any man ever could the blinding clearness of his intuitions. Sometimes he illuminates but a point in the midst of a deep obscurity; sometimes what he reveals is a secondary element in history and not a primary; the conception of history he imparts is one which simplifies and exaggerates and even at times distorts; but Carlyle has the faculty of catching the essential forms of objects and reproducing them in an unforgettable illumination. In each of his studies, whether of an individual or of a group, of an age or of a mode of heroic activity, there is a wealth of divining genius, an intuition of spiritual realities. It is not very important that in some cases, with Rousseau for example, he has not sufficient sympathy for insight, when in so many cases the intensity of his sympathy and the penetration of his insight enable him to re-create the spiritual realities of the past.

From his gallery of portraits one can derive the moral complexion of the hero, identical in all the variety of its forms. The prophet is really and potentially a poet; and the poet is potentially and really a prophet. In a memorable passage in the lecture on *The Hero as Poet*, Carlyle defines heroism as a superiority in intellect. By intellect he understands sympathetic intuition or spiritual instinct, —the faculty to which all the "faculties" of scholastic psychology may be reduced, in which the will, the emotions and the intelligence merge in an intensity of soul and a depth of spiritual life. The pure intelligence, the analytic reason, is but a secondary, incomplete aspect of the intellect, the central faculty: by itself it can know nothing, for love is the prerequisite of knowledge; it can seize only the husk of a thing and tear it to fragments, but the interior reality, the vital reality, of a thing it cannot seize. Inward spiritual realities must be sought by a moral faculty, illuminated by a desire for justice and virtue. Therefore the characteristic attitude of the hero, face to face with this obscure realm of appearances, is one of energetic intuition, inspired and directed by a moral need of sincerity.

Passionately the hero strives to penetrate through and beyond the shams and impostures of appearance, to attain to hidden truth. Mahomet was such a hero, a destroyer of idols, a soul intensely devoted to the solution of the terrifying enigma of this mysterious universe. The hero is not however content with the perception of the spiritual reality which lies behind appearances. The hero grasps the relations between appearances with a perception more vivid and concrete and complete than that of other men. He is a great man of action as well as a great visionary. His practical sense, his sense of realities, of the humdrum realities to which our acts relate, is as potent as his sense of the mysterious background and foundation of our being. Carlyle solves the principal problem of English moral idealism, and solves it without even analysing its terms, when he identifies the faculty of transcendental illumination with the robust grasp of useful realities. For example he refers Cromwell's genius in politics and war to the superior quality of his religious life: "Everywhere we have to note the decisive practical *eye* of this man; how he drives towards the practical and practicable; has a genuine insight into what *is* fact. Such an intellect, I maintain, does not belong to a false man: the false man sees false shows, plausibilities, expediences: the true man is needed to discern even practical truth." In this profound intuition the very instinct of the British race is apparent, with its obscure but powerful consciousness that beneath the superficial divergence of its religious and practical activities, there is an interior unity.

Such are the heroes: sincere, strong, earnest, intuitive, mystical, active, practical. A final trait may complete their characterisation; just as analytical intelligence has an unimportant part in the life of their mind, and as their thought does not seek to formulate and explicate itself; so speech, the instrument of analytical reason and madness, the instrument of formulation and explication, is not one of their talents. They employ it as seldom as they can, even if they are writers, even if they are orators! They belong to "the great Empire of Silence: higher than the stars; deeper than the Kingdoms of Death"! In silence they labor and meditate, and they are the salt of the earth. "A country that has none or few of these is in a bad way. Like a forest which had no *roots;* which had all turned into leaves and boughs;—which must soon wither and be no forest. Woe for us if we had nothing but what we can show or speak. . . . I hope we English will long maintain our *grand talent pour le silence.*"

These men have a divine right to rule and the duty of all others is to obey them. The theory of heroism supplies Carlyle's social gospel, now in a state of development and moving toward greater precision, with the practical principle it required, the element of imperious authority which was henceforth to be its essential trait. Liberty, democracy and all other idols of the modern age will be thrust from their pedestals by the higher obligation to obey the Divine will, interpreted by its commissioned heroes. Can it be said that the political theory of Carlyle issues in a theocracy? In a sense it can, and Carlyle does not shrink from the word: "That right and truth, or God's Law, reign supreme among men, this is the Heavenly Ideal . . . towards which the Reformer will insist that all be more and more approximated. All true Reformers, as I said, are by the nature of them Priests, and strive for a Theocracy."

Nothing could be more deceptive than to relate this doctrine to individualism. The spirit of individualism is alien to Carlyle's political thought, and any confusion of his meaning with that doctrine, in which an anarchy is implicit, is a perversion. Only the heroes are privileged, in his conception of society: and they are an exceptional caste, a class definitively superior to the remainder of humanity. It is true that the conception of the hero is among the materials from which the conception of the superman was to be forged. But Carlyle's ideal converges with Nietzsche's only in the most commonplace and superficial applications: the spirit which informs them is very different. With Nietzsche the individual is the centre and the summit; he acquires knowledge and power in order fully to realize his possibilities; his egoism spurs him to an activity of which he is the beginning and the end, the cause and the effect. Carlyle, on the contrary, begins by proclaiming the essential inequality of men, so that he may more surely compel all men to bear a common yoke, the yoke of what one might term a moral collectivism. The hero is not an end in himself, he is the instrument of a transcendental will; and to realise his possibilities is not to achieve a harmonious development of his whole being; it is to transmit the divine inspiration which is passing through him; it is to annihilate his self, through its crushing exaltation. Whatever germs of individual pride and irresponsible egoism there normally are in the doctrines of the great intuitive seers, these had been destroyed in Carlyle by the absolute commands against them in the Old Testament and by the asceticism of the Puritan spirit. In his conception of the Universe there was a superhuman fate to control both the heroic leaders and the worship-

PHILOSOPHY OF HISTORY 179

pers they lead. At the very heart of his idea is the strict conscience of the hero, the source of his force and the warrant of his sublime selflessness. And Carlyle's stubborn faith in an overruling Providence blinded him to the contingency that energy and inspiration might not always be conjoined.

The heroes are a chosen few, the salt of the earth. Are we to understand that the privileges Carlyle accords to them are theirs exclusively, theirs without the least extension to others, theirs because there is no gradual transition, but a sharp break, between them and other men? Is there no participation in their sacred character? Is there no democratisation of the conception of heroism? There are passages which permit us to entertain the supposition that Carlyle's doctrine is not so drastic as first appears. He seems at times to suggest that by their strenuous zeal for the victory of the right, and more particularly by their obedience to the heroic leaders, the entire army of worshippers participates in the moral glory that emanates from them; that between the leaders and the rank-and-file there is a complete hierarchy of officers, who receive their authority and delegate it, adding the weight of their individual will. For the ordinary honest man to follow the hero's decrees is in a sense to resemble him. Carlyle never stresses this aspect of his teaching; he is more interested in making sure of general submission to the hero; and his mind, passing quickly over the dream of universal brotherhood, fastens upon the need for inspired despotism.

The doctrine of worship culminates in a doctrine of obedience; and what we are summoned to obey substantiates its claims not by convincing our reason but by achieving tangible success. It is a far cry to the intellectual idealism of Fichte, to the sublime seer revealing to men the Divine Idea. By pressing his theme to the extreme point of a voluntarist mysticism, Carlyle comes to deny the rights of the intelligence and of consciousness, if consciousness is an effort of the human spirit to possess the world by understanding it. Carlyle falls here into the fatalism, the trust in nature and the unconscious, that he had partially expressed in *Characteristics*. The hero reveals not ideas but merely a transcendent will; and the seal of his divine mission is the success he achieves in his activity and his life; hero-worshop—like all Carlyle's religious and moral teaching—is, at bottom, merely a superior form of utilitarianism. And just as with Hegel Fichte's idealism expanded into a realistic theory of the metaphysical identity between right and might, so Carlyle, following out his thought to its ultimate implications, proclaims that all that exists has a right to exist, that all that succeeds has a right to succeed. He proclaims, in a word, that the force and the will to conquer are the sole criteria of right: "I care little about the sword: I will allow a thing to struggle for itself in this world, with any sword or tongue or implement it has, or can lay hold of. We will let it preach, and pamphleteer, and fight, and to the uttermost bestir itself, and do, beak and claws, whatsoever is in it; very sure that it will, in the long-run, conquer nothing which does not deserve to be conquered. What is better than itself, it cannot put away, but only what is worse. In this great Duel, Nature herself is umpire, and can do no wrong: the thing which is deepest-rooted in Nature, what we call *truest*, that thing and not the other will be found growing at last." A formidable conclusion, but a just and inevitable one, to issue from a moral and psychological theory in which the idea of justice does not emerge from a laborious ratiocination, but springs immediately from an intuition, furnished by the rough instinctive forces of life. The eternal course of the divine will is no longer distinguishable for Carlyle from the blind process of nature; and in his glorification of human energy the prophet ends by refusing to the highest and purest perceptions of the soul their holy privilege of passing judgment upon the deeds of mere natural might.

CHAPTER III

SOCIAL PHILOSOPHY

WE have seen how the march of events, together with the march of his thought, brought certain changes to Carlyle's first formulation of his social doctrine in *Sartor Resartus* (1831) and the paper on the *Corn Law Rhymes* (1832). The triumph of Liberalism had been followed by bitter disappointment; the leaders of a party which had posed as the bulwark of democracy had used their tenure of power merely to add to the privileges of classes already privileged; and henceforward the "philosophical radicals" were to be out of popular favor. Carlyle had from the very beginning inveighed against the dry rationality of their theories: his antipathy was now reinforced by their failure in practice. Poverty was becoming more acute every day; disappointed in their hope of better conditions of living, the "poor-slaves," as Carlyle named them in *Sartor*, were commencing to stir, were organising for the pacific vindication of their civil rights, were perhaps contemplating active rebellion. Chartism was born at the very moment when Carlyle was resurrecting the riots of the French Revolution; and history seemed to threaten England with a sinister recurrence.

In *Chartism* (1839) and in *Past and Present* (1843) Carlyle's social philosophy finds complete utterance. The two works utter the same series of ideas; but a separation

SOCIAL PHILOSOPHY 183

of the two is imperative, since there is a slight evolution from the first to the second.

I

To an astonishing degree Carlyle had the faculty for coining memorable formulae, formulae which impress upon a reader's mind the general tendency, the profile so to speak, of new ideas; and along with this faculty went a penchant, early developed, to repeat his formulae with some obstinacy. With his imaginative and historical talent and his prophetic genius he was able to draw from what was, after all, a very simple process, effects of remarkable power. In the *French Revolution* Carlyle usually defines his "characters" by one dominant trait or one picturesque feature; and by recalling this trait or feature on every occasion when they appear, he makes them extraordinarily vivid and vital, and lends to what would otherwise be but a reported conflict something dramatic and personal. By such recourse to his imaginative memory, such confidence in the force of symbols, such insistence upon the saliencies and angles of reality, Carlyle adds to his propaganda one of its distinctive excellences. By suggestive words some part of his fund of ideas penetrated into the public mind; and about this nucleus there grew up a vague conception of his teaching, a conception which was to have its slow action upon the masses.

The political writings of Carlyle are extraordinarily rich in formulae of this kind. *Chartism* opens with the enunciation of one of them: "The Condition-of-England Question," says Carlyle, "is the most ominous of all practical matters whatever." At one flash, this quiet challenge overthrew the facade of official optimism: it held readers, gave a specific form to their vague anxieties, and set before public opinion the social problem in all its breadth.

Whatever the press might say, in the autumn of 1839, Chartism, despite the failure of the first solemn petition, was far from dead. It was, on the contrary, profoundly alive in the unjust privations which soured the disposition and fired the will of the working classes. "It is a new name for a thing which has had many names and which will yet have many." Is the lot of the English people endurable? asks Carlyle. The essential function of their government is, according to him, to answer this question; and if the answer is no, it is the essential duty of their government to remedy the evil. Against this imperative intervention, Carlyle sees a band of hostile principles arrayed. Political economy is opposed to any interference with the course of natural laws. Political economy claims to have for its basis a precise and rigorous knowledge of fact; but the statistics on which it relies are uncertain and unstable. Suppose that the average length of human life has increased: of what account is this if human wretchedness is as widespread, as devouring, as before? Carlyle suggests that calculations which are merely arithmetical do not cover all the data in the social problem; between the meshes of statistics, a part of reality slips out of sight and is lost from consideration. Anticipating the tenor of the arguments which were later to destroy dogmatic economics, Carlyle affirms, against the deductions of a science too eager to affirm, the right of the concrete, of the close observation of facts in their total complexity.

To be sure, in the method which does not go beyond observation, there is also danger: incomplete data always lead to false conclusions. Carlyle looks forward to the day when social investigations will be conducted with a sound method, the day when the will of the State will press them to the finest result that patience combined with precision can attain. Then, and then only, he thinks, shall we have a scientific knowledge of what is wrong with society. Carlyle is far from denying the possibility of a science of economics: what he denies is the validity of the narrow deductive method of the economists of his time. Carlyle calls attention to some essential data they have overlooked: to the inquiries into the rate of the workers' pay must be added inquiries into the regularity of their employment; and along with the guarantee to them of a living wage must go the establishment of stable relations between employer and employee. "What constitutes the well-being of a man? Many things; of which the wages he gets and the bread he buys with them are but one preliminary item." In these matters Carlyle shows a quick perception of real facts, through which his idealism brings him nearer to the heart of the matter than all the theorists of rational economics could get.

One great law, he finds, has absorbed the attention of Parliament ever since the Reform Bill: this is the new Poor Law of 1834, in which public charity was reorganised. That this law was justifiable, Carlyle does not dispute, but he finds in it a clearing of the way for a negative policy singularly open to criticism. The new Poor Law corrected many abuses and affirmed sound principles—the necessity of work, the anti-social aspect of idleness. Carlyle's first question is—does the government imagine that by suppressing the "dole," by creating the work-houses in such a way that any healthy man would prefer the hardest work outside them to the rough gloomy life within them, its social duty is fulfilled? The law states that no man who will not work, has a right to live; but the law does not take account of unemployment. And, Carlyle continues, what of Ireland? Ireland, even more than England, suffers from the scourges of unemployment and famine, the products of long centuries of injustice and exploitation. Despite his pharisaical English pride, Carlyle achieves nobility in his confession of English tyranny in Ireland and the evil it has done: "For the oppression has gone far farther than into the economics of Ireland; inward to her very heart and soul. The Irish national character is degraded, disordered; till this recover itself nothing is yet recovered." It is a fatal outcome of a solidarity too long forgotten that the poverty of Ireland has its repercussion upon England: the Irish working class, forced to leave their home by imminent starvation, are crossing to England; and their competition with English labor will be fatal. The ultimate result will be the fall of the two islands to the same low level of economic and moral decay.

The suffering masses are restive and in their wrath they can appeal to their characteristic weapon—might. Chartism is the terror of the possessors. Has it right on its side? This is the question asked and answered by Carlyle in the bold chapter *Rights and Mights*. In his *Heroes*, composed the next year, his answer was to be complete; but here he already reveals the basis of his thought. If the masses rise in revolt and prove their might, they will, in so doing, prove also their right: might and right are parallel concepts, diverse by accident, in essence akin. The drama of successive revolutions, the seizure of power by one class after another, expresses the exact relations of struggling forces, the very will of the universe and of God. If the poor are really oppressed, then they are capable of crushing their oppressors; as they shake off the yoke, as they affirm their might, they create their right, too, inseparable from it. The course of history is, then, the fated disappearance of successive iniquities and their replacement by new formulae of justice. We are back once more to the metaphysic of *Sartor:* injustice is an unreal appearance, a symbol void of content; and the world has done with it, finding it a garment covering no body.

Is the state of the English people a just one? Does the English people accept it as just? Chartism is its reply to these questions; and against the sincere conviction which is the heart of Chartism, nothing less sincere can prevail. The authority of the upper classes can be legitimated only by real power and real activity. Otherwise revolution is assured. How, Carlyle inquires, can this catastrophe be averted? In spite of his fatalism, he remains the prophet of energy; if the universal will is a mystery and reveals itself only at its chosen time, the individual, the human community, can become conscious of their might, realise all the potentialities of their being, and even question the edicts passed upon them by destiny. A Chartist revolution would be a disaster: the establishment of an absolute democracy would be a demented dream. Showing England the extent of her danger, Carlyle also points to the means of escape. Let the ruling classes affirm together both might and right. Were they really to rule, their empire would never again be threatened by rebel wills; they might laugh at Chartism, for they would have destroyed its source—the fact of injustice. Two chapters follow in which the problem of legislative interference is frankly discussed. In these chapters (*Laissez-faire* and *Not laissez-faire*) Carlyle, who for ten years had ridiculed the current system, ventured upon a more spirited attack: in its most cherished formulae he smote the established orthodoxy.

To appreciate the prestige enjoyed, at the time when Carlyle attacked it, by the negative formula of *laissez-faire*, we must remember the unanimity with which it was upheld. The instincts of the triumphant middle class and the dogmatism of the economic theorists were alike behind it. It was an expression of the elated assertiveness of modern industry and modern individualism, free at last from the fetters and the routine of the dying feudal order. It represented the reality of the immediate past, and, as such, exercised a tyrannous authority over the new and opposed truth as yet merely in becoming. Carlyle was among the first to perceive this new truth—the need for organisation to correct the anarchy implicit in the unlimited freedom of individual appetites. Many another thinker, following in his wake—Ruskin for example—drew from this perception of Carlyle the tenor of their social doctrine. Carlyle is their precursor and instructor and need share this honor only with the socialist theorists and the warmest hearts of his age. Amid all the disorder, the persistent incoherence, of his writings, among the repetitions, the digressions, the oscillations, of his thought, he is able almost always to seize upon the critical points in his problem; and with a sure sense of expression to clothe them in formulae, poorly placed sometimes but in themselves sharp and striking—formulae which mark the passing order and the order that is to come.

Laissez-faire, says Carlyle, was the doctrine of the 18th

SOCIAL PHILOSOPHY 189

century; its fruitfulness is past; for new times and new needs a new doctrine is required. In itself, what is *laissez-faire?* It is a confession of impotence, a theory grounded in fatalism. Necessary at one moment in the national history it has outlived that moment: Chartism is the certain urgent proof of an opposite reality, it calls for intervention. But intervention supposes a government strong, capable of activity, free from all paralysing controls. What will become of democracy in this new order? Shaking off the aura which surrounds this word, Carlyle defines his attitude toward the principle it embodies, a principle which he finds to be merely negative and, worse, opposed to the irresistible needs of the new age. Democracy is for him merely a transitional and empty form; denying the older authorities, and so far acceptable, democracy, to please Carlyle, must limit, and indeed deny, itself in an acceptance of the authorities of the new order, alone legitimate, competent and beneficent. On the foundations of the new order, the social edifice must be built; and these foundations are a real aristocracy, an *élite* which shall rule in fact, a Church worthy of the name, which shall supply men with the moral direction for which they call. As he evokes the sovereignty of real temporal and spiritual authorities, Carlyle's mind is naturally brought back to the ages in which they were really authoritative; regret for the passing of the Middle Ages becomes strong in his mind, and he touches on the theme he is later to explore in *Past and Present.*

From the past, his mind glances forward into the future; a tremor of pride and hope inspires the chapter on *New Eras* where Carlyle writes in the epic mode the paean to English greatness. He celebrates the great destinies of the race of divine predilection as it passes through the phases ordained for its development. The epic is ascribed, according to his favorite fiction, to the pen of a German professor, one Sauerteig. The theme of universal becoming had already held a great place in *Sartor;* here the prophetic vision of ages yet to be, ages for which social transformations are reserving England, brings Carlyle once more into the presence of this theme. He sets out to find in the remembrance of England's safe transformations in the past an encouragement for the timid conservative men of his own time. Sixty years before Kipling, he celebrates, in language which resounds with his enthusiasm for empire, the achievements and the glories of the Saxon race, from its dark and sanguinary beginnings to its magnificent expansion through the achievements of commerce and the feats of war. To England conquered races remain subject, and this is because her greater might is greater right; her conquests have been lasting and this is the proof that they were just. As for William the Conqueror and his Normans, the memory of their coming is but a glory the more; for, says Carlyle, they were German to the marrow.

For the privileged English race he finds two tasks ordained: government and industry—the elaboration of political justice and the victory over raw matter. The British Constitution is not yet complete; the middle class has won its place in the State; but the working classes clamor for their share and Chartism threatens. This threat the spirit of the British Constitution will dissipate, resolving new problems by tried formulae; there are moments for capitulation to might. As for the industrial problem, it is close to its final solution; everywhere the energy of the

English race has been victorious over matter. And Carlyle sings the beauty of Manchester, the greatness of the immense factories of England, whirring and hurried: "Hast thou heard with sound ears the awakening of a Manchester, on Monday morning at half-past five by the clock; the rushing off of its thousand mills, like the boom of an Atlantic tide, ten thousand times ten thousand spools and spindles all set humming there,—it is perhaps if thou knew it well, sublime as a Niagara, or more so." It was left for Ruskin to tell, with no less eloquence and emotion, of the horror of the English cities, smoky and noisy; Carlyle, more responsive to the activity than to the harmony of forces, his heart open to every robust energy, felt the poetry of modern industry even in his denunciations of its murderous selfishness.

A policy of reform is sketched in his final chapter. Chasing indolence and dogmatism to their very last entrenchments, Carlyle denounces the argument of every weakling—"This is impossible." He has two remedies. The first is education. At the very moment when he writes, the attention of the government is turned to the necessity of this national service. In 1833, for the first time, Parliament had voted a sum, the meagre sum of £20,000, for the building of schools; in 1839 the sum rises to £30,000, and a committee of the Privy Council is created to direct its distribution; this is the humble beginning of the Board of Education. Carlyle's vibrant appeal coincides with this significant initiative; if he did not inspire it, he at least contributed to the public opinion which sustained and developed it. Already, cutting across the educational problem, the religious question is alive; and Carlyle with a prophetic clearness calls for a separation of the functions of Church and State, and the constitution of an educational system which shall be universal, secular and obligatory, the basis of national culture. On this principle, discreetly applied, the reform of English primary education in 1870 reposes.

Carlyle was no less a prophet in pointing, as his second remedy, to emigration. It was his distinction to discover and reveal the Empire as a magnificent reality, a living organism becoming conscious of itself and calling for the surplus of English life to feed it, an immense fraternal community flung to the uttermost parts of the Earth's surface. "Is it not as if this swelling simmering never-resting Europe of ours stood, once more on the verge of an expansion without parallel; strangling, struggling like a mighty tree again about to burst in the embrace of summer and shoot forth broad frondent boughs which would fill the whole earth. . . . Canadian forests stand unfelled, boundless Plains and Prairies unbroken with the plough; on the west and on the east green desert spaces never yet made white with corn; and to the overcrowded little western nook of Europe, our Terrestrial Planet, nine-tenths of it yet vacant or tenanted by nomads, is still crying, Come and till me, come and reap me!"

When Emerson read the treatise on Chartism, he wrote to Carlyle, the 21st of April, 1840: "All that is therein said is well and strongly said. . . . And yet I thought the book itself instructed one to look for more. We seemed to have a right to an answer less concise to a question so grave and humane, and put with energy and eloquence. I mean that whatever probabilities or possibilities of solution occurred should have been opened to us in some detail. But now it stands as a preliminary word, and you

SOCIAL PHILOSOPHY

will one day, when the fact itself is riper, write the Second Lesson."

II

In 1840 the Camden Society had published the Latin chronicle in which Jocelyn of Brakelonde wrote the history of the Monastery of St. Edmunds. In this old work Carlyle found what he had been seeking: a simple case of the elementary virtues necessary to his contemporaries. He had already found such an example in Cromwell and the Puritans of the seventeenth century; and he had written to Emerson, inveighing against the ailing age in which they lived, saying that the only hope for the salvation of the age lay in the emergence of new Cromwells and new Puritans. But he kept back the example of Cromwell, waiting until he should have finished his biography of the great Puritan commander. He seized instead upon this unexpected opportunity.

His social ideas were entering their ultimate crystallisation; and his political ideal was finding its directive principle. Not only was contemporary liberalism repugnant to his instinct, but in ages past he could discover the image of an organisation wise, just, stable. From the contrast between past and present, it was perfectly clear that the progress so proudly asserted had been, in many respects, not a progress but a decadence. The remedy for the evils of the present would be in a spirited effort to remount the stream of time. Carlyle in his desire for a better future, sought to instruct the present in the great school of the past.

The theme of a return to the past had for half a century been a power in the sentimental and imaginative literature of England and of Europe as a whole. In the romantic confusion it had been mingled with revolutionary aspirations. A retrospective ideal, a regret for a better age apparently gone forever, it had set before a people intoxicated with iconoclasm the dream of a golden age in the irrecoverable past. Now in England the Tory reaction had been assailed by the impatient and victorious attacks of the middle class: the dominant mark on public life from 1815 to 1835 had been that made by industrial pretensions and liberal theories. Inevitably the hostility of the nineteenth century to the spirit of the eighteenth, defeated in the fields of action, concentrated in the fields of art and thought. In those sobered romantics, Wordsworth and Southey, in Walter Scott, seized by the picturesque charm of superseded manners, in Coleridge, too, now the mystical prophet of a religious philosophy, there were to be found the scattered elements for a new system which was to be hurried into birth by the play of economic forces. Eighteen thirty-three marks the Anglican revival at Oxford, destined to grow apace into a Catholic revival. The aspiration for a return to forsaken forms and beliefs, religious and civil, was indeed in the air. But it was the radical Thomas Carlyle who gave to the Toryism of the time, already furnished with a superficial sketch of a programme by the Young England party, its strongest, best articulated doctrine. Carlyle brought into harmony the silent recriminations of the populace, ground down by the selfish expansion of the middle class, and the resistance and resentment of the aristocracy supplanted by that same middle class. He left to the middle class its due place and part in the national life, and dreamed of a progress which, restoring

SOCIAL PHILOSOPHY 195

the old organic order of society, would establish a broader justice, allowing scope to the new forces of industry, but imposing on them a discipline transmitted from the past. It will be seen that the axis of his social philosophy was the yearning of his age for a return to the golden past.

The first book, the *Proem*, of *Past and Present* is a preface to the work. Carlyle returns to the facts and doctrines already expounded in *Chartism;* he describes with spirit and sobriety the state of England and the urgency of the crisis. What remedies can be applied? In his answer to this question we perceive how much his social doctrine has broadened since 1839, how much of the complexity of the social problem he has discovered. The remedies are difficult and will take time to act: there is no panacea, no Morrison's Pill, to cure the diseases of a society. Emigration and education are palliatives, not remedies. A profound regeneration of minds and hearts is necessary; social reform must follow moral reform or not come at all. The doctrine of the hero and the worship of the hero is the frame of all specific reforms: moral progress may be compressed into one abstract formula—government by the wisest. An aristocracy of talent will be the salvation of England; such a régime would commit the nation to the practice of hero-worship, and would bring the English to conform with the divine will of the universe. Hero-worship, however, presupposes purity of heart. It is difficult to choose the wisest, difficult to constitute an authentic aristocracy. The rule of such an aristocracy is not only the cause of a state's well-being but its effect: justice must animate the citizens before they consent to choose the wisest masters. . . .

Accordingly, we are in a circle. Oppressed by a

poignant sense of this, of the interdependence of the primary conditions and the consequences of just government, Carlyle will hereafter be a social pessimist. His pessimism will not be absolute, but quite incomplete, capricious, subject to every spurt of his humor. To the very end messages of hope, sometimes ecstatic and inspired, sometimes nearer to a savage, almost desperate, energy than to the normal forms of hope, will stand side by side in his writings with the bitterest irony and contempt for the mediocrity of his age and the frivolity of his fellows. Why should he continue to preach, we may ask, if all preaching is vain? Here is the escape indeed from the maddening circle; in stirring the souls of men, in rousing there the powers of conscience and of faith, the Heroic Man of Letters, a prophet pregnant with a divine message, will give men the power of choosing the wisest masters who shall lead them to the absolute good. The proem ends with an image of a star shining in the darkness and an image of the tree Igdrasil, a mystical symbol uniting the past, present, and future, even as the eternal and ever-novel universe. The way of salvation is a rough one; and the imagination of Carlyle in suggesting it combines the tragic vision of the earliest Saxons with the austerity of the Bible. It is a road "over steep untrodden places, through storm-clad chasms, waste oceans and the bosom of tornadoes; thank Heaven if not through very Chaos and the Abyss."

III

The second book is entitled *The Ancient Monk:* it is the image of the past.

The simple Chronicle of Jocelyn of Brakelonde seized

Carlyle's imagination with such force because it reveals an age of faith, of beneficent and venerated authority. Religion was no hypocrisy in that day, no verbal formula, no cant like the Puseyism of Oxford, to which Carlyle's uncompromising hostility will concede no sincerity whatever. Neither was it a morbid torment of the soul, an anxious care for one's personal salvation, like Methodism, where the same uncompromising hostility finds no authenticity. Religion was then a valiant joyous trust; God was in heaven, heaven was near, the devil was never far away. For this simple faith, men lived and died like martyrs; witness Edmund, patron of the monastery, martyred by the Danes and justly canonised. Was he not a saint, being a hero? Carlyle finds an ingenious solution of a teasing conflict between his affection for the age and his subject, and his bitter hatred and contempt for the Catholic notion of intermediaries between the soul and God.

The temporal powers as well as the spiritual powers were in those times a reality: the feudal aristocracy exercised over its vassals an authoritative control, founded on authentic might—the might of energetic mind and valiant arm. This aristocracy, says Carlyle, supervised the exploitation of nature and "less consciously," the distribution of her products; "judging, soldiering, adjusting; everywhere governing the people." Royalty could point with pride to Richard the Lion-Hearted, the hero-king; and against the extortions of a John Lackland the common people found their natural protectors in their bishops and their barons.

There is yet another virtue in this simple chronicle: it indicates the mediæval solution of the problem difficult beyond all others: the wise choice of guides and shepherds.

Jocelyn is a Boswell: he has a Johnson in Abbot Samson. In the midst of the dangers which threaten that monastery, we witness the election of a new abbot; the sound instinctive justice of the monks, men ignorant and narrow, but sincere; capable of believing and discerning the guide sent them by God, the hero set amongst them, the energetic, serious, patient governor who should save them, and who has submitted to the long hard apprenticeship of suffering silence and obedience. In very truth, this silent man, massive and virile, is the type of Carlyle's heroes. "The reader is desired to mark this Monk. A personable man of seven-and-forty; stout-made, stands erect as a pillar; with bushy eyebrows, the eyes of him beaming into you in a really strange way; the face massive, grave, with a very eminent nose; his head almost bald, its auburn remnants of hair, and the copious ruddy beard, getting slightly streaked with gray. . . . A thoughtful, firm-standing man; much loved by some, not loved by all; his clear eyes flashing into you, in an almost inconvenient way."

We see the abbot at his task; and the plain narrative of his valiant, authoritative, beneficent activity, set down in all simplicity, vivified and pointed by Carlyle, places before our eyes the labors and the struggles, the performances and the benefactions, of government in its ideal state. To great and little alike, Samson dispenses perfect justice; he renders due homage to the powers established by God, but, in defence of his rights, he can resist them. His firm government does not scorn to be suave and supple on occasion. His heroic career has its lesson on its very face: he knew how to govern because he had known how to obey;

SOCIAL PHILOSOPHY

he got others to obey him because the rule of all his actions was an inflexible devotion to a moral law.

Nowhere is Carlyle's genius in making past events live more marvelous than in these chapters lit by a passionate intensity, a vividly sympathetic imagination. His mind, like the path of light falling upon a dark night, illumines at a distance of seven centuries the outline, the strong, homely, spirited truth of an age gone beyond recovery. The thought of an irretrievable reality intoxicates him; he lingers over his evocation of a past age, savoring to the full his poignant sense of a reality so near and yet so far, a reality which once was, is no longer, and yet in a mysterious sense will never cease to be: "Beautifully, in our earnest loving glance, the old centuries melt from opaque to partially translucent, transparent here and there; and the void black Night, one finds, is but the summing-up of innumerable peopled luminous Days. . . . Why *there*, I say, Seven Centuries off; sunk *so* far in the Night, there they *are;* peep through the blankets of the old Night and thou wilt see! King Henry himself is visibly there; a vivid noble-looking man, with grizzled beard, in glittering uncertain costume; with earls round him, and bishops, and dignitaries, in the like. . . ."

Suddenly Jocelyn's Chronicle stops: in an instant, with a sound of dissolution perceptible to one's spiritual ear, all the real fantasmagoria is cast back once more into the midst of the twelfth century. "Monks, Abbot, Hero-worship, Government, Obedience, Coeur-de-Lion and St. Edmund's Shrine, vanish like Mirza's Vision."

Such is Carlyle's pursuit through the abyss of time—the spectral chase that he speaks of in *Sartor*—of the fantastic cortège of human history, a chase in which he clears like a flash the shining zone of existence to plunge again into those dark depths from which the sharp activity of the mind raises him for moments only. Thus the last chapter of this second book, takes up again one of the principal themes of *Sartor*.

After the past, the present. The third book, *The Modern Worker*, is built upon a contrast of what is with what was. Carlyle opposes the shame and the wretchedness of an individualistic state with the old order at once stable and organic. Nowhere does he succeed so little in attaining continuity in the development of his ideas. An oppressive richness of thought leads him into undue haste: or rather, his directive ideas, few and simple, become infinitely ramified and interlaced. As he criticises the present order, his burning conviction persists in introducing comments which are hortatory rather than analytic. Inextricably mingled with his picture of the evil state of society are his projects for remedying that state. The presentation of these projects had been the object of the Proem, and was to be the object of the Conclusion; but here, into the very body of the book it also intrudes.

We cannot hope to summarise the prophetic denunciations in which Carlyle passes judgment upon the society of his contemporaries. We can merely point to the most striking formulae in which his criticisms are concentrated, words which have impressed themselves upon so many minds and led them to doubt the social forms in which they live. Nowhere is there a greater abundance of such formulae.

The evil plight of society, Carlyle had already claimed, has a moral origin. Here he defines it: it is the impiety,

SOCIAL PHILOSOPHY

the materialism, of the age. By losing his faith in God, in the law of duty, in immortality, man has, as it were, lost his own soul. Is it astonishing then to find that his body, that the collectivity of human bodies, the community, is disintegrating? Impious doctrines, brutal catchwords, have superseded the Christian religion; and here Carlyle has not to coin new formulae: he has only to take over those coined by the economists and the Utilitarians. *"Laissez-faire, laissez-passer,"* "Supply and demand," "The greatest happiness of the greatest number"; he juggles with those phrases like a mad giant brandishing the weapons of defeated opponents. But he creates new formulae too; and in these he gives the facts an altogether different cast. In the age in which we live all the moral and emotional bonds which used to link men are destroyed; the only valid relation between them is the cynical material payment of prices and wages; to put together and keep together the dusty human atoms of our time there is no other force but "Cash-payment, the sole nexus between man and man."

This is the practical gospel of the doers—the active vital class of manufacturers and merchants, the middle class which Carlyle pursues with a hatred and contempt mitigated only by his respect for its laboriousness and its might, which is in some sense a right, and which secures to it, whatever its failings, the fields of the future. It is from this class, as the remainder of the book makes it evident, that Carlyle expects the essential elements of social regeneration. But as long as this class continues to have but the one crass goal—to apply the laws of competition, turning them roughly to its own advantage, "selling cheaper than any other people"—it will be living according to a materialistic gospel; and upon this gospel Carlyle fastens the Biblical name, already haunting for ages the imagination of the English people—"The Gospel of Mammonism." Beside the middle class fondling their golden calf, is the elegant scepticism, the selfish indifference of an indolent aristocracy, an "Unworking Aristocracy." Its creed, also an issue of modern impiety, is "Dilettantism," a general formula which replaces here the "Dandyism" of *Sartor*. Interested only in its scandalous privileges, it defends the Corn Laws with might and main, the Corn Laws because of which the common people are dying of hunger.

From the lowest classes, inaudible in former times, angry voices are now rising, voices which call for just wages, just work, "a fair day's wages for a fair day's work." No demand, says Carlyle, was ever more just than this. We must distinguish and honor those who practise the religion of labor. Admirable in its wisdom is the old Chinese rite in which at the spring of every year the Emperor in the sight of his people and under the eyes of invisible powers turns over in the earth, once more alive, the first furrow. Where the solemn meaning of the act is perceived and applied, error will not rule unchallenged. The representative of Mammon, the symbolic manufacturer Plugson of Undershot, is but a modern buccaneer without the leisure to become civilised, to adopt chivalry which is the beauty of the brave. He must learn to organise work, as the French say; he will learn too, and his energy which has been victorious over matter will be victorious over itself as well. Individual initiative will bear its fruit. But political democracy, the creaking motion of a great machine which merely collects and registers anonymous wills, is hopeless. All Carlyle's inexhaustible scorn and disgust is turned upon Parliamentary government, a mere rattle of words. Sir Jabesh Windbag is relegated in passing among the grotesque and superfluous.

The way is clear, now, for the positive doctrine of social reconstruction; and to it is devoted the Fourth Book, *Horoscope*.

IV

Carlyle appears reluctant to leave his general formulae for the more dangerous ground of detailed programmes. In the first and second chapters of this Fourth Book, he lingers over certain preliminary affirmations. England, he says, must have a new and authentic aristocracy, and this can, and must, emerge from the manufacturing class, the force of the future. Parliamentary government is the prey of corruption, of bribery. How then shall we reconcile democracy, the survival of which is inevitable, although democracy is impotent, with the authority we require? How shall we organise labor, so long as at this task there are no collaborators other than selfish appetites?

Our reply is furnished by the one institution in which the principle of order continues to live. This "one institution" is the army, a clear example of the fruitfulness of discipline. The genius of the army, once perceived, will throw light on every aspect of the social ideal: the true spirit of the army is one of obedience and hierarchy: and government has only to organise on the military model. The officers of the state, disciplined and directed by genuine leaders, moved by an apostolic zeal, will be the foes of vice, crime and ignorance. They will procure for England a national efficiency; and the age-old question of rights and duties will be solved when a national will is clearly manifested, accepted, and obeyed. Carlyle goes on, after making a few qualifications of minor importance, to solve the greater difficulty, that implicit in the intervention of the State in matters economic. The State, he says, will extend the scope of its activity farther and farther: its hand will be felt in every domain. Labor inspectors will visit every factory and mine, every building, every field: they will satisfy themselves that the salaries of every worker and the sanitation are as they should be. They will miss none of the oppressions which harm the toiling masses. "Such things," Carlyle proclaims, "cannot longer be idly lapped in darkness and suffered to go on unseen: the Heavens do see them: the curse not the blessing of the Heavens is on an Earth that refuses to see them. The legal order need not be disturbed but merely realised; baths, free air, a wholesome temperature, ceilings twenty feet high, might be ordained by Act of Parliament in all establishments licensed as Mills." Official investigations of the various matters mentioned by Carlyle had already revealed monstrous abuses current in the practice of those times: Carlyle in the reforms he preaches merely follows the lines already traced in the Blue Books. Modelling their methods upon those of the army, with all the precision and discipline of a military force, the civil officers will stretch their supervision to cover education and emigration. Carlyle concedes that his hints are not adequate to a complete regeneration of society; he insists that his intention is not to elaborate in its details a programme of social reform. Rather it is to stimulate and direct the efforts of reformers; once these efforts are trained, every aspect of social injustice will, by the pres-

SOCIAL PHILOSOPHY 205

sure of irresistible necessity, find its remedy. "The 'way to do it'—is to try it, knowing that thou shalt die if it be not done."

"State-socialism" is the true definition for the doctrine of social reorganization that we have so briefly sketched. Such is, at least, the ideal toward which Carlyle's suggestions point: intervention, centralisation, supervision of all national activities. It is also toward this ideal that, for almost a century, the forces of English life have been evolving. No moral force has made a more effective contribution to this process than the vigorous impulse Carlyle gave to the English mind, appealing to the nation's instinctive sense of how to preserve its force.

State-socialism is a form of government quite opposed to individualism: it supposes either a democracy or a monarchy, having to do with the collective will and mass activity, and relying upon elaborate and complex organisation. There is no scope under State-socialism for the authoritative enterprise of heroes, men inspired by special missions. State-socialism can be reconciled with the dominance of a benevolent despot, a modern Cromwell, but it excludes the possibility of a governing *élite*. Later, in his *Latter-day Pamphlets*, Carlyle will appeal to heaven for an inspired minister, a savior and a ruler: but in *Past and Present* his hope is still pinned to an effective aristocracy, an *élite* of heroes. Therefore he is obliged to correct the socialistic tendencies just developed, and in the concluding chapters he defines the rôle of the ruling classes in the ideal state, disciplined, organised and planned for effective life.

Carlyle's first concern is with the captains of industry: the name itself suggests the military model he has in

mind. He appeals to them with the deepest feeling; he would rouse their spirit, lead them to transfer the magnificent energy they possess from the conquest of matter to the quest of ideal justice; he would have them imitate the virtues, as they already have achieved the power, of the feudal lord and the knight. "Awake, ye noble Workers, warriors in the one true war: all this must be remedied. It is you who are already half-alive, whom I will welcome into life; whom I will conjure, in God's name, to shake off your enchanted sleep, and live wholly!
. . . Let God's justice, let pity, nobleness and manly valor, with more gold-purses or with fewer, testify themselves in this your brief Life-transit to all the Eternities, the Gods and Silences. . . . It is to you I call: ye know at least this, That the mandate of God to His creature man is: Work! The future Epic of the World rests not with those that are near dead, but with those that are alive, and those that are coming into life.

"Look around you. Your world-hosts are all in mutiny, in confusion, destitution; on the eve of fiery wreck and madness! They will not march farther for you, on the sixpence a day and supply-and-demand principle: they will not; nor ought they, nor can they. Ye shall reduce them to order, begin reducing them. To order, to just subordination; noble loyalty in return for noble guidance. Their souls are driven nigh mad; let yours be sane and ever saner. Not as a bewildered bewildering mob; but as a firm regimented mass, with real captains over them will these men march any more."

To stabilise the precarious economic life of England, a life disintegrated to a dust of atoms by the free play of individual appetites, the captains of industry must accept a state-control hitherto unknown. Contracts must be permanent: if they are for brief terms, there is none of that mystical confidence between man and man, that consent of the spirit, which is the only solid basis for the fragile edifice of social life. There can be no health, no happiness, where there is no permanence. Carlyle proposes, to secure economic stability in industry, that the employees share in the direction and perhaps even in the profit of their companies.

This is his solution of the problem which had surged up to puzzle him: the reconciliation between liberty and despotism lies in a despotism which shall be just. He goes farther, investigating the moral bases of the social order, and reaches formulae which are purely idealistic and point to the economics of Ruskin. Take for instance his definition of value in such terms as these: "the wealth of a man is the number of things which he loves and blesses, which he is loved and blessed by!"

To the other aristocracy, the Landed Aristocracy, Carlyle leaves its present authority and its present rôle in the social order. The land, he perceives, the necessary source of all material life, as of all social dignity, is the requisite basis for social authority. The Landed Aristocracy has its duties: the duty of charity material and spiritual, the duty of government and the imperative duty of showing the best example. But whatever his concessions to the conservative and traditional spirit, Carlyle's sympathy for the landed proprietors, the captains of agriculture, is a sympathy without real trust: his Scottish lower middle class instincts control him still and determine him to a hostility toward the landowner. In the struggle between the two powers, the power of the castle and the power of the factory, Carlyle cannot suppress his sympathy with the latter, the stronger and more vital. The scandal of the Corn Laws is to him a greater scandal than the existence of factories which take the lives of men. There are, he finds, but rare exceptions to the rule of selfishness in the landed aristocracy; for one Ashley (Lord Shaftesbury), how many lords there are who are idlers and fribbles, mere card-board men from whom life has long departed. There is no Duke of Weimar among the landed aristocracy of England.

Higher than captains of agriculture, higher than captains of industry, is the place of the great seer, the prophet, the creator of ideas and emotions. His part is to sustain the two social armies and their leaders at their work, and to provide society with a soul. The seers are "The Gifted Ones," the genuine priesthood of the new age. The modern hero appears as a man of letters, or a philosopher, perhaps, or a great seer. Their disinterestedness is absolute, sublime, their life a solitary one, their word rich in results. They have a love and pity inexpressibly tender for their fellows; but they evoke no love in return, for their soul is in the distant vast spaces of the universe.

It is with a cry of hope, then, that the arraignment of modern society in this great book closes. In his last pages Carlyle admits the signs of a dawn soon to rise, whose rays already mitigate the darkness. He affirms his invincible faith in the profound and living genius of his nation. His prophetic gift leads him to discern the vague promise of a spiritual regeneration; and here for the first time he describes the glory that is to be: "A deep feeling of the eternal nature of Justice looks out among us everywhere." With a sure intuition he finds the hidden source of a great

SOCIAL PHILOSOPHY

shifting of moral values. Humanity has not yet consented to its death. "My opinion is, that the Upper Powers have not yet determined on destroying the Lower World." A final appeal to all who have faith and to all who labor; and the social gospel, as Carlyle preached it in his richest prime, closes with an unwearied energy, a mystical enthusiasm stronger than the strongest doubt or the bitterest despair, stronger even than all the wrath that indignant spirit ever knew.

BOOK III

THE VEHEMENT REITERATIONS

CHAPTER I

CROMWELL AND FREDERICK

Past and Present completes the expression of Carlyle's doctrine; the subsequent works are not, however, to be neglected. If henceforward vehement reiteration is their principal characteristic, it is not an altogether new one; from the time when Carlyle first acquired a faith, he sacrificed to it everything else, the literary graces included. The natural temper of his mind was one uncongenial to the rational organisation of ideas; and equally uncongenial to their artistic and harmonious arrangement. Beginning with *Sartor Resartus* he ventured to be fully himself, and his boldness was an expression of his sense that his power was increasing. His first essays, in which he still was timid, were marked by simplicity, ease and balance in their development; but with *Sartor Resartus* impulse begins to rule his work, and the play of his mind is vehement and readily becomes aggressive as it moves forward in a series of leaps. Retaining a centre of thought, which is scarcely ever displaced and from which his gaze takes in the immense panorama of life and history, Carlyle is forever leaping forward, now in this direction, now in that, always regaining his usual position, and then leaping forward once more. Sometimes he carries the war into the enemy's camp; sometimes he expresses his admiration for a man or an event, an admiration which is that of a fighter, fastening furiously upon its object and embracing its cause against the rest of the universe. Whenever he regains contact with the sacred soil of his mystical beliefs, a flood of vigor reanimates him and overflows into unvarying triumphant affirmations. As in a choir, the bass now dwindles to the almost inaudible, without ever becoming silent, and then rises above all the other voices; Carlyle's philosophy is a hymn which stubbornly celebrates the same gods.

The primary interest of his later works is in the occasions which gave rise to them, the points to which his doctrine is applied, rather than in the doctrine itself. The plan of this study leaves them a subordinate place. Still, for the history of ideas, they retain their importance as gestures, their massive energy, their rôle as influences—for as moral and social influences they are not at all inferior to the works which went before. Furthermore, it would be unjust to deny them all doctrinal significance. Carlyle's thought, fixed in outline at the time when *Sartor Resartus* was written, successively develops its several aspects; it may be said that this thought evolves as it realises its implications; his books continue to express a living mind. Once the prophet has traversed the general aspects of man and the external world, the past and the present, specific chapters of history and politics attract his attention; he writes the biography of Cromwell and then of Frederick the Great; and in the intervals of composing these longer works, he addresses himself to the errors of the time, throws forth the series of *Latter-day Pamphlets*, or tranquillises himself in the composition of the *Life of Sterling*. None of these works, none of the briefer ones contemporary with them, adds anything essential to Carlyle's doc-

CROMWELL AND FREDERICK

trine; but in reading them one grasps the essential movement of that doctrine—a movement which has slowed down but not ceased. Carlyle continues to move over new ground along routes he had already determined. As he moves, some of his ideas are ratified by his experience, others are imperceptibly modified. The years Carlyle spent in intimacy with the spirit of Cromwell gave a slightly oblique direction to his social philosophy; and the *Latter-day Pamphlets*, revealing the influence exercised on the writer's mind by the great Puritan, witness also a new orientation of his political criticism. The sermons and satires that they really are have such a richness of power, and such a confusion of arrangement, that one has to free one's self from their seductive eloquence to appreciate the monotony of their doctrine; however quickly one wearies of their sustained intensity, one's curiosity as quickly recovers its edge; and each new formulation of a wisdom already twenty times expressed maintains its hold upon the reader's sensibility, if not upon his cold intelligence.

I

Carlyle's choice of a method for his *Cromwell* was, as has been said, a matter of chance and frustration. As he conceived it according to a traditional form, the work refused to shape itself; when he reduced it to an annotated collection of letters and speeches, it turned out to be the most vivid, the most engaging, of biographies. What Carlyle's vehement genius unintentionally achieved here was objective history, history as subsequent investigation and reflection has revealed it—the preference for the concrete, the respect for the simple document, which preside to-day at the most learned and the most admirable reconstitutions of the past. All Carlyle's instincts were opposed to the scientific spirit of research, but in practice his method here coincided with it; his imagination and intuitive temperament, starting from directly opposite beginnings, conducted him to analogous conclusions. For him life contained within itself the whole causality of the universe; the individual drama which constituted it was the peak of history and of ethics; and to reveal in activity a heroic soul was to give an adequate response to every noble curiosity of the mind. The struggle of such a soul against itself and against the elements of the external world lights in the centre of the past the only flame of authentic explanation, and gives to the observer the lessons in conduct without which all knowledge is in vain. Obscurely Carlyle's instinct was directed by his powerful sense for concrete reality—the faculty of his race—and by his obstinate love for the fact, for the human fact in especial, and by his eager, pious perception of the infinite meaning of the fact. Here his motives, if they were still different from those obeyed by the modern historian, were not so distant from them. For many years before the composition of *Cromwell* this mental inclination had been asserting itself; in his article on the *Parliamentary History of the French Revolution* (1837) it was expressed. To Thiers and Mignet he preferred the compilation of Buchez and Roux. And he added: ". . . One of the most interesting English biographies we have is that long thin Folio on Oliver Cromwell, published some five-and-twenty years ago, where the editor has merely clipt out from the contemporary newspapers whatsoever article, paragraph, or sentence he found to contain the name of Old Noll, and printed them in the order of their dates. It is surprising that the like has not been attempted in other cases."

The first chapter of the introduction is a manifesto. In it Carlyle proclaims the exceptional interest of the Puritan period, the last of the heroic ages, and savagely criticises the ideal and the methods of scholarship. Upon both subjects he had already spoken his mind; in the lectures on the hero as priest and the hero as king he had sketched an apology for Puritanism and for Cromwell; and the pedant Dryasdust had long figured in the gallery of Carlyle's nicknames and abominations. Never before, however, had he employed in the exaltation of the one, or in the vilification of the other, such a passionate certitude, such a savagery in satire. In the course of his preparatory studies he had explored the principal sources for the history of the Commonwealth; and from his conscientious examination he had derived, and retained, a horror of human fatuity and a resentment at an arid task. Lumping in a single hatred the mediocre chroniclers, the devoted, scantly endowed excavators of forgotten works, and the innumerable ephemeral writings which echoed the religious and political controversies of the seventeenth century, he declared war upon scholarship and upon the materials which are its usual nutriment. In his view only the texts in which a spark of human life, some trait of heroism or of character, shines out have the right to survive (even the right to moulder on library-shelves), the claim to occupy the attention of the historian. Of all other texts the wise historian would merely make a bonfire. The division of materials into living documents and hateful scribblings would apparently be left to the infallible decision of an inspired seer. It is too simple a conception of the value and interest of evidence, a conception which marks the distance between objectivity as Carlyle understands it and that to which modern historiography aspires. What he seems never to have perceived is that the dryest of documents, when sifted by a patient technician, may be rich in vitality.

Nevertheless, Carlyle's vision was remarkably clear. If he summarily condemned the genuine scholarship with the spurious, if he attacked the philosophy of history without appreciating its legitimacy and its merits, the general trend of his criticism and his practice was profoundly right. Two centuries had left their obliterating traces upon Cromwell; scholarly commentaries and rational explanations had merely obscured his personality and his performance. Edited without due system, or conserved in confusion in the British Museum, the documents of Cromwell's age crushed under their shapeless bulk even the most tenacious courage. The Civil War was the ground of predilection for the mediocre, well-intentioned zeal of amateur scholars. To make matters even worse, the rationalists of the eighteenth century had fostered the growth of a hostile legend about the Puritan hero, a legend composed of dislikes, prejudices, rancors and bigotries. For some of them he was the rebel and the regicide, for others the traitor and common man of ambition; his enigmatic figure was vaguely outlined against the sinister grotesque background of an age of madness of which England was secretly ashamed, which England asked only to forget. Was Cromwell sincere? Very few would have dared to affirm it. There was no longer any direct contact between his soul and the present age; he was no longer intelligible.

To reestablish such a contact Carlyle made a strenuous effort of sympathetic penetration. All his talents helped him in this effort, the natural trend of his imagination and his heart, the habits of his intelligence, his moral preferences, his sense of an affinity of which he had long been aware. "Here of our own land and lineage, in practical English shape, were Heroes on the Earth once more. Who knew in every fibre, and with heroic daring laid to heart, that an Almighty Justice does verily rule this world; that it is good to fight on God's side and bad to fight on the Devil's side. The essence of all Heroisms and Veracities that have been or will be." This is the cardinal truth, failing to perceive which an impious age cannot understand the distant fact of Puritanism. The Puritans are, for such an age, not merely extinct but incredible. Their ardent aspiration evokes no answering resonance in the frivolous hearts of modern people. They are as dead in spirit as in body: still they must be brought back to life. If we desire to remain alive ourselves, faith must be resurrected in us; once resurrected, it will illuminate for us the mystery of their believing lives; and the lofty lessons one may take from their lives will lend new strength to the meagre renewal of our spiritual being. Carlyle pursues a double aim; to disperse the darkness which hides a magnificent epic, the epic of conscience struggling with evil; and to accomplish a prophet's task in teaching and in presenting to minds at last opened to such a revelation, the mighty expression of an example which has the quality of inspired wisdom. Nothing could be less disinterested than his curiosity about the past. "Truly," he says, "the Art of History, the grand difference between a Dryasdust and a sacred Poet, is very much even this: To distinguish well what does still reach to the surface, and is alive and frondent for us; and what reaches no longer to the surface, but moulders safe underground, never to send forth leaves or fruit for mankind any more: of the former we shall rejoice to hear; to hear of the latter will be an affliction to us."

Guided by such motives, instincts and desires as these, Carlyle goes right to the mysterious core of the past as of the present—the human personality. His talent for psychological divination, his moral intuition, his imaginative energy, unite to evoke the real shape and form of bodies and souls. His method is built upon these bases, and if it was the result of chance, the chance in question was guided by some premonitions. The letters and speeches of Cromwell are collected and arranged in their actual order; in themselves they are a remarkably vivid commentary on the history of the time; and they are introduced, accompanied and explained by a moral interpretation as tactful as it is penetrating. The events reflect light upon the great soul who undergoes and indeed directs them; and that soul in turn reflects light upon the events; but the brightest illumination is in words, in the direct expressions of a conscience which in our very presence we observe feeling and acting. So suggestive, so brilliant, is the manner in which Cromwell reveals himself, that the rôle of the historian seems to be secondary, and the eclipse of his interpretation by his subject is the very effect at which Carlyle was aiming. On close examination, however, the effective presentation of the documents is seen to be the essential condition of the historical and artistic interest of the work. The texts themselves would only too often have been insignificant or obscure if their value had not been underlined by the editor; furthermore, the antiquated style and the sometimes confused eloquence of Cromwell would not always be intelligible without a commentary. Signs of life, indications of the soul, are collected from all sides: such and such a gesture, such and such a deed, such and such a facial expression, as related by Cromwell's contemporaries, adds a new element to the fascinating problem. Solidly developed, growing ever surer of its validity, Carlyle's solution of the problem imposes itself upon us without violence, finding its proof in the immense field of facts and words. Although the investigation is centred upon the figure of Cromwell, it does not exclude from its scope the other actors in the drama, his friends and enemies, soldiers and members of Parliament, Puritans and Cavaliers; each actor is illuminated by his relation to the hero, the centre of the whole. Such and such an episodic personage, such and such an officer unknown to history, once involved in the narrative is forever unforgettable, a profile fixed eternally by the piercing, searching gaze of the investigator.

As this gallery of moral portraits surrounds the dominating figure of an heroic character, the setting of space and time surrounds all the souls, completes their reality, gives to their actions and reactions their concrete expressions. Carlyle minutely followed the day-to-day course of events in the tragic years of which he was writing, making the fullest possible use of his texts; and his evocative power makes the events live again. He declined to separate from the superficial appearances of things the spiritual struggles and decisions, the efforts of wills, the agonies of souls which an indestructible convergence joined with them. He had visited Cromwell's native county; he had meditated and dreamed in the very places on which those eyes, disturbed by mystical emotions, had rested; from patient study of every detail, every episode, he had come to know the battlefields on which destiny had given its pronouncements; he had ransacked the old chronicles, the letters, newspapers, pamphlets, records of meetings and of victories, to find the particular facts, the picturesque traits, the line and color which should animate his narrative and clothe it with reality and life. Over the entire drama, thus restored to its human and physical setting, he casts the spell of the rich and powerful poetry of nature and the march of the seasons. The great spectacles of heaven and earth, the elemental forces, the play of light and shadow, starry nights, the roar of the waves, the rough breath of storms, suddenly surge up from the indistinct obscurity of the past to set quivering in us the same strong emotion which long ago other men have undergone. Here there are imaginative effects which put the final touch to the historical truth and lend it a deeper accent of intense reality; here, too, are the effusions of a sensibility obsessed by the cruel enigma of time and memory; here, too, is the spontaneous soaring of a religious mind toward the grandest aspects of a universe impregnated with the Divine Presence, and heavy with suggestions of the infinite.

II

The figure of Cromwell becomes more and more definite as his career develops. The introduction summarises the history of his family and the events of his youth. We see him, sprung of robust ancestors, leading in the green low-lying plains of Huntingdon and Saint Ives, the calm, monotonous life of a country gentleman. ". . . How he lived at St. Ives: how he saluted men on the streets; read Bibles; sold cattle; and walked, with heavy footfall and many thoughts, through the Market Green or old narrow lanes in St. Ives, by the shore of the black Ouse River—shall be left to the reader's imagination. There is in this man talent for farming; there are thoughts enough, thoughts bounded by the Ouse River, thoughts that go beyond Eternity—and a great black sea of things that he has never yet been able to *think*."

Beginning with January, 1635, Cromwell is known to us directly; the first of his letters that Carlyle gives is dated the eleventh of that month. ". . . These words, expository of that day and hour, Oliver Cromwell did see fittest to be written down. The Letter hangs there in the dark abysses of the Past: if like a star almost extinct, yet like a real star; fixed; about which there is no cavilling possible. That autograph Letter, it was once all luminous as a burning beacon, every word of it a live coal, in its time; it was once a piece of the general fire and light of Human Life, that Letter! Neither is it yet entirely extinct: well read, there is still in it light enough to exhibit its own *self*; nay, to diffuse a faint authentic twilight some distance round it. Heaped embers which in the daylight looked black, may still look *red* in the utter darkness. These letters of Oliver will convince any man that the Past did exist! By degrees the combined small twilights may produce a kind of general feeble twilight, rendering the Past credible, the Ghosts of the Past in some glimpses of them visible!"

Except for a few insignificant notes, all the extant letters of Cromwell appear in Carlyle's collection. These letters have the value of direct expression and fullness of matter;

there is value also in their reticences, in what they conceal or cannot utter. ". . . Dimly we discover features of an Intelligence and Soul of a Man, greater than any speech. . . . Cromwell, emblem of the dumb English, is interesting to me by the very inadequacy of his speech." The inadequacy of speech is purely comparative. It is not unfair to Cromwell, "emblem of the dumb English," to find some of his harangues unconscionably long.

Cromwell is a believer, and his time a time of belief. Cant was not yet born, says Carlyle, every one then said what he thought. For the last time, man's conception of the universe was determined by a belief in God. From the very outset we find Cromwell's spirit occupied by ideas which are as infinite as eternity, filled with an immense sea of ideas which he has not yet been capable of thinking through. It is a disturbed and tormented soul experienced in moral anguish, a soul, too, which blesses the divine grace which illuminates it, while it reproaches itself with being the prince of sinners and the persecutor of saints. Cromwell's simple confessions had served the malevolent zeal of some of his biographers only too well. Carlyle with the triumphant certitude of his intuitive mind discerns in those confessions the trace of the eternal crisis, the crisis of self-renunciation, through which he himself had passed.

Meanwhile events were following one another in haste. The absolutism of the King, the religious policy of Archbishop Laud, were stirring men everywhere to resistance or even rebellion. The Scots were up in the name of the Covenant; the Long Parliament was in session; the trial of Stafford was beginning. Cromwell, member for Cambridge, was in the foreground, forced on by destiny, and by the vigor of his will, the fervor of his faith, the in-

CROMWELL AND FREDERICK

fallible exactitude of his "seeing eye." Then came the first Civil War; consciences were divided by the claims of the Crown, divine right, tradition, on one side, and on the other the imperious demands of the religious instinct. Cromwell was a captain, and later a colonel, in the army of the Roundheads. ". . . How a staid, most pacific, solid Farmer of three-and-forty decides on girding himself with warlike iron, and fighting, he and his, against principalities and powers, let readers who have formed any notion of this man conceive for themselves." Through the confusion of marchings and counter-marchings, of multitudinous episodes, of ceaseless surprises, the sure undeviating activity of his heroic personality opens a clear, direct way for his fellows; men and facts are more and more grouped about him and governed by him; his troops are the model of the parliamentary army with their formidable fusion of mystical enthusiasm and unvarying discipline. Cromwell's effort was entirely absorbed by the holy daily task; and his figure was becoming that of the soldier of the Lord.

His speech is humble, full of Biblical jargon; his action is authoritative and pitiless. Neither relations of friendship nor any other human affections make him hesitate; a strange insensibility to suffering gets possession of him; and yet in his letters there are moments when his heart seems to melt, and the pathos of the Psalms affords him heartrending expressions for his griefs. Is the opposition an impossible one? Is the man a sphinx or a hypocrite? Not at all, says Carlyle. Beneath the frigid surface, there is profound tenderness in this Saxon soul; the faith of Cromwell, in its passionate vitality, its ecstasies and terrors, its inexpressible emotions, is nourished by the deep feelings which flow through his soul; but this is an ordered and a governed faith, the whole moral energy of which is directed toward the sublime egotism of duty.

Cromwell became Lieutenant-Governor; every day saw an increase in his popularity and his power; destiny took a hand and made him the master of the moment. He proclaimed himself the obedient tool of Parliament; he condemned the Anabaptists; and if he preferred the Independents to the Presbyterians, he still kept his preference a secret. The enthusiast is not without a policy; but his policy is an unconscious one, the expression of the will-to-live, the elementary inevitable opportunism of an energy so fully its own master, as to be able to accept the conditions necessary for success. Neither duplicity nor calculation is a part of Cromwell's prudence; the instinct of the race is too wise for him to weaken his spirit by dividing it; to his conscience Cromwell commits the clear perception of ideal ends; to himself he reserves the obscure but efficacious sense of what accommodations, what compromises, must be accepted. In his contention that Cromwell's sincerity was absolute, Carlyle was himself sincere and psychology supports his contention. How can one smile at formulae, incessantly repeated, which attribute to God the whole glory of victory, and seem to have as scrupulous care to preclude the jealousy of Heaven as to respect the susceptibilities of Parliament? Dictated by a just sense of the moral laws which regulate mental health, these formulae are not false, for they are useful. After Naseby, Cromwell writes of Fairfax in these terms: "The General served you with all faithfulness and honor: and the best commendation I can give him is, that I dare say he attributes all to God, and would rather perish than assume to himself. Which is an honest and a thriving way. . . ." Cromwell's humility finally became more dogmatic and more dangerous than pride. His successive triumphs were, in his view, the Lord's doing. Nothing could be more patent; and only an unbeliever could deny it. Every fresh favor of Providence fortified his mystical sense of his divine mission; and the spirit of a man who had been modest and troubled took from the stubborn confidence of Heaven a tendency to the dizziest kind of self-assurance.

We may safely concede what Carlyle requires of us. The legend of Cromwell's Machiavellianism was the superficial error of short-sighted rationalists. All the Protector's words and actions harmonise with the simplest of all hypotheses, the hypothesis of his good faith. His very contradictions, the denials of his own positions which were forced upon him by the nature of things, the several stages of his conquest of power, his struggle against the logical necessities of his rôle and of history, are softened, and melt into the genuine pattern of life; and a will which was always bent to promote the coming of a heavenly régime, which was always guided by a burning zeal for impersonal ends, has assumed the appearance of a schooled and calculating ambition. The reading of these letters and speeches of his reveals to us Cromwell the man; the God-inspired executioner had bowels of compassion; the stern avenger was a good husband and a good father; he did nothing which was not authorised by the disinterested command of his conscience; and a deep faith, a faith intensely felt and lived, was the support, the nourishment, the very substance, of his every action and his every thought.

The expressions of his piety are irresistibly conclusive. Some of them have the flaming intensity, the mystical quality, of a Pascal. To one of his daughters he writes: ". . . Happy Seeker! happy finder! Who ever tasted that the Lord is gracious, without some sense of self, vanity and badness? Who ever tasted that graciousness of His, and could go less in desire—less than pressing after full enjoyment? Dear Heart, press on; let not Husband, let not anything cool thy affections after Christ." More often than by affection, he is dominated by a faith which is an appeal for strength addressed to the supernatural source which tempers men for action. Take, for example, the meeting of the military leaders early in 1648, a time when a thousand dangers threatened—the King always a menace, royalist feeling reviving, rival factions in the Parliamentary party at grips with one another—while these rough men, determined to win back the Divine favor which has deserted them, pray anxiously, examine their consciences, beat their breasts in penitence, searching for whatever crimes they may unwittingly have committed: ". . . Which we found to be those cursed carnal Conferences our own conceited wisdom, our fears, and want of faith had prompted us, the year before, to entertain the King and his Party. . . ."

"And in this path the Lord led us, not only to see our sin, but also our duty; and this so unanimously set with weight upon each heart, that none was able hardly to speak a word to each other for bitter weeping, . . . in the sense and shame of our iniquities; of our unbelief, base fear of men, and carnal consultations (as the fruit thereof) —with our own wisdoms, and not with the Word of the Lord—which only is a way of wisdom, strength and safety, and all beside it are ways of snares . . . and presently we were led and helped to a clear agreement amongst ourselves, not any dissenting, That it was the duty of our day, with the forces we had, to go out and fight against those potent enemies, which that year in all places appeared against us. . . . With a humble confidence, in the name of the Lord only, that we should destroy them. . . . And that it was our duty, if ever the Lord brought us back again in peace, to call Charles Stuart, that man of blood, to an account for that blood he had shed, and mischief he had done to his utmost, against the Lord's Cause and People in these poor Nations." The despairing appeal of the exhausted wills of those men to the energetic principle which could restore their vigor is once again hearkened to; the vigor regained, their souls leap forward in consonance with instincts and desires; just as the weakening of their activity was the work of sin, the reflux of divine grace was a torrent which bore them toward activity. War to the bitter end, the death of the King—these were the issues of the tragic examination of conscience in which, in the silence of their hearts, the natural and the supernatural merged their voices.

Still, if Carlyle has firmly grasped the psychological truth in the case of Cromwell, can we accept the spirit in which he exalts and glorifies his hero? If his historical thesis is acceptable can we say as much for his social and philosophical thesis? In *Cromwell* he adds nothing to the fund of ideas upon which his gospel reposes; of these ideas Cromwell is a grand example, a magnificent and uncompromising application. The essence of the gospel remains a fatalism conjoined with an assimilation of right to might. Cromwell's faith was a simple one; his exemplary value is easy to formulate—it is the absolute obedience of conduct to the suggestions of a conscience which seeks light from mystical intuition alone. Many of his friends, many of his enemies, resembled Cromwell in this. His success is here also the one sure mark, the consecration, of his heroism. The poor Levellers, the enthusiasts who dreamed of a Biblical communism, were also listening to a supernatural voice; if Cromwell was right in destroying them, was it not, in the last analysis, because Cromwell was mightier than they? The secondary motives for their destruction which Carlyle presents derived from principles foreign to his pure gospel, from the limits which his temperament imposed upon necessary revolutions. Carlyle implies a divine judgment in all the pronouncements of destiny, and in this judgment is the only real superiority to be found in the victor. From Naseby on, he says, God in the whirlwind of battles appears to speak and testify in an unmistakable voice. It is surely the part of wisdom to confess under these circumstances that God's designs are impenetrable; and in any event Carlyle's moral system is brought to coincide with these designs only at the price of extremely arbitrary affirmations. All Carlyle's self-trust is needed if one is to refuse to the Catholic faith of the Irish an intrinsic right to overcome the Puritan faith of Cromwell; and if God has made the Celts a radically inferior race, as Carlyle believed, the religion of the wretched Irish, hunted, massacred, by the justice-loving Cromwell is not at fault.

Carlyle may fairly be charged with lacking humor now and then. When the Scottish Covenanters in arguing with Cromwell very aptly quote certain texts from the Scriptures, Cromwell replies: "I am persuaded that divers of

CROMWELL AND FREDERICK

you, who lead the People, have laboured to build yourselves in these things; wherein you have censored others and established yourselves 'upon the Word of God.' Is it therefore infallibly agreeable to the Word of God, all that *you* say? I beseech you, in the bowels of Christ, think it possible you may be mistaken." The reader is sorely tempted to an ironical smile. In such a religious assault-at-arms, Cromwell's only advantage is in his pikes and muskets. His adversaries, loyal to the best element in the New Testament, are unwilling to make the event the criterion of the justice of the cause; and Cromwell's only reply is that such a term as "event" is an insult to his victories, which are indeed the evidence of God's handiwork.

It is an extremely doubtful claim; but behind it are massed, one feels, arguments of a factual sort. The absence of moral criticism, voluntary or involuntary, gives an element of cynical brutality to Carlyle's work for all its attempts at edification. The moments in which Cromwell is preparing his mystical *coup d'état*, parting from his loyal friends of long standing devoted to the republican cause, accepting the honors and the wealth that came unsought, looking after his private fortunes like a good father, and alternating at his own caprice the defence and the destruction of order—maintaining, for example, with the instinct of a country gentleman, the sacredness of real property—these moments are for the mind which thinks in purely human fashion irresistible motives for suspicion that self-interest was present. To resist such suggestions successfully, to accept and venerate the tyrannous and bloody deeds of the savior of Puritanism, the long series of well-intentioned acts of violence which placed Cromwell at the head of the State and kept him there, the chain of circumstances by which such a scorner of hereditary right chose his own son as his successor, one must be obstinately contemptuous of any system of thought save that which blindly and stubbornly assimilates what is to what ought to be. Carlyle was soon to discover in the Jesuitical spirit the principle of the moral decadence of modern times. Still, if the maxim that the end justifies the means is nowhere explicitly stated in this work, it is its very essence: as is the sinister image of a Nemesis in history revealed in the impact of race on race, a Nemesis which conducts men toward the Kingdom of God through blood and through tears. It may be that such an image is the final revelation concerning the destiny of mankind; others have thought that it was, and some of these have conceived of themselves as idealists; but none of these had such an invincible confidence that this doctrine was in agreement with the inner meaning of Christianity, and the noblest efforts of the human conscience.

III

The History of Frederick the Second of Prussia, called Frederick the Great, is the longest of Carlyle's works; he struggled with it for fourteen years. By 1851 he had chosen it as the subject of his next history and begun to read; in the autumn of 1852 he went to Germany to collect material and visit the fields on which Frederick had fought. When he got back to London, he immersed himself in the torturing work of composition. "The elements of our task," he writes in his journal, "lie scattered, disorganised, as if in a thick, viscous chaotic ocean, ocean illimitable in all its three dimensions; and we must swim and sprawl towards them, must snatch them, and victoriously piece them together as we can." He forgot what tortures he had endured in preparing *Cromwell;* never, never, had impatience, uncertainty or exhaustion wrung from Carlyle such complaints. Slowly, however, his task did get done. In 1858 the first two volumes came out; and in this same year Carlyle was obliged to undertake a second visit to Germany; the third volume came out in 1862, the fourth in 1864, the fifth and sixth together in 1865. During fourteen years Carlyle's whole life had been absorbed by his single preying task; all his power of physical resistance, all his moral energy, all his faculty of feeling, had been preempted by it. The success of the history was immediate and it completed his glory. Translated forthwith into German, the history became a classic in the land of its hero.

There is none of Carlyle's works which has not passionate enthusiasts bent upon giving it the first place; and *Frederick the Great* is no exception. Neither the general public nor the lovers of Carlyle refuse it a respectful esteem, but it would be absurd to say that it now finds many readers. Along with its admirable qualities one must accept some serious defects: the plan is too vast and it seems uncertain, the internal harmony is insecure. The subject is always expanding; expanding from the biography of the hero to the history of German aggrandisement, from the record of the Prussian monarchy to the mirror of German relations with the rest of Europe, and little by little of eighteenth century Europe as a whole. The first book relates the hero's birth and situates him in a family-group; in the second book the reader is abruptly thrust eight centuries backward and is the spectator of the slow, stubborn progress of the two forces which went to the making of Prussia, the March of Brandenburg and the Hohenzollern dynasty. In the third book the two forces are brought together, the Elector of Brandenburg becomes a King; and in passing Carlyle reveals the historical meaning of the Reformation. These three introductory books show a patient, laborious scholarship in the writer, a scholarship animated by the sense that the beginnings described are those of great things and by the exaltation natural to the discourse of a prophet. Still, only national patriotism could prevent one finding these books dry. Carlyle's specific subject is new but his theme, his gospel, is the same as of old: once again we are told that it is the religious laws of life and the decisions of Providence which connect the success of nations with certain moral attitudes of reverence and perspicacity, with the fear of the invincible powers before which man must bow, and of the visible facts which he must accept, or, denying, perish. ". . . It is the history of a State, or Social Vitality, growing from small to great; steadily growing henceforth under guidance: and the contrast between guidance and no-guidance, or misguidance, in such matters, is again impressively illustrated there."

Finally, the narrative of Frederick's education begins, but Frederick is still secondary; the picturesque personality of his father, Frederick-William, is still in the foreground, and Carlyle is reluctant to have done with him. The Sergeant-King merely paved the way for his son's victories; but his rough simplicity was more in consonance with Carlyle's profoundest unavowed preferences than the character of his son; and the painful history of the rela-

CROMWELL AND FREDERICK

tions between Frederick-William and his heir is told in such a way that, for all his violent acts and words, it is the father who comes out better. Indomitable and obstinate he dies with dignity and "slept with the primeval sons of Thor." "No Baresark of them, nor Odin's self, I think, was a bit of truer human stuff;—I confess his value to me, in these sad times, is rare and great. . . ." From this point on, the story has its unity and its fixed centre; explored in its least details, the figure of Frederick takes on extraordinarily sharp relief; but the evocative realism of Carlyle recalls the art of Richardson in which the reader is spared nothing. Vivid and intense as the epic is, it requires a boundless courage to read it right through without weakening. As one reads, one understands the complaints and outcries of Carlyle when he was writing it. His historical conscience is admirably scrupulous, but he presses his passion for the concrete, for the fact, to the point where the resurrection of the past becomes a veritable victory and a veritable torture. Opposed as he was to the simplifications which others have accepted as inevitable, in writing his histories he declined to deal with wholes. If his penetration enables him to be objective, still his angle of vision is highly personal to himself; light and shade are distributed according to his prejudices; and the subjectivity of his angle of vision makes it impossible for him to renew the sources or the perspective of the story, and leads him to sacrifice Frederick the organizer to the soldier and the diplomat. Never were narrations of battles studied with more care or written with more affection for the subject. Perhaps, too, Carlyle makes excessive use of the anecdote, precious and significant as it is, in the re-vitalisation of the past. A very substantial chapter of the work is given over to the relations between Frederick the Great and Voltaire, but it cannot be admitted that Carlyle satisfied his ambition of saying the last word on that troubling problem. The portrait of Voltaire reveals an effort to be impartial and a more balanced art than one might have expected. Carlyle's instinct for the humorous fastened upon Voltaire as an incomparable subject for its play. It may even be said that he experienced some actual sympathy with Voltaire; sensible as he was, and he was only too sensible, of all Voltaire's defects, he ascribed to him a rôle in history which was, in its own way, providential. Voltaire had contributed to the destruction of sham and empty falsehoods, and his arid railing heart had known generous inspirations. Carlyle had uttered practically the same opinion of Voltaire in the essay of 1829; but now his opinion has become more definite, more complete, and in so doing, it has acquired an added severity. There is a subtle and perilous injustice in these two estimates of Voltaire, an injustice which is the result of a bias deeply, ineradicably, set in Carlyle's temper, of a too dogmatic judgment passed upon the French intelligence of which Voltaire is taken as a symbol, and of a whole hierarchy of intellectual and moral values as narrow as they are fixed.

Frederick himself is not a hero after Carlyle's own conception; and nothing is more curious to watch than the adept idealisation of Frederick, and the addition of nuances to his figure, with a view to combining a recognisable likeness with a character acceptable as a vehicle of divine inspiration. Two elements entered into the formation of Frederick's moral being. One was French and borrowed from Frederick's Huguenot governesses, from the culture he acquired, from the language he spoke; and Carlyle does not

CROMWELL AND FREDERICK

attempt to deny the extent of this French influence. He prefers to recognise its force and connect with it all the failings of Frederick's character. In the Calvinistic discipline Carlyle's Puritanism could take some satisfaction—"It might have been a worse element; and we must be thankful for it." Nevertheless Calvinism has its logical quality, its dialectic and critical aspect; and the French language was only too well fitted to accentuate the evil consequences of these. ". . . Not a bad dialect; yet also none of the best. Very lean and shallow, if very clear and convenient; leaving much in poor Fritz unuttered, unthought, unpractised, which might otherwise have come into activity in the course of his life. . . ." Despite its mighty virtues, the Teutonic spirit could not efface the early imprint upon Frederick, all of whose grave and earnest qualities are, however, its doing. He continues the tradition of "long lines of rugged ancestors, cast in the same rude stalwart mould." These German sons of nature have bequeathed to their descendant a fibre too tough for it to be corrupted by his French masters, the sons of art and theory. ". . . Remarkable men, many of those old Prussian soldiers; of whom one wishes, to no purpose, that there had more knowledge been attainable. . . . Grim hirsute, Hyperborean figures, they pass mostly mute before us: burly, surly; in mustaches, in dim, uncertain garniture, of which the buffbelts and the steel are alone conspicuous. Growling in guttural Teutsch what little articulate meaning they had: spending, of the inarticulate, a proportion in games of chance, probably too in drinking beer; yet having an immense overplus which they do not so spend, but endeavour to utter in such working as there may be. . . ."

Alas, their heir has not quite their primitive simplicity: he writes elegant verse in the French manner, he covets the reputation of a man of wit, he coquettes with M. de Voltaire and believes, to be frank, in neither God nor Devil. Even so; he is of his age, could not be of another, and he has been infected by its damnable diseases. But plumb the depths of his spirit, of his actions, and do you not get the Germanic earnestness, the gravity masked by irony? But can you say that he who believed in facts was an unbeliever? How can you deny his belief in them when his hold upon them was so strong? Do you not see him, like his will, supple and commanding at once, moulding things and persons and divining the hidden point upon which force may effectively centre? Alone against Europe, beset with mortal dangers, he holds his ground, and victory smiles upon him; for in his education the chief factor was the unconscious apprenticeship to which he had been subjected by that incomparable instructor, the Sergeant-King. He has a genius for war, and a genius for peace as well; he knows how the prosperity of a State is built up and fortified; order and authority emanate from him and pass through a thousand channels down to the daily tasks of his humblest subject. This is the true life of Frederick, his creative activity; and what guides him is his Germanic sense of the real. He may have played the fool in the world of appearances, but never was he taken in by it: he is a "sincere" man. Exhausted by his prodigious activity, he dies a stoical and solitary death, feared rather than loved, and giving to the Divine little thought; but he dies with his task completed and time will confirm his work.

Nothing could be simpler than the philosophy of this last of Carlyle's histories; no element in it had not already

CROMWELL AND FREDERICK

been said and said again in the *Heroes* and the *Cromwell* among others. The novelty is in the necessary adaptation of Carlyle's doctrine to an example not too well-suited to it; the necessity for such an adaptation accounts for the expansion of the subject and the plan. Voltaire and the eighteenth century had to come in, to explain, and in some measure, to excuse, the sceptical and frivolous aspects of Frederick; and the completeness of the narrative, the infinite detail with which war and negotiations are described, was necessary to reveal the essentially realistic genius of Frederick in action. As a creator of an empire, he would participate in heroism by his intuition of the secret will of the universe. The supreme judgment of the event would set his achievement beyond criticism; and if the means Frederick used were not always irreproachable, the investiture of Providence would hallow all his deeds, making him a collaborator with destiny. Conquered without very good title, Silesia found its place and its part in the new edifice of the Prussian monarchy; and there, too, Silesia found its happiness. A robust agent of order, a destroyer of anarchy, Frederick brought to their fine maturity the seeds of Germanic greatness; he made ready the way for German unity and for a German hegemony of Europe—in Carlyle's view, a welcome certainty of the future. Carlyle was a great prophet; but he did not foresee everything that was to be; and, to-day, his enthusiasm seems to his compatriots to have been a little excessive.

CHAPTER II

SERMONS AND SATIRES

I

AMONG the later writings of Carlyle it is the *Latter-day Pamphlets* which most emphatically strike a new note. All the works which follow them have a larger measure of indignation and denunciation, a greater bitterness, a less vivid hope, than those which had gone before. If Carlyle ever breaks off from his persistent criticism of the present it is only to recall with characteristic tenacity the rules of wisdom—only to replace the satire by the sermon. *The Life of Sterling* stands apart from the other works, a moment of calm amid a stormy voyage. If from 1850 to 1865 Carlyle seems to have forgotten his time and to be abandoning it to its incurable ailments, this is because the consuming task of his *Frederick* was leaving him no leisure, no peace.

Even more than that of his earlier works, the style of the *Pamphlets* is distinguished by its intensity. Indignation, contempt, irony flame forth and take all regularity, all rounded grace, away. For Carlyle is impatient of regular construction, of useless connectives; he sacrifices everything to gain force. Words packed with meaning are pressed together and seem to jostle one another in their passionate haste: the most vigorous, the most essential, word takes the key position; and the others distribute themselves about it as best they can. Sudden leaps of feel-

SERMONS AND SATIRES 241

ing are forever moulding the sentences, and modifying their movement. The stops, the impacts, the broken rhythms, inarticulate, tortured fragments of sentences—all have an extraordinary suggestive and evocative power. Carlyle takes his opponents to task; he provokes and apostrophises them; his raillery passes into insult, while vulgar, familiar, comical nicknames are flung out with the most unexpected and picturesque effect. From the whole the reader gets an impression of feverish ardor.

However sincere and spontaneous this originality of style may be, however securely and intimately it may be bound up with the writer's temperament, one cannot banish the suspicion, even the certainty, that there is an element of the deliberate in it. There is art, there is even artifice, one feels; or if the style has become habitual, automatic, in the beginning it was consciously adopted. Carlyle has several idioms; for his literary work he chose the most emphatic, the idiom which corresponded to the most violent tone of his sensibility and of his entire being, the idiom which brought into the strongest relief his intellectual personality. An admission which is to be remembered without being overstressed, throws light upon that artistic exaggeration, in which there is in some sense a transposed and exalted sincerity. As early as 1825 he notes in his journal: "In my speech concerning them I overcharge the impression they have made upon me, for my conscience, like my sense of pain and pleasure, has grown dull, and I secretly desire to compensate for laxity of feeling by intenseness of describing." Through the complex of Carlyle's later style runs an unbroken vein of humor inextricably mingled with indignation. Here as everywhere the humor issues from the conjunction of an original temperament with a certain set of processes, a mental attitude, an æsthetic mechanism. Dogmatic and ardent, Carlyle was none the less capable of indirect expression; the opulence of his nature, his characteristically Scottish faculty of self-scrutiny, the entire background of his philosophic speculations, equipped his mind with the duality of planes, so to speak, without which no preacher could be a humorist. He had, in addition, the shrewdness of his native country, the talent for concrete observation, the vivid perception of the distinct elements in things. His imagination fed upon fresh, clear impressions scarcely at all elaborated by his understanding: it shared in the general characteristics of normal Anglo-Saxon perception, characteristics so emphatic and remarkable in the Puritan masters of the imagination, men like Bunyan and Richardson. Finally he had what those others lacked—a gift for fantasy, an extraordinary freedom of invention, mental agility, a faculty for unexpected associations, a fund of verve and drollery.

One thing more is needed, transposition, the special trick of the humorist; and Carlyle's humor flows according to principles but instinctively divined and obscurely understood. A meticulous minuteness in his descriptions creates the illusion of a scientific tone; and the ostensible gravity with which he always proceeds gives to his jests a remarkably sharp savor. Sometimes he pretends to abandon his moral criteria and in his new cynical guise he is able to shed a stronger light, and a more various one, upon the baseness of the vices with which he is concerned. Sometimes, more often, indeed, he conceals all emotion behind a transparent mask of indifference. Again, he adopts cer-

SERMONS AND SATIRES 243

tain of Richter's processes; an apparent disorder, a temporary suspension of logical method, or of good taste; what ensues is a bewildering jumble of incongruities and contradictions. Most of these modes of humor take on a sharper edge by marked contrasts, violent juxtapositions and surprising comparisons. The celebrated account in the *Latter-day Pamphlets* of the Pig-philosophy illustrates all of them.

But this mechanism, so far as we have described it, is impersonal; it remains to characterise its operation in the particular case of Carlyle. Carlyle's humor is remarkable for the unique pitch of its feeling and for the unique color of its picturesque imagination. This imagination is violent, often indeed crude and brutal, becoming more and more crude and brutal as Carlyle's career goes forward. It is the imagination of a Flemish painter, rich in baroque realism and gross spirit: the smells of the London gutters are among Carlyle's favorite images along with the varieties of dead dogs. As for the emotional pitch of Carlyle's humor, the strained tone, the obviousness and the copiousness of the devices, the nature and the quality of the effects sought, all suggest and diffuse a fierce and contemptuous scorn, a boiling indignation at the prophet's age and mankind in general. Carlyle's humor is akin to Swift's, setting force above sweetness, subtlety or delicacy. It is a humor which knows nothing of the cunning, refined manipulation of shades, or the caressing iridescent effects, of a mind like Lamb's. Carlyle's humor rapidly comes to the point where humor ends and satire begins: and there are times when the rush of his wrath shatters all barriers of reserve; and the effect is that of a volcano in blazing eruption. So intense, so contagiously intense, is Carlyle's humor that it is not amusing so often or so profoundly as it is touching, gripping, dominating.

II

The study of *Doctor Francia,* published in 1843, is written in the spirit which animated the *Cromwell.* Carlyle presents the life and work of the terrible dictator as worthy of emulation—for Francia was strong to govern, to command, to execute, to provide—was able to banish from a still primitive people the seven deadly sins and, by the use of simple authoritative methods, sometimes harsh but never gratuitously so, to make Paraguay a prosperous contented nation. The striking paper on the *Nigger Question* (1849) is the natural preface to the *Latter-day Pamphlets:* most of their themes and formulae are announced in it. The root of this virulent satire is Carlyle's irritation at the political and social chaos of 1848. Europe appeared to him to be speeding toward destruction; and the sentimental fatuity, the nonchalant levity, of so many of her governors led them either to ignore the danger or to deal with it by applying strange and ineffective remedies. The liberals and the economists, with their indefatigable optimism, congratulated themselves upon the irresistible progress of democracy and minimised whatever setbacks it encountered as purely temporary; the English humanitarians, whom ten years of national misery had stirred to nothing but the mildest protests, were still in tears before the moving spectacle of the negroes at last assured their freedom. To the general satisfaction Lord John Russell had proclaimed that the freed slaves in the British West Indies were comfortable and happy. Carlyle pictures them reclining in the shade, on the edge of fields of sugar cane rotting away for lack of men to cut them; and his imagination plays ironically upon these black brothers with their sturdy jaws operating upon calabashes, the free gift of nature. In Ireland, meanwhile, famine rules and kills; in London the Chartists' indignation continues to rumble; and the slave system of English industry chains to machines the huge armies of the English proletariat. Carlyle flays the soggy humanitarianism which refuses to see, to feel, to accept, the divine laws of reality: humanitarianism is but a sham, a hypocrisy, a monstrous aberration. The abolition of slavery or of compulsory work is tantamount to an abolition of pain, an abolition of the tears whose necessity the Bible wisely asserts. The horizon of man upon earth is dominated by a single inevitable fact: the idle man must be provided with work to do and, if he decline to do it, he must be constrained, for a benevolent authority has the right and the duty to constrain him. The heroism of the English people was able to conquer and control a luxuriant virgin soil; the riches that soil may produce are the right of that race; the title to their possession has the sanction of Providence itself. If the black slave trade is indeed the shame of mankind, that trade must cease; should there be other evils, other shames, crying more loudly to heaven, the wills of men should turn first to the eradication of these.

The same angry spirit informs the *Latter-day Pamphlets*. Lulled to sleep by the recent discomfiture of the revolutionary and subversive elements in Europe, England was in 1850 giving herself up to a feverish pursuit of material prosperity and luxury. It was a false security, based on tentative compromises; and the solutions of political and social problems upon which it counted left untouched the indispensable task of organising labor.

The Government of the day was dominated by mediocre, undecided minds. Lord John Russell's tenure of office was dependent upon the support of the Peelites. Peel, who had been driven from power in the popular furore caused by his repeal of the Corn Laws in 1846, was, in Carlyle's opinion, the only politician of the time with anything of the hero in his make-up. Foreign policy was determined by the personal caprices of Palmerston. The bonds which knit England and her Colonies together were growing looser, and no one was aware of the need to maintain and even to strengthen them. Civil government was at a loss, quite incapable of coping with the emergent needs of an age when a gigantic economic development was always presenting unexpected problems. The Irish question was farther than ever from solution. Two successive harvests had been failures; these failures had been aggravated by half-measures and tergiversations, with the result that famine was daily depleting the Irish nation. Under the stress of emigration and famine the Irish population had declined by three millions. In 1849 Carlyle went to Ireland, bent upon seeing and knowing the reality of the peril; he returned to England heart-sore, gloomy, and terrified by the prevision of imminent upheavals. Early in 1850 he began to write, and continued on into July; the title he selected when he came to reprint his articles in book-form is instinct with the apocalyptic spirit which pervades them with the threat of divine retribution.

The first article, *The Present Time*, is one of those general conspectuses so dear to Carlyle, dear because they are invitations to launch upon all his main tendencies of thought, and so demonstrate that all questions are connex,

SERMONS AND SATIRES

the only valid arrangement being the inextricable confusion of reality itself. He achieves in this paper, indeed, a new expression of his complete social philosophy, new because of the intensity of his feeling and the acerbity of his anger. A fierce indignation settles upon the prophet as he looks out upon a continent shaken by all kinds of disturbance, with thrones crumbling and nations rising from slavery only to relapse into a shameful disorder. The hour is a fateful one; either a new era of hope or a final ineluctable catastrophe is at hand, says Carlyle. Democracy is a palpable fact, terrible but true; against "sham Kings" the peoples prevail or shall prevail. But democracy is not a form of government; democracy is anarchy; the example of the ancient Greek republics is not imitable; neither is the example of the United States—a nation with a materialistic and corrupt public life, a nation of eighteen million fools satisfied with themselves—bores, as Carlyle calls them somewhere else. The universe is a monarchy, a hierarchy; the sole safety for the British régime is in a recognition of heroic leaders whose duty is to command, as the duty of all others is to obey. Only by such a recognition is there a cure for the horrible abscess of Irish poverty and the social scandals published by the press, the scandal, for instance, of thirty thousand London needle-workers on starvation wages. In a humorous harangue, Carlyle presents an ideal prime-minister preaching to a disheartened army of workers the value of enrolment under the beneficent authority of captains of industry.

Meanwhile the liberated slaves and the grotesque misconceptions of sentimental philanthrophy had cropped up again; and in the second essay, *Model Prisons*, Carlyle turns bitterly upon false remedies and quack doctors. Humanitarian sentimentalism he dismisses as a sham, and does so for two chief reasons—it fails to cure the evil it attempts to cope with, failing to perceive where the root of that evil is; and it aggravates the evil because of a morbid pity for the fact of crime. The model prison of Pentonville, the last word in a penitentiary system which is ostensibly the product of enlightened conscience, offends Carlyle's scrupulous sense of justice, offends it so gravely that its shadow spreads over all other aspects of humanitarianism. In the model prison Carlyle discovers an essential element of contemporary disorder, an alarming symptom of anarchy. To know how to punish is, in his opinion, the first duty of a just government, a government, that is, which couples benevolence with firm authority: not to know how to punish is to have parted company with the conception of justice: the charity lavished upon the guilty is stolen from the innocent. Following his idea to its extreme implications, Carlyle defines Christianity as a religion of hatred, "a healthy hatred of scoundrels." With this strange dogmatism of his, this *simpliste* intelligence seeking and finding everywhere in reality sharp antitheses, antitheses without a single nuance or qualification, Carlyle affirms that in England there exist "a worst man" and "a best man," and that the security of society depends upon hanging the one and investing the other with absolute authority. The doctrine springs from a profoundly mystical temperament, akin to those of the leaders in the Wars of Religion and to those of the fanatical many, closer akin perhaps to that of Cromwell himself.

In *Downing Street*, the third pamphlet, Carlyle shows himself an imperialist rather than a socialist, concerned not so much with the establishment of social justice as with the national efficiency—the rectification of political and administrative shortcomings. He appears as a realist demanding that the national machine turn out its best product. Is there contradiction between the position he occupies here and his previous denunciations of mechanism, his diatribes against the modern fetish of automatic and complex organisation? To some extent there is, no doubt; but above the machine he requires leaders. He would have at the head of the State ten men, ten Ministers whose will and initiative shall be supreme; and from ten he passes to one—one supreme reforming prime minister. Sir Robert Peel shall be the new Hercules: the task of cleansing the Augean stables, suppressing the red tape, the cumbrous useless routine of the English public service, shall be his. Once again, Carlyle sings the glories of "intellect"—by which he means the intuitive faculty through which men perceive the true and achieve the good. He enquires why should not a sovereign or a prime minister endowed with this precious faculty choose his advisers, and the chief agents, without submitting to the ineffective control, the feeble initiative, of Parliament? Carlyle would inflect the development of the British Constitution toward past stages—returning gladly to rule by the ruler's pleasure.

The sketch of reforms immediately practicable is completed in the fourth pamphlet, *New Downing Street*. Here Carlyle presents a programme broader, and at the same time more exact, than he had previously devised. Since 1843 his sense of what is possible in politics and what is necessary in government, had grown much richer. The organisation here described is still one in which the State has high and broad functions. But Carlyle is still less of a socialist here than in his preceding works. The idea of necessary authority, and that of a larger national output, replace the notion of the just distribution of wealth. The sole survival of the democratic ideal is in the accessibility of any office to the man of talent, in the possibility that the hero may be chosen by his fellows, whatever the level of his birth. Carlyle's doctrine remains authoritarian in essence: the agent of power may be one man or more, a reforming minister controlling the national activity with his single sovereign will, or a band of ministers chosen by co-optation. In either case, Downing Street must be peopled with talents, and its energies bent upon real and vital achievements.

It is a significant fact that Carlyle first considers the Foreign Office, the organ for the international activity of England and for her political defence. His imperialistic eye, looking to the expansion of England, requires in the Foreign Office a nice adjustment of means to ends. There must be no more erratic intervention in the affairs of other peoples, there must be instead a tightening of the imperial tie, a grouping of the colonies and dominions in closer unity with the Motherland. The Home Office must have the primary place in domestic affairs. It must be reorganised, and lead in the struggle against poverty and unemployment. Looking into the future, Carlyle foresees the formation of new organs to deal with national problems not yet appreciated at their real importance. "A Minister of Works; Minister of Justice, . . . Minister of Education. . . . To-morrow morning they might all begin to be." Always the practical realist in such matters, Carlyle dares to turn a critical glance upon the Public Schools and the old universities. He goes further, he criticises their antiquated curricula, their preoccupation with extinct civilisations and dead languages, and he argues for some better training for life.

In the last four articles, less exciting problems are taken up. *Stump Orator* is in praise of the virtue of silence, although the praise is uttered with a feverish abundance of words. The vice which corrupts modern societies is, Carlyle claims, the power of words: the superficial brilliance in speech is our criterion of talent, the condition of success, of access, even, in our public life. Wisdom is not voluble, but silent. If one generation lost the power of speech, humanity would be purified. Worth reading are Carlyle's counsels to the youth of England, as he tells of the mysterious fruitfulness of ideas on which the mind broods in secret, of the loss to these ideas when they are expressed and circulated. Deep counsels based on a very penetrating perception of the phenomena of mental life, they are unhappily contradicted by the entire span of Carlyle's life, by his effort at ceaseless expression of himself, and by the relief he invariably found through that expression. This contradiction may not deprive Carlyle's counsels of their intuitive value, but how much richer and suppler, how much farther from dogmatism, had Carlyle been aware of the clash in himself! *Parliaments* takes up a theme already threadbare. Still, Carlyle states his case with greater precision here: he shows how parliaments are now vitiated by two new and fundamental facts: the existence of the daily press, through which political debates are communicated into every part of the country, and the ceremonious encounters of parliamentarians shorn of their usefulness; and the absence from Parliament of the Sovereign, formerly the chief executive. The former function of parliament was to advise the executive; but now it combines with the right to deliberate the right to act. *Hudson's Statue* applies the doctrine of the Hero. Hudson, a railway king, was about to have his statue in bronze, gigantic and symbolical, but Cromwell still waits in vain for his. Carlyle draws from this contrast a distinction between the genuine and the spurious hero, and preaches the power of the ideal to a generation mired in materialism.

The content of the final paper is richer. Here writing on *Jesuitism* Carlyle repeats some of his oldest ideas, states once again the social philosophy which during the past twenty years had come to relate all his work to the metaphysics of *Sartor*. The old lesson of truth and reality is taught again: the old hatred of sham as the vilest of spiritual crimes, as the denial of the supreme veracity of the universe, bursts forth with undiminished strength. The influence of his casual reading, coupled with Carlyle's rancor against the growing power of the Catholic revival and Puseyism, led him to crystallise about the Jesuit ethic and the personality of Loyola all his distrust of the insincerity to which modern life owes its profound corruption. There is nothing in the entire range of Carlyle's work which shows more clearly his strength and his weakness, his sectarian vehemence, his obstinacy and narrowness, along with the depth of his moral intuitions, his creative fertility, the vast cosmic spaces through which his thought passes, the grandiose beauty of his visions. Just as all his power in humor and fantasy comes out in "Pig Philosophy," all the poetic sublimity of his soul appears in the last page where he pictures the inexorable torment of modern society, followed in its fevered speed and its mad

SERMONS AND SATIRES

progress by the sigh of the boundless ennui that it carries in its heart.

It is interesting to enquire whether the doctrine of Carlyle might have escaped from its formulae, and renewed itself. There is some ground for thinking it might, although one hesitates to claim this with confidence. Twice in these pages, at once so admirable and so perverse, Carlyle appears to see beyond the limited horizon of his fixed monotonous certitudes. He appears to see the waters of uncharted seas, but he stops short; and if he celebrates the eternal march of humanity, if he is confident of its immense and inconceivable promise, his confidence results merely in his attaching all the wonder of the future as well as of the past and the present to the immutable standards of his principal beliefs. Rarely did he speak of the fine arts; at their appeal to the senses his Puritan character was acutely uncomfortable. We still find him, in the *Life of Sterling*, describing the gospel of art as one of the "Windy gospels addressed to our poor century." In this last of the *Latter-day Pamphlets* the theme of universal Jesuitism leads him to sketch, unexpectedly, a theory of artistic decadence and regeneration. Ruskin did not go any farther in his comments on the moral law of sincerity in art and on the dignity of the æsthetic mission. We wonder if Carlyle will add this rich ground to his province of conduct. He pulls up short, and the secret cause of his hesitation can be fathomed: he has no warm love, no genuine regard, for art, and his loathing for shams, for cant, in this field which remains to him unfamiliar, stifles in him the taste and the joy of the beautiful, even the need for it. Farther on in this paper he returns to the bold, symbolical phrase coined two years before: "Exodus from Houndsditch." The untrammeled prospect of a religious evolution with no *term,* leaving behind all the outworn forms of Judaism, is here pictured in a few words: "If it please Heaven we shall all yet make our Exodus from Houndsditch, and bid the sordid continents, of once rich apparel now grown poisonous *Ou' clo',* a mild farewell! Exodus into wider horizons, into God's daylight once more; where eternal skies, measuring more than three ells, shall again overawe us; and men, immeasurably better for having dwelt among the Hebrews, shall pursue their *human* pilgrimage." Out of date, impregnated with germs, the clothes of the Jewish traders will be burned: the immense tree of the Christian Church, nurtured during forty generations by the best spirits of humanity, is already rotten in its roots and shaken by the strong winds of fate; soon it will bend and fall: and then the stars of heaven, long hidden by its dense foliage, will shine again upon man, and freeing him from the vain terrors of superstition, guide him in his unending march. But the prophet expresses himself here in brief symbols; his thought is held back by a sense of restraint, inspired not by the established orthodoxies so much as by the imperious veto of his own deep instincts. The moment he points to these vast expanses of the future, he forsakes them. We come back to the clear, definitive, immutable orders of conscience: good and evil revert to the old familiar forms of the Bible and the heart; and Carlyle, frightened, it seems, in some obscure way by his accepting the possibility of some new religion, denies his vision. Truth, he concludes, is already complete, it cannot be renewed or enlarged. "My friends," he exclaims, "you will not get this new religion of yours; I perceive you already have it, have always had it."

Two years later, in 1852, Carlyle wrote the fragmentary paper that Froude was to publish, "Spiritual Optics." The formidable old subject is again approached. The relativism of the modern world has displaced the axis of the moral as well as of the physical world; just as the sun is no longer conceived as rotating about the earth, the dogmas of religion are no longer conceived as emanating from God,—man originates them and applies them to God. Will the religious ideas of the Jews, created by that people and for it, be eternally valid? Here again the prophet pauses and leaves us with an incomplete knowledge of his thought. This is of little consequence; we know that his final word would have been an affirmation, not a negation; and we have this final word in his repeated emphasis upon the complexity of the universe, and the simplicity of the sanctions it imposes upon the moral conduct of men.

III

Sterling died in 1844, confiding to Carlyle and Archdeacon Hare conjointly the task of literary executor. In 1848 Hare published a biographical sketch of Sterling as an introduction to an edition of his works. Carlyle did not accept Hare's sketch as a true image of his friend. Sterling, after a short period in orders, had left the Anglican ministry: his religious ideas were fresh and daring, and in Hare's account the question of his orthodoxy was too much in the foreground to suit the mind of Carlyle, always a scorner of outward forms. Stimulated by his disagreement with Hare, Carlyle set quickly to work, and without laborious preparations composed a portrait so animated and so revealing that the painting of souls has known no greater triumph.

The *Life of Sterling* (1851) has often been likened to a quiet sunny spot in the midst of the angry storms among which in these later days Carlyle seemed to live. It is indeed an attractive oasis; and its peculiar softness and melancholy, very close to tenderness, has a charm without a parallel in Carlyle. One must not exaggerate the calm of this book, however: the distant rumblings of thunder prove the authorship of Carlyle, and now and then a flash of angry lightning gives a more impressive warning. Carlyle could give up his hates in his absorption in a pious obligation; but he was far too self-centred to forget for long his own personality. The analogies between his subject's life and his own, as in his much earlier study of Schiller, hold his interest and control the perspective of the book. Sudden outbursts into satire or sermon reveal this egoistic preoccupation: and nowhere have the hopeless moral confusion of a century deprived of faith, the ugliness and the baseness of that century, and the harrying doubt of its greatest souls, led here and there by the witchfires of false doctrines, been expressed in a more gripping way.

In spite of that intrusion, Sterling is drawn with the sense of emphasis, the vigorous decisive hand, the gift of seizing upon the characteristic detail, which make Carlyle so great a painter of men. That lively, fresh, immediate perception of his gave him the power of reproducing character with marvelous concision and expressive force. Some critics relate this freshness and quickness of perception to the peasant stock from which he came, and it is true that all his long life of letters and abstract thought could not impair his peasant instincts. His genius rather added to the power of these, casting a spiritual light upon the objects he describes and, for all his absorption in the vast syntheses of transcendentalism, bringing out specific details against the background of impenetrable mystery. To search the secrets of a soul, as Carlyle does, in the *Life of Sterling,* a powerful sense of the inner life is necessary; and to reproduce the lines and details of a spiritual being, there must be a rare discernment of psychic reality. The portrait of Sterling is among Carlyle's greatest achievements; but to appreciate the full force of his pencil, the subtlest accent of his rendering, one must go beyond his formal works and dip into his *Reminiscences.*

Affectionate, brilliant, full of dash and enthusiasm, mobile, many-sided, Sterling is brought back to life; and our sympathy is won for the warmth of his character, the nobility of his too short life. There is now and then the very faintest suggestion that Carlyle involuntarily dominates his friend and feels and notes the limits of his abilities. But even more interesting to us than the delineation of Sterling is Carlyle's admirable portrait of Coleridge, and his endeavor to define his true relation, in the history of English ideas, to his great precursor. No chapter in Carlyle's work shows us more clearly than that on Coleridge, the essential bias of his mind, and the curious contrast between his perceptiveness and his blindness. In his eagerness to mark the difference between Coleridge's moral attitude and his own, he makes what he regards as his own intellectual disinterestedness the principle of an absolute opposition between Coleridge and himself. He thus presents Coleridge as a man only partially sincere, too weak to attain a genuine sincerity even with himself, seduced by a half-desired mirage in which reason and faith are reconciled. Coleridge's effort to renew the philosophic bases of Anglican belief is presented by Carlyle in a very doubtful light. On the other hand, Carlyle the uncompromising prophet of ethical certitudes which he proudly confessed to be indemonstrable, the scorner of the dry light of the intellect, the apostle of the supreme claims of life, presents himself as the passionate pilgrim moving toward the one truth. This egocentric feeling is an element of the greatest importance in Carlyle's personality: it decides for his thought and teaching at what point the bold sincerity of his mind gives place to the subtle spell of his instincts.

IV

In April, 1866, Carlyle, elected Lord Rector by the students of Edinburgh, delivered his inaugural address. Edinburgh was all agog; all of England, and indeed the entire Anglo-Saxon world waited to hear what he would say. A new generation had matured, a generation in which the common people, as well as the *élite*, were attuned to Carlyle's spirit and persuaded of his prophetic authority. The task of Carlyle was now accomplished; the seeds he had so tirelessly sown had now sprouted; and Carlyle could look with confidence to a public fully capable of appreciating his message because of the rôle that message had played in its formation. And a fate once bitter, now friendly, held in store a compensation for him. Born out of due time, he had wrestled with a hostile age and come off victor: he could be sure now that the influence of his work would survive him. Better yet, he was still alive and active, when the immortality of his work was secure.

In his inaugural address, he preached his old sermon, stressing the duty of sincerity, urging the fruitfulness of conscience and the religion of labor. He evoked once more the old heroic figures, the founders of modern England and Scotland, Knox and Cromwell above all. He lauded knowledge and the moral fibre without which knowledge is a dead thing; and to a forward-looking youth he pointed out the uncertainties in the immediate social future. But his pessimism grew softer under the influence of their young energy; and he held out to the earnest heart, to the honest effort, the assurance of spiritual peace and physical health, its corollary. To be holy is to be healthy, says Carlyle; there can be no better definition of holiness. Reminded of the destinies of the Germanic peoples as Providence has determined them, he closed his speech with Goethe's hymn, that marching song with its lofty sweeping movement rising to the last words: labor and hope; in this movement and in these words he found the very voice of the Germanic genius.

The success of this address was triumphant: the depth, the salutary virtue, of the doctrine were celebrated far and wide. And Carlyle could not refrain from entering his bitter complaint in his *Reminiscences:* "No idea, or shadow of an idea, in that Address, but what had been set forth by me tens of times before: and the poor gaping sea of Prurient Blockheadism receives it as a kind of inspired revelation. . . ." In the following year Carlyle's anger came back upon him, more violent than ever. The Second Reform Bill was about to be passed, far more liberal and therefore far more hazardous than the first; and to add fuel to the flame, it was the Conservative party that sponsored it, giving up its dignity and its traditional platform. An irresistible current was pulling England toward absolute democracy: Nothing could hold her back from the cataracts ahead; and among all the millions who were speeding with a light heart toward the abyss, how many individuals even speculated on what was coming?

Shooting Niagara, and After is a fulminating and caustic sermon. Carlyle finds three cataracts ahead: the people will govern, the Churches will break up, trade and commerce will be absolutely free. The course of destiny is quick and disconcerting: the unity of Germany under the hegemony of Prussia will be a phenomenon of to-morrow; a Civil War in the United States has brought the shedding of oceans of blood, merely to break the salutary contract which bound the negro worker to his master; a mere political adventurer, Disraeli, has committed the fate and future of England to the ocean of democracy; and if the people tires of a sham royalty, who shall stop it in its course? Where shall we find the authority which will then be more than ever necessary, the chiefs we shall obey, the centres of social initiative and discipline? Shall we find it in heaven-sent heroes, reborn of the greatness of their works? Carlyle looks elsewhere: more clearly than ever before he expresses confidence in the age-old aristocracy of England. The prestige of this aristocracy is greatly enhanced by its political liberalism: the great Barons have granted the vote to the people, and the people answer the gift with a more lively respect and renewed trust. Where in the entire range of society shall one find a class comparable to the families which are firmly settled in their influence and fortune, as in the patriarchal dignity of their mode of life? Unsuspected potentialities are here: generosity and idealism may come from them ample to redeem the vulgar materialism of the middle class, and the unspeakable complacency of a material civilisation.

The hero has a nobility conferred by God: but the baron has a human nobility, the outcome of generations of fastidious breeding. Our nobles, human and divine, should be united, for is not the problem of securing a noble group of chiefs day by day more difficult? The hob-nailed boots of the crowd threaten to destroy all that is distinguished and elevated. The sacred band—the heroic spirits, the great captains of industry, the active barons: every member of this band will have his part to play. Carlyle's confidence in the man of letters, however, has fallen far. Writing is a dangerous task and insincere: before the vast flow of empty books, feeble thoughts and false imaginations the prophet feels sick, and his faith in an intellectual priesthood weakens. He proclaims that within half a century literature will be a sham and no great soul will remain in its precincts. The leaders of industry, too, have disappointed his hopes: their sway has brought with it the brutal insolent lordship of gold. Irresistibly his hope goes out to the castles, the manors of the original aristocracy: and to these he addresses his last appeal in the name of society. The aristocracy might go beyond the vague function of benevolence and protection that it fulfils in modern life. Its guidance would be fruitful in education: in reforming the schools and the spirit of pedagogy; the English aristocracy, adopting military discipline for its model, would be able to reconstruct English life to a form at once effective and coherent. The boundless swarming of modern England calls for a strong organising will; each citizen must be set in his proper place, fixed within the salutary forms of living, trained to the regular activities of body and mind; such an endeavor, the necessary corrective to democratic anarchy, is the task of the future. Parliaments are powerless and helpless before the need to bring order out of chaos: but the Peers, the viceroys of England, are naturally equipped to meet it.

The "radical" of 1830 had, as one sees, followed the habitual course, and reached in his old age all the traditional forms of conservative wisdom, putting order above all other things and respecting the existing aristocracy as the natural guardian of order. In the absence of the hero, the hereditary lord seemed to him in the depths of his doubt, a genuine force, a substantial principle of social good. Without giving up his mystical bases, in political thought Carlyle was becoming more and more of a realist. In this sermon, the last of his social gospels, he not only repeats all his old doctrines—the necessity of State intervention, the duty of the State to check the appetites and instincts of the mighty, and to protect the losers in the industrial war; but he rouses himself to new aspects of the social problem—denouncing the forces which defiled the rivers of England, infected its air and dirtied the divine face of the earth. In these points he is very near to Ruskin who in these same decades was writing *Unto this Last* and *Ethics of the Dust,* books which Carlyle read with approval and delight, recognising in their author the greatest talent for preaching of any man alive. Carlyle followed with deep sympathy the crusade his disciple was leading against the individualistic economics of the day. Carlyle saw Ruskin's æsthetic significance not so

SERMONS AND SATIRES 263

much in the worship of beauty that he preached as in his attack upon the old notion of art as something dead, rather than the fruit of intense spiritual energy.

Only once more did Carlyle lift up his voice to praise or blame his contemporaries. In November, 1870, English sympathies, appalled by the disasters that had befallen the French, and immensely surprised by the German victories, were still uncertain. Pity for France and a vague fear of the Germans in their intoxicating success were inclining many Englishmen to sympathise with the French, when Carlyle wrote to *The Times* a letter so effective that the German soldiers in the trenches encircling Paris read it in translation, and despatched to Carlyle simple statements of their gratitude. Under the guise of an implacable seer exhibiting the retribution of the Most High, Carlyle was able to express a love and a hate of long standing. Alternately in this letter he lauded the nobility and greatness of the German genius and denounced the frivolous corruption of France. He jeered at the tender spirits who pitied the nation that was being chastised for her crimes: he went far back into the past, enlarging on the irreparable wrongs inflicted on the Germans in the age-old duel, by Richelieu, Louis XIV, and Napoleon. On the other side, he hailed the birth of a German empire, rich in the promise of a future grandeur, and of destinies too great to be detailed: and joining the Saxon and the Teuton branches of the German tree, he claimed that the "Germanic" race possessed the future of the world. "That noble, patient, deep, pious and solid Germany should be at length welded into a Nation, and become Queen of the Continent, instead of vapouring, vainglorious, gesticulating, quarrelsome, restless and over-sensitive France, seems to me the hopefulest public fact that has occurred in my time." And Carlyle's prestige determined the attitude of his wavering countrymen—England remained officially indifferent to the ruin which befell France. The authority of facts, in which Carlyle discerned a divine revelation, does not to-day, in the eyes of the British themselves, confirm all the inferences he was so ready to draw.

CHAPTER III

LAST YEARS

NEITHER his youth nor his maturity had brought happiness to Carlyle: too noble for the complacent vulgar happiness of the majority, he was too sensitive, too restive, to find happiness in love or in private contemplation. But in both these periods of his life, there came sudden flashes of light, days of pure repose, moments, too, of joy, and even whole months which brought him peace when they would have brought any one else the airiest, most exuberant pleasure. The old age of Carlyle was one of unrelieved gloom: it was darkened by one overwhelming sorrow. A great remorse, intensified by the generosity of his heart, took from his last years every prospect of joy, and plunged him up to his death in a gloom that nothing could beguile.

The catastrophe was preceded by many warnings, but it was not in Carlyle's temperament to heed or even to note such warnings. His will, perpetually intent upon his mission and the activities it required, led him to make light of trouble and so spare his energy for his great task. Jane had grown old without his perceiving it, stoically faithful to the duties she found so empty, large-hearted enough to appreciate the sincere but silent affection of her husband, but not heroic enough to endure moral solitude without suffering or to hide her suffering from her intimate friends. After Lady Ashburton's death in 1857 the Carlyle household became calmer. Frequent separations strengthened the tie between Thomas and Jane: for Carlyle expressed his warmest feelings better in the pages of a letter than by word of mouth. When they were together, Jane was sorely tried by his ill humor. Her rapidly growing weakness was no obstacle to her taste for little gatherings in Cheyne Row where all were friends and there was good talk. Her wit and vivacity, as brilliant as ever, gave a great charm to her simple entertainments, in which the master's beloved disciples took their parts. Younger men were coming: Froude, Clough, whose untimely death was a cause of sorrow to Carlyle, and Ruskin whose social apostolate made up in Carlyle's eyes for his æstheticism. Some of the older friends no longer came: John Stuart Mill, for example, was repelled by the authoritarian strain growing stronger in Carlyle, and by his vindication of slavery. The contact between Mill and Carlyle had been close and genuine, and if they grew old apart, the living symbols of two tendencies henceforth irreconcilable, they kept, none the less, all of their esteem for each other.

But Jane was suffering from racking pains and from insomnia; she could no longer move about with ease. Carlyle got better servants and arranged for two drives a week in a carriage. The remembrance of these little kindnesses was later to be a precious consolation. Then toward the end of October, 1863, as she was waiting for a bus in a crowded street in the City, she fell in an attempt to get out of the way of a cab, and in the fall hurt herself very badly. Weeks of cruel pain followed before she could limp about the house. Her neuralgia became more

LAST YEARS 267

painful and she could get scarcely any sleep. The country, the sea air, the bracing climate of Scotland, were of no help. With smiling fortitude she hid her worst sufferings from her husband; and he, incessantly absorbed, tyrannised, indeed, by his work, made merely spasmodic and clumsy efforts to sympathise with her. In 1865 the last volumes of *Frederick* came out and Carlyle fell at once into a new disquiet,—the reaction from a long task finished and the restlessness at nothing left to do. Jane was growing stronger however and was able to go out; Carlyle, to his last breath, blessed the inspiration which prompted him to offer her a brougham of her own. "Never was soul," he says in his *Reminiscences* "more grateful for so small a kindness; which seemed to illuminate, in some sort, all her remaining days for her."

In November, 1865, Carlyle was elected Rector of the University of Edinburgh; at the end of March, 1866, he left London to deliver the customary address, an address awaited, in this instance, with the greatest impatience. He bade Jane good-bye at their threshold and he never saw her again. On the twenty-first of April as she was driving in Hyde Park, her little dog, running beside the horse, was hurt by another carriage. She got down, took it in her arms, and, once back in the carriage, fainted. The emotion she had felt at the pain the dog suffered was so intense that she died from it. It was found, too late, that she had felt symptoms of a diseased heart. This sudden stunning blow reached Carlyle in Scotland, where he was resting. He hastened to London in bewilderment; his affection welled up in all its force, excited by a sense of the irreparable and by a deep regret that he had not voiced his feeling more fully and more often. He collected all that he could find of his wife's writings; and in her letters and diaries the broken-hearted old man came upon the trace of her unhappiness and the lifelong bitterness which had eaten into her soul. He fought in vain against the evidence: he was obliged to admit it. And he satisfied his obscure feeling that expiation was called for by a long and terrible remorse.

He set down on paper the character of Jane, the history of her family and of his relations with her. It is a moving piece of work, penetrated by Carlyle's belated regret and his indelible pain at understanding what Jane had meant in his life only when he had to live it without her, at having lost so many irrecoverable opportunities by his engrossing devotion to his task. Sometimes the pain is quieted; and, absorbed by the interest of his materials, Carlyle's imagination flowers with a melancholy delight in the years that have gone. The spirited, intense descriptions and portraits, the deep feeling which traverses the work and pierces to its surface ever and again would make these *Reminiscences* the most admirable confession in litterature, were it not that their sacred object prevents our attending to their beauty.

At Mentone, where the second Lady Ashburton was his hostess, he drank the bitter cup of memory to the dregs, and, led on by the new direction of his mind, he noted down his recollections of Edward Irving and Lord Jeffrey. Under the cloak of these remembrances of others, he was unconsciously writing his own biography; almost without realising it, he was always speaking of himself, introducing himself as the friend of the central figure. Long before, he had expressed the wish that his life should not be told in the usual way of biography. Since his wife's death, however, he had wavered; a desire more or less vague to expiate his wrong by hiding nothing of the cruel truth, a feeling that he could not escape what had been the common fate of famous men, and a wish to explain, to extenuate by the very fact of an explanation, what had been painful in his relations with Jane: from all these motives and desires came acquiescence. Carlyle wrote his *Reminiscences* and gave to Froude his wife's letters, almost all of his own, and other documents.

On these Froude based his absorbing and penetrating study, a study vitiated however by a hidden intention to dramatise his story. The history of the relations between Froude and Carlyle, of the commands and desires which appeared to Froude to authorise his book, of the spirit in which Froude fulfilled his task, all this belongs to a controversy which is not yet closed, a controversy of which the interest is too highly special for it to be treated here at any length. It will be enough to recall the constant presence beside the enfeebled old man of the disciple, unquestionably sincere in his devotion, and erring perhaps only when he was dominated by an admiring pity for the brilliant woman who had not found happiness in the companionship of the prophet. Through Carlyle's last years, Froude was his habitual companion in his walks. Carlyle's mind did not become infirm; his physical force was greatly weakened, however, and his right hand trembled and then was paralysed; he was unable to hold a pen in hand and far too impatient to adapt himself to dictation. In Kensington Gardens, however, and along the quays of the Thames, that face ravaged by thought and age still passed, intent upon some train of speculation or animated in the denunciation of the age's errors. The citizens of Chelsea would recognise with a feeling compounded of veneration and fright, the man who had known so many bursts of holy wrath and whom the world revered as much as any king. He did not live in absolute solitude; his brother John made an attempt to dwell with him but gave it up; and then his niece Mary Aitken came and served him with the most devoted care. Still a man of independent mind, he declined the Order of the Bath and a pension offered him by Disraeli; but he did accept the Prussian Order of Merit. Glory had brought him the riches that he had never sought; and he was capable of a very delicate generosity with them. In his will, remembering his hard youth, he bequeathed the revenue of Craigenputtock to the University of Edinburgh, directing that it be used for bursaries for indigent students.

His mind, self-absorbed, was still active: it clove firmly to the essential doctrines it had formulated, and occupied itself in defending these against the audacious criticism of an age which went farther and farther every day in its negations. He was able both to gauge what his influence had been, and to realise where his labor had been futile. The tone of social life had changed; the spirit of selfish brutality, the cynical materialism, against which he had led the attack, had softened. The spirit of moral rigor, of Puritan respectability, of middle class decency, had penetrated society from its highest to its lowest strata. The worst scandals in the public and personal life of the country had been rooted out; virtue had come into fashion and the Ten Commandments received the official homage of England. There were other great changes. The economic individualism which had ruled absolutely in Carlyle's youth had been checked by a more sensitive national conscience and by the rebellion of the interests it chiefly damaged. Confronting the rational formulae in philosophy and industry there were now mighty forces inspired by idealism. English art had been regenerated. The Churches had been strengthened by a new religious fervor. A nation-wide spirit of philanthropy was changing the face of English life. There was a new sense of solidarity quickening the relation between the mother country and her overseas possessions: and from it came a more conscious, a more articulate, imperialism than England had ever known. In the profound transformation of the country many forces had been at work: unconsciously collaborating with the *élite*—the preachers, prophets, poets, painters—were the great middle class committed to Puritanism and the lower classes vivified by the influence of Methodism; and, consecrating their collaboration, there was the silent decision of the national genius that these things should be. Still, the rôle of Carlyle in this transformation was one of inestimable importance; and of this he was confusedly aware. In every walk of life, active or reflective, he could point to his disciples; young men used to write to him as a moral counsellor, and prize his opinion as that of an oracle. He could feel setting toward him a current of national gratitude as England appreciated what momentum he had given to the nation's activity, what sanity he had brought back to its soul. Almost all the leaders of the age openly confessed their debt to his influence; Ruskin was his continuator and this relationship was steadily becoming more patent; Dickens and Kingsley, who had touched the hearts of their readers and fed the flame of philanthropy, owed him their essential tenets. Disraeli, even, borrowed some of his ideas. The face that the century wore at its closing differed greatly from that with which it had begun; and in the difference Carlyle could, and did, recognise the trace of his handiwork.

It was in his temperament, however, to attend rather to the features he had failed to change. He was not to be deceived by the appearance of a rapid, widespread, moral-progress: it was too rapid, too widespread, not to excite his suspicion, not to let him know that it was a varnishing, not a cleansing, of the soul. Carlyle's greatest battle, his battle against sham and cant, was a defeat: the weakness of human nature was stronger than all his strength. In his bitter disappointment he would even lose his sense of justice, miss the true spirit in the words and gestures of his contemporaries, where there was a genuine if modest gain in virtue and sincerity. He was oppressed to the stifling of every hope and joy by a feeling that the life of England was an immense lie, a conscious hypocrisy in which the entire nation conspired. The hostile currents of rationalism had not, he knew, been choked off at their poisoned sources: they had merely been checked here and there and made to flow in less powerful courses; and they still continued to undermine the foundations of belief necessary to life and blessedness. The higher criticism was continuing its destructive work; and Carlyle, who had foretold and enjoined the shattering of all Biblical forms, was unable to excuse the higher critics for moving faster and farther than himself. Bishop Colenso roused his aversion and so did the authors of *Essays and Reviews*. His mind, once supple, but now long closed to new ideas, stiffened into a violent hostility toward the enterprises of scientific research. He made no attempt to understand Comte or Darwin: the mind which had been open to every movement in human life and thought, offered a passionate resistance to the theses of evolution. Utilitarianism was dead as a doctrine but it was as vital as ever in the invulnerable optimism of the middle class; and Carlyle grieved to see his enemy rooted in the manners of his people, a part of their very lifeblood. Should science validate her promise to explain the moral world by resolving it into simple physical elements, the future would hold for England and the world no better prospect than that of an ever-widening positivism and materialism, an ever-deepening corruption of mind and soul.

Against these new enemies, Carlyle had not the strength to fight. He could only cling more and more closely to his little sheaf of certitudes, those he had won for himself in the moral crisis of his youth and kept unimpaired by the wear-and-tear of life. These certitudes were those of Kant: the categorical imperative, the distinction between good and evil, the freedom of the will, the eternal sanctions, and the existence of God. Not relaxing in his Puritanism, maintaining his severe judgment upon all formal religions, he was capable in these later years of unexpected tolerance. One day, in St. Paul's, as he listened for the first time to a solemn choral service, he was moved to tears. One may suppose, perhaps, that an instinct of conservatism in matters religious, the parallel of his instinct in social matters, led him to perceive a value in exterior tradition, hierarchised religion, disciplne. It would be imprudent, however, to assert this dogmatically. His conception of prayer was almost identical with Meredith's: powerless to modify the will of God, impious if it aspires to do so, prayer is legitimate and necessary, as well as natural, if it is considered as a cry of appeal, an aspiration of the soul in pain, a confession—better silent—from the heart only. The last form of Carlyle's attitude toward the highest questions anticipates that of the pragmatists. Endless discussion of the source and basis of faith in God and in the good is as empty as it is mischievous; this faith is not a product of the intelligence but of life and action. Act and you will be brought to believe.

To scientific atheism one must reply by an obstinate affirmation of the ideal—the truth of God and of the spiritual life in man must be maintained by the will. This is Carlyle's position at the end of his life, as it is that of the anti-intellectualists who triumphed twenty years later with the concept of the intuition.

Carlyle died peacefully the 4th of February, 1881, Foreseeing that an offer would be made to bury him in Westminster Abbey, he had expressed the wish that this offer be declined. He preferred to lie beside his wife at Haddington. There is however a symbolical justice—whatever his personal preference may have been—in the final choice of the old cemetery of Ecclefechan where he lies with his father and mother, finally reunited with those who were closest to him in life.

CONCLUSION

HE was the supreme utilitarian. Other men, coming before him and of his own people, had usurped this title and laboriously constructed a miserable concatenation of ideas in which proofs of the utilitarian doctrine and formulae for its practice might be found. For these arid, abject pedants Carlyle had nothing but ironic scorn; he rent their system to pieces, and liked nothing better than to toss its wretched fragments to the winds. He knew very well that for all their pretensions to realism the followers of Jeremy Bentham were but naïve intellectuals, stubbornly devoted to the quest of a futile ideal, since it was a disinterested one—that of a rational harmony among ideas, and of a remote, austere kind of beauty. These men were taking to themselves the name utilitarians, and they were forgetting that life, health and peace are the first concerns of man, and the necessary presuppositions to the realisation of any human value! Their short-sighted wisdom was wrecking the very foundations of the human happiness they were engaged in defining and regulating. With his broad, deep, sure, perceptive power Carlyle recognised that it was he, not they, who stood for the laws of life and the true conception of utility. From the subconscious processes of thought to the acts and gestures of the social being, Carlyle grasped all the internal elements of these laws of life, inextricably bound with the network of human actions and reactions, with all their aspects, and all their rules as well. In faith, moral health, the normal play of the emotions, the security and the discipline which strengthen, exalt, refresh and renew the soul for its daily battles; in the practice of duty, without which the will dissolves and a consuming appetite gnaws the energy of the individual being; in the exercise of the salutary loves and hates codified and deified by the experience of the race; in these, he knew, were the indispensable conditions of a self which should be organised, homogeneous, effective, the conditions, too, of joy and success. Only at this price could the world be won; at this price, too, unless some of our finest visions were to be falsified by eternity, another and a better world could be won. The individuals, the nations, the races, who were sufficiently supple in their intuitions, sufficiently reverent to the incomparable majesty of the real, to submit their conduct to the supreme laws of life in the dark way in which men see them, received from Providence the Kingdom of the Earth—and history was there to bear startling witness to this! Appalled by the horrible vision of an England which was blind and negligent of the sacred laws, given over to the fevers of vain ideals, to the whims of the "understanding," to the sensualities of art, and above all, to the crass pleasures and the brutal appetite of wealth, Carlyle felt his prophetic wrath rising, and alone among the nation, he madly cried out in protest, pointing to the abyss, to the imminent destruction of all, to the unfailing penalties of outraged nature, to the vengeance of God.

His cry was that of an idealist. He refused to admit the existence of the body, allowed it at best a shadowy life. He affirmed that in the universe in which space and time build a stage for the narrow life of man, man must live according to maxims of a noble prudence, maxims to which the difficulty of moderating human passions and of conceiving supernatural ends has always associated an essence of loftiness and nobility; he preached the ideal, morality, religion, and preached so passionately that he fell foul of the churches and focussed his view directly upon the Divine, upon the correspondences established by an immanent justice between certain attitudes of the soul on the one hand, and life or death on the other. The admiration and the gratitude of men went out toward this independent, heroic figure, defying their anger and their mockery to reveal to them that they would die if they did not sacrifice everything to the will to live.

His, then, was the only deep and genuine utilitarianism, the utilitarianism of the will and the instincts, not that of the understanding. He knew enough of the secret laws of moral health not to present moral health as an end in itself, not to clarify to the final point the consciousness of self; clear consciousness, he thought, was the dangerous foe of effective reflex action. He let the full intensity of the desire which animated him attach itself to remote ends, spend itself in *élans* toward the ideal conditions of life; and in so doing he won the supreme force of generosity, the intoxicating conviction of disinterestedness. Of all beliefs, the worship of the truth, as he felt, had the singular attraction, the inspiring virtue, of sacrifice; and having felt this, it was not enough to associate the religion of truth with the religion of life; the second was forgotten, swallowed up by the first, and Carlyle proclaimed that truth alone is the assurance of life, that falsehood leads to death; he went farther, crying out that the surest duty of men is to seek the true; to slay in themselves all voluntary falsehoods, all illusions nourished by laziness and cowardice. More than the wicked or the depraved he denounced hypocrites, men who pretend to believe or men who believe they believe. And so his words came to resemble to a strange degree the exhortations of other sages, the denunciations of the very rationalists whom he so intensely hated.

As soon, however, as the search for truth began to result in dangerous conclusions, began to imperil the moral certitudes on which our balance depends, began to threaten the sacred securities to which Carlyle attached the greatest importance, it was clear that truth was not the supreme deity for him. He raged against the imprudent men, the insane men, who had merely been doing what he had urged upon them. He was merciless to Darwin and the positivists who, he thought, were following the devil of science to the bottomless pit in which humanity would lose its faith. Their doctrines were weakening the moral energy of man; and their doctrines must therefore be wrong in some way. It was clear that if Carlyle conceived the search for truth as the chief duty of man, it was on condition that it was compatible with life; on condition that the truth was what Carlyle believed.

Such was, roughly, the deep-laid relation within Carlyle's doctrine between his fundamental utilitarianism and those incentives to activity to be found in morality, religion and science, incentives indiscriminately recognised and honored by men as noble and pure. Carlyle made these incentives his own, assimilated their force, made use of them in order to reduce them all to his specific aim. Another noble activity has won the enthusiastic respect of men—art; but Carlyle did not even attempt to relate art to his aim. In his transcription of his visions, beauty often added its halo to the silent activities of immanent Deity; the poetry of the imagination lent an epic grandeur, a vehement and wild splendor, to the moral doctrines of man and the landscapes of the earth. Still, for all his sense of the beautiful, Carlyle had no æsthetic theories: his Puritanism was too insurgent against the sacred sensuousness of art. Carlyle lived, thought and prophesied outside the sanctuaries of art as outside those of established creeds. He made no effort to deflect the sources of spiritual energy and happiness which the artist's self-sacrifice brings into play, to the unique and all-absorbing activity of the will-to-live. Ruskin was to make the effort and to succeed in it. So far as all other forces are concerned, Carlyle's doctrine, and his work, can be summed up in just such an attempt toward an absorption and integration; a sincere endeavor, since vital energy is to him the measure of all value, and every compromise it demands is thus sanctioned by the divine will of things; a fruitful endeavor, since it has fostered and developed the psychological conditions of strength and health in the soul, not only of a nation, but of a race.

Carlyle's constructive activity should not be obscured by the temporarily destructive influence his doctrine may have had, with its devastation of shams and antiquated convictions. His constructive activity was essential and central. Through it he has been the supreme life-giving force for modern England. His doctrine is infinitely greater than he: it is ancient, it is as traditional as the genius of England, of whose genius, at a moment of grave crisis, he became the bitter and indignant expression. He is the spokesman of an anonymous inarticulate multitude, of the soldiers of Cromwell, of the Puritans who left England to preserve the integrity of their conscience and practice, of the Calvinist and Methodist miners and small farmers, of mystical, practical, conquering England, which after three centuries of silent activity at last finds in Carlyle a voice worthy of itself.

Latent in the heart of the common people of England there has been, as there still is, an incomparable active power, a passionate preference for action over thought, a hatred for whatever cloak disguises the real, disguises the fact, together with a profound feeling of the help necessary to success which can be had by reverence for supernatural or spiritual causes. These elements, united in an indissoluble synthesis and representing, as they do, the firmest, most vital fibre of a race, of a collective soul, rose to a consciousness of their nature in Carlyle's mind; and his work is an indefatigable affirmation, an instinctive demonstration of them. He not only developed them to a conscious form, he elevated them to abstract philosophic expression; and in so doing he broadened their scope, tightened their hold upon the real, and entered into a superficial opposition with their then current forms and expressions.

Thus Carlyle came to be considered in England as an iconoclast, a heretic, a prophet of revolution. Nevertheless his function was not to combat the religion of his compatriots, but to confirm it, and to strengthen its position by relieving it of a useless burden of antiquated formulae. The whole subsequent affirmation of the moral being of England, all the Nation's reactions undertaken to enrich her life and her being, emanate from him: for it was he who, disengaging the main principles of the national tradition, throwing a strong new light upon them, imposing them upon the attention of the people, provided the national activity with a new and powerful nourishment. Carlyle it was who gave the signal for the revenge of the instincts; the crusade for social justice, the rise of Imperialism are related to his teachings; pioneer and soldier, statesman and businessman alike live by his doctrine, as it has been assimilated in different forms. The Ruskins and the Kiplings are the heirs of Carlyle's thought, developed and enriched with secondary variations. No achievement is of more importance than his; he fashioned and tempered the soul of an age. If England has avoided the abysses of moral corruption and economic individualism, a large share of the credit must go to him.

Some observers of our own time (1913) are in fear lest England fall into quite other abysses, abysses which Carlyle did not see and toward which his very teaching has led: national pride, the cult of mere energy, a pharisaism more subtle than hypocrisy, a narrow Hebraic culture, a desiccating selfishness. Despite the bitterness of his destructive criticism, the present revision of moral values is following a trend opposed to his; his thought lacks the very principle of self-renovation, because the limits of its tolerance are too firmly and clearly fixed. Even some of his disciples, Meredith for example, will eventually count in the history of ideas as forces opposing his influence. The Puritanism of Bernard Shaw has nothing in common with his; and Galsworthy, among others, is suggesting to the national conscience lessons which Carlyle would not have understood. It is still possible to accept the spirit of his message, but not the application he himself made of it. Only the spirit is enlarging, the rest is deceiving and confusing; the influence of Carlyle is fruitful only for those who seek in him an example of independence and moral courage.

Rich, but not inexhaustible, his doctrine is not of the future but of the past, to which he passionately connects the present and subjugates the future. One may go so far as to say, that in raising to consciousness a tradition whose virtue lay in its very unconsciousness he imperiled its survival. He galvanised Puritan England, but, in so doing, he more clearly brought out its weaknesses quite as much as its force; and if it is difficult to imagine that the religious and moral energy he formulated and defined should ever die, one may well fear that it may be enfeebled by the stimulus given to contrary tendencies, by the pricking of the self-criticism from which only instinctive activities are free. Here again the point of perfection is perhaps, as so often, very close to the decadence.

Fortunately the pragmatists, professing a philosophy harmonious with Carlyle's influence, came to correct in good time the most evident of its weaknesses. Carlyle affirmed on the one hand the primordial duty of being sincere, searching for truth, refusing to be blinded by the illusion of truth; on the other hand he tirelessly reiterated, making the welkin resound with all the thunders of destiny, that without piety and faith in God neither nation nor person had lived or prospered. A scrupulous mind, faced with the two commands equally dogmatic, might, in certain circumstances, experience some embarrassment. The pragmatists' doctrine which equated truth with the exigencies of life and action, gave a timely solution to the problem which the prophet had set without solving, or, at least, without doing more than foreshadowing the solution. The primacy of the practical will and of vital values is the very core of his doctrine; contemporary anti-intellectualism, if it is not a product of his teaching, is the natural expansion, the final evolution, of his thought. One may say that the philosophic success, if not the specific survival, of his influence, is bound up with that of the powerful doctrine of the pragmatists, which for a time submerged all habits of reflection and displaced the axis of intellectual integrity.

II

If we judge Carlyle the thinker to have been less a creator of ideas than a mighty echo of a tradition which before he wrote had been active rather than speculative, how shall we judge the man and the writer? The man is great, so great that he can never lose our sympathy; he wins that sympathy by the depth of his affection, an affection which so often he failed to make articulate, and by the suffering which, if he could not endure it in silence as he commanded others to bear suffering, he bore with admirable courage. He was not a hero. He was not a saint. He was as fallible as other men, and the inner light in which he trusted led him astray as often as aright. The violence he would do to the freedom of our minds and our consciences has its source in error as often as in the assurance of truth. His character had its weaknesses, his life its stains and its pettinesses. Other masters have had a larger share of sweetness, of charity, and of justice; other masters have added more to the fund of spiritual knowledge, or opened fresher, more sparkling springs of inspiration for the heart. Even if we do not love him beyond other men, still, none of us will deny him greatness, sincerity, and a certain form of self-sacrifice. He gave the admirable example of a life entirely devoted to the service of the ideal, in the guise in which he conceived the ideal—the guise of the national respect and the dutiful observance of sacred laws. In the impersonality of that great desire, all alloy disappears from his doctrine: he dreamed of a supreme victory of life in which his own powerful will-to-live would lose all consciousness of itself.

It is tempting to find in his one misfortune—which crushed his old age with a bitter remorse—an immanent logic, a just and natural retribution. He lived his theories intensely and they bore their proper fruit—a rigorous concentration upon a search for inward energy—in the present instance, for a spiritual and intellectual energy—so rigorous a concentration that everything else was sacrificed, the expansion of his instincts and his senses, the broadening of his sympathies, the happiness of his associates and of himself. Over the ruins of his own happiness, he marched triumphantly on to the realisation of his aim. He was incapable of regretting it; he was achieving what he was most eager to achieve. An inexorable destiny condemned to suffering whatever life might be linked with his. Jane Welsh was herself responsible for half of the disappointments she was obliged to endure; the cause of the others is in the austere gospel to which Carlyle sacrificed her as he sacrificed himself. It is an instructive and a salutary commentary upon Carlyle's doctrine to find its first fruits in himself and his own home: in one life—his own—fortified for incessant activity, for the daily resumption of its tasks, we have a striking proof of the health-giving force of the doctrine; in another life—his wife's—mutilated beyond her real and free consent, deprived of the joys which would for her weaker nature have been the most authentic, the most certain, of satisfactions, we have a proof of its perils and inadequacies. The practical virtue of his wisdom, and the limits of this virtue, could not be better symbolised.

The greatness of the writer imposes recognition even by those who withstand the thinker and the man. Carlyle is one of the most spirited poets of modern England. When his words have exhausted all their practical effects, Carlyle will continue to live as a poet. The imperfections of his artistic instinct, the failures of his sense of rhythm, precluded his writing verse; but all other qualities of poetry, the essential qualities of poetry, were his. His vision of the world is that toward which the poets of the romantic generation had striven: a perception of the spiritual in the material. But the universality, the might and the lofty vistas of German idealism gave to Carlyle's vision, while he was at the very beginning of his literary career, a breadth and a clearness beyond comparison. His imagination lived so freely under the sense of the unreality of time and space, that every spectacle he pictured had its double aspect of reality and dream. To his eyes, hazy depths revealed themselves behind the configurations of nature and history; the particular details are bathed in haze, and, of a sudden, they melt into it and disappear; and from the darkness of death, the past surges suddenly into view, still alive. Such swift appearances and disappearances intoxicate the mind with a penetrating, magnificent obsession; and the poetry and the mystery of the beyond flow into all the aspects of the real more intimately than with any other writer. No poet has had in a higher degree, sublimity of imagination; no poet has with greater power evoked the infinite, or the eternal silences which lie behind the transitory sights and sounds of life.

To its unexampled power of metaphysical dissolution, Carlyle's imagination joins the specifically English gift of concrete force and picturesque energy. It is as capable of concentrating its shining rays upon picture after picture, as of dissolving these pictures. The intellectual vigor of narrative and description, the precision of detail, the expressive richness of idiom make Carlyle's style one of the most intense there are. His style is as effective upon the senses as upon the intelligence, upon those senses, at least, which are not, in the narrow connotation, sensual, those senses which are a part of the mind and of the muscular energy. The sudden relaxations and irruptions, the broken rhythms of this style, its discordant harmony, its profound congruence with the vehemence, the bitterness, the irony and the humor of the thought it conveys, make it a unique instrument, the work of a unique temperament, an instrument which adds an unforgettable note to the choir of English prose. Like his doctrine, Carlyle's art has its weaknesses and its limitations; in both art and doctrine, the deepest quality, the quality which will best assure the duration of Carlyle's work, is force, that energy which is capable of violating ideas, of subjugating them without inducing them to obedience or discipline; but capable, too, without striving for or achieving the perfectly beautiful, of eliciting from the world and from the soul fragments marvelous in their beauty.

INDEX

Ashburton, Lady (see Baring)

Badams, Dr., 118
Baring, Mrs., 144, 266
Bentham, Jeremy, 54, 275
Berkeley, George, 108
Boswell, James, 198
Browne, Sir Thomas, 131
Browning, Robert, 139
Buchez, 216
Buller, Charles, 257-258
Burke, Edmund, 98
Burns, Robert, 90, 173
Byron, George Gordon, Lord, 46, 54, 115

Carlyle, Alexander, 58, 76
Carlyle, James, 4, 5, 6, 8 72
Carlyle, Jane (see Jane Welsh)
Carlyle, John, 8, 101, 129
Carlyle, Margaret, 4, 5, 6, 151
Carlyle, Thomas, birth, 3; schooling, 10; at Edinburgh University, 11; schoolmaster at Auran, 12; at Kirkcaldy, 13; love for Margaret Gordon, 15-16; writer for encyclopædia, 18; knowledge of French culture, 29-32; knowledge of Kant, 35-39, of Goethe, 42-47, of Richter, 47-51; tutorship in Buller family, 57-58; first meeting with Jane Welsh, 59; courtship, 60-71; marriage, 72; life in Edinburgh, 72-77; at Craigenputtock, 77-83; *Sartor Resartus*, 82-84; removes to London, 84; first essays and studies, 86-99; *Sartor Resartus* (style and ideas), 100-133; life in London, 134-151; public lectures, 145-146; *French Revolution*, 153-167; *Heroes and Hero-Worship*, 167-181; *Chartism*, 147-148; 182-193; *Past and Present*, 193-209; *Cromwell*, 214-232; *Frederick the Great*, 232-239; *Latter-Day Pamphlets*, 239-255; *Life of Sterling*, 255-258; election to Rectorship of Edinburgh University, 267; disciples, 270-273; death, 274; general estimate of Carlyle, 275-286
Characteristics, 95-98
Clough, Arthur Hugh, 266
Colenso, John William (Bishop of Natal), 272
Coleridge, Samuel Taylor, 32, 53, 54, 58, 110, 132, 257, 258
Comte, Auguste, 272
Cromwell, Oliver, 148, 173, 176, 193, 214-232, 248, 252, 259
Cromwell (Letters and Speeches of), 149, 214-232

Dante, 173
Danton, Georges, 165
Darwin, Charles, 272, 275
Desmoulins, Camille, 165
Dickens, Charles, 139, 271
Disraeli, Benjamin, 259, 270, 271

Emerson, Ralph Waldo, 84, 95, 105, 138, 139, 168, 192, 193

Fairfax, Thomas, Lord, 226
Fichte, Johann Gottlieb, 39-42, 46-49, 52, 108, 111, 168-169
Fox, George, 120

INDEX

Francis, Dr. José, 244
Fraser's Magazine, 84, 101
Frederick the Great (II), of Prussia, 214, 232-239
Frederick the Second, History of, 232-239
Frederick William, of Prussia, 234-235, 238
French Revolution, History of the, 153-167
Froude, James Anthony, 255, 266, 299

Galsworthy, John, 281
Gibbon, Edward, 14, 30, 89, 94
Goethe, 33-34, 42-47, 49, 52, 61, 69, 76, 84, 100, 115, 117, 126, 173, 259
Gordon, Margaret, 15-16, 114
Grimm, Jakob, 172

Hare, Julius (Archdeacon), 255-256
Hegel, George Friedrich Wilhelm, 47, 112
Herder, J. W., 51-52, 94, 112
Heroes and Hero-Worship, 167-181
Heyne, Gottlieb, 88
Hoffmann, Ernst Theodor, 34
Hume, David, 30
Hunt, Leigh, 138

Irving, Edward, 13-14, 15, 16, 57, 59, 70, 119, 129, 132, 138, 268

Jeffrey, Francis (Lord), 75, 77, 268
Jocelyn, of Brakelonde, 193, 197, 199
John (King of England), 197
Johnson, Samuel, 90, 173, 198

Kant, Immanuel, 33, 35-39, 40, 43, 106, 107, 108, 109, 111, 273
Kingsley, Charles, 139, 271
Kipling Rudyard, 190, 281
Kirkpatrick, Kitty, 58, 66

Knox, John, 173, 259

La Fayette, 165
Lamb, Charles, 243
Lamotte-Fouqué, Friedrich de, 34
Latter-day Pamphlets, 150-151, 240
Laud, William (Archbishop), 224
Legendre, Adrien Marie, 29
Loyola, Ignatius of, 252
Luther, Martin, 173

Macaulay, Thomas Babington, 94
Mahomet, 173, 174, 176
Malthus, Thomas, 125
Maurice, Frederick Denison, 139
Meredith, George, 273, 281
Mignet, François Auguste, 216
Mill, James, 54
Mill, John Stuart, 54, 138, 139-140, 266
Milton, John, 131
Mirabeau, Gabriel Honoré, 165
Montaigne, 29
Montesquieu, Charles Secondat de, 29, 101

Napoleon, 163, 165, 173, 263
Necker, Jacques, 29
Nietzsche, Friedrich, 92, 178
Noralis, 34, 51, 112

Palmerston, Lord, 246
Pascal, Blaise, 29, 228
Past and Present, 148, 193-209
Peel, Sir Robert, 150, 249, 271

Raleigh, Sir Walter, 92
Rembrandt, 38
Richard I, King of England, 197, 199
Richardson, Samuel, 235
Richter, Jean Paul, 34, 47-51, 52, 89, 101, 102, 103, 112, 130, 243
Robespierre, Maximilien, 163, 165
Rousseau, Jean Jacques, 30, 161, 173, 175

INDEX

Ruskin, John, 188, 191, 253, 262-263, 266, 271, 279, 281
Russell, Lord John, 244, 246

Saint-Just, Antoine Louis de, 165
Saint-Simon, Claude Henri, 30, 95, 126, 127
Samson, Abbot, 198-199
Sartor Resartus, 100-133, 139, 213-214
Schelling, Friedrich von, 47, 106, 111, 112
Schiller, Johann Friedrich von, 33-34, 45, 51, 256
Schiller, Life of, 87-88
Schleiermacher, Friedrich, 52
Scott, Sir Walter, 32, 194
Shaftesbury, Lord (5th), 208
Shakespeare, 131, 173
Shaw, George Bernard, 281
Signs of the Times, 94-95
Southey, Robert, 139, 194
Spenser, Edmund, 131
Staël, Madame de, 32, 53
Sterling, John, 45, 107, 138, 151, 255-258
Sterling, Life of, 253, 255-258
Sterne, Lawrence, 51
Stewart, Dugald, 11
Strafford, Thomas, Earl of, 224
Swift, Jonathan, 51, 243

Taylor, Jeremy, 131
Taylor, William, 32
Tennyson, Alfred, Lord, 139
Thiers, Adolphe, 216
Tieck, Ludwig, 34

Voltaire, 29, 336, 239

Welsh, Jane Baillie, pupil of Irving, 13; learns German, 33; life before meeting Carlyle, 59; courtship, 60-71; marriage, 72; early life in Edinburgh, 72-77, at Craigenputtock, 78-82; relation to Blumine, 114; life in London, 134-145; death of mother, 151; illness, 265-266; sudden death, 267
Welsh, Mrs. John, 59, 64, 69, 72, 75, 77, 140, 151
William the Conqueror (of England), 190
Wordsworth, William, 54, 113, 139, 194